Introduction to VAX/VMS

3rd Edition

Introduction to VAX/VMS
3rd Edition

David W. Bynon
Terry C. Shannon

pb

PROFESSIONAL
PRESS BOOKS

Cover design by Michael Cousart

Trademark Acknowledgments

The following are trademarks of Digital Equipment Corporation:

A-to-Z, ALL-IN-1, applicationDEC, CDA, CDD, CI, DATATRIEVE, DCL,
DDCMP, DEC, DECalc, DECconnect, DECgraph, DECmail, DECmate, DECnet,
DECserver, DECstation, DECsystem-10, DECsystem-20, DEC/Test, DECUS,
DECwindows, DELNI, DEQNA, DIBOL, Digital, DNA, ESE20, EVE, FileView,
FMS, GIGI, HSC, IAS, IVIS, LAN Bridge, LAT, LA50, LA100, LQP02, LSI-11,
MASSBUS, MicroPDP-11, MicroPower/Pascal, MicroVAX, NAS, PDP, PDT,
P/OS, Q-bus, Rainbow, RALLY, RAxx, Rdb/VMS, RdbExpert, ReGIS, RSTS/E,
RSX, RT-11, TAxx, TEAMDATA, ThinWire, UDA50, ULTRIX, UNIBUS, VAX,
VAXBI, VAXcluster, VAX DIBOL, VAXELN, VAXFMS, VAX LISP, VAX SCAN,
VAXserver, VAXstation, VMS, VMSmail, VT, Work Processor, WPS.

X Window System is a trademark of Massachusetts Institute of Technology.

Library of Congress Cataloging-in-Publication Data

Bynon, David W., 1959-
   Introduction to VAX/VMS / David W. Bynon, Terry C. Shannon. —3rd ed.

      p.   cm.

   Includes index.
   ISBN 1-878956-05-1
   1. Operating systems (Computers) 2. VAX/VMS. 3. VAX computers-
-Programming.   I. Shannon, Terry C. (Terry Craig), 1952- .
II. Title.
QA76.76.063B96 1991
005.4'44—dc20   91-21070
                                                  CIP

Please address comments and questions to the publisher:

Professional Press Books
101 Witmer Road
Horsham, PA 19044
(215) 957-4287 FAX (215) 957-1050
Internet: books@propress.com

Contents

Chapter 4 — Files and Directories

Chapter 9 — Command Procedures 9-1

Chapter 10 (continued)

This book is an extensive introduction to Digital Equipment Corporation's VAX computer systems that use the Virtual Memory System (VMS) operating system. It is intended for users of all experience levels as supplemental documentation to the VAX/VMS documentation set. This book brings together a vast amount of information found in numerous Digital Equipment reference manuals.

Introduction to VAX/VMS is designed so you can learn VMS in a classroom or on your own. Each chapter begins with a discussion of what you'll learn, and offers guidance on how to proceed and where to find additional information. *Introduction to VAX/VMS* takes a step-by-step, hands-on approach, with examples you can try at your terminal. If you're a new VMS user, you're encouraged to use this book as a tutorial. After your initial learning experience, you can continue to use it as a reference guide.

New in the Third Edition
This edition is current through VMS Version 5.4. If you're working with a different VMS version (5.5 or higher), there will be slight variations, although most VMS user commands will not change.

This edition of *Introduction to VAX/VMS* expands on the information in the second edition with a full chapter devoted to DECwindows, Digital's powerful graphical user interface.

Although DECwindows will adopt the OSF/Motif look and feel in 1992, its functions will remain the same.

While EDT continues to be a favorite text editor for many VMS users, we've received a large number of requests for information on the Text Processing Utility (TPU). So, for those of you who prefer TPU, Chapter 6 has been expanded to cover EVE, the default TPU editor.

Finally, the third edition includes more examples and provides more in-depth information in many areas. A good example is Chapter 9, "Command Procedures," which includes twice as many examples as in the second edition.

How This Book is Structured

This book contains an Introduction, 10 chapters, eight appendices, and a glossary. The chapters progress logically, but it is not necessary to read them in order.

The Introduction provides a brief overview of the VAX family of computers and the VMS operating system.

Chapter 1, "Getting Started," explains to the first-time computer user how to begin using VMS. You will learn about your terminal, how to log in to your VAX account, and the HELP command.

Chapter 2, "Introduction to DECwindows," explains to the workstation user how to begin. If you will be using a VAXstation or a VT1000 (X Window terminal), you should read this chapter first. In it you'll explore the DECwindows graphical user interface.

Chapter 3, "The Digital Command Language," describes the Digital Command Language (DCL), the link between you and the VAX computer. A handful of commands are demonstrated to support the text.

Chapter 4, "Files and Directories," discusses the VMS file and directory system. You'll learn to create files and directories, and the commands to manage them.

Chapter 5, "The VMS User Environment," introduces you to the VMS user environment. In this chapter, you'll explore your user account, learn to modify characteristics of your terminal, define function keys, and understand VMS security features.

Chapter 6, "VMS Text Editors," details EDT and EVE, the two VMS text file editors. Although they are not word processors, EDT and EVE provide features for easy text entry and text editing.

Chapter 7, "VMS Utilities," covers three important utilities: Mail, Phone and FileView. Mail and Phone enable you to communicate with other VAX users. FileView is a useful tool for VAXstation and VT1000 users.

Chapter 8, "Symbols, Data, Expressions and Lexical Functions," introduces symbols and explains how to use them to customize your user environment.

Chapter 9, "Command Procedures," explains the ins and outs of writing command procedures. Command procedures enable you to automate routine tasks.

Chapter 10, "Advanced VMS Features," contains advanced topics for VMS users who have mastered DCL commands. In this chapter, you'll explore using more than one process, batch processing and DECnet.

Acknowledgments

Every now and then, I run across a memento that makes me recall special events. Recently I came across an old Western Union message from Professional Press Editor Dave Mallery asking if I would review Terry Shannon's *Introduction to VAX/VMS* for an update. From this message, my relationship with Dave Mallery and Professional Press began.

While I thank Dave for involving me with this book, all of the Professional Press crew deserve praise. Their dedication to creating a quality product is beyond reproach. Special kudos go to Annette Nelson for her editing expertise, and to Lee Willis for never failing to be critical of my work.

— David Bynon

Symbols and Conventions

This book uses the following standard symbols and conventions.

Symbol	Explanation
$	When at the beginning of a line, the dollar sign indicates the user prompt. This means that the VMS operating system is ready to receive commands. All example commands in this book begin with the dollar sign.
<key>	All key names are enclosed in angle brackets.
<CTRL/x>	For some functions, a two-key keyboard command sequence is used. These are called *control key commands* and are issued by simultaneously pressing the <CTRL> key and an alphabetic key, indicated here by x.
SMALL CAPS	All commands the user enters, such as PRINT, and all keyboard keys, are shown in small caps.

Symbol	Explanation
[,...]	This annotation, used in Appendix A, indicates optional or additional parameters. For example, the DCL COPY command can be used to copy a multiple input file into a single output file. The command would be explained as follows: $COPY input_file_spec[,...] output_file_spec
spec	This term, used in the appendices, is an abbreviation for *specification* or *file specification*. For example, in the above COPY command, input_file_spec refers to the name of the file being copied.

About the VAX and VMS

Digital Equipment introduced the first VAX computer, the VAX 11/780, in 1978 as an extension of the popular PDP-11 series of computers. PDP-11 customers easily migrated software and hardware from PDP-11 systems to the VAX 11/780. Using special software, PDP-11 programs continue to run on VAX computers.

Digital Equipment committed numerous resources to create the VAX computer architecture. Its goal was to create a software-compatible family of computers that serves a wide range of applications from the desktop to the mainframe. The VAX goal was to provide a rich computing environment with increased capabilities, yet be friendly enough that it could be used by people with less specialized training.

Although the VAX and its VMS operating system are more than 13 years old, they continue to enjoy notable status. They are used in every major industry and have a reputation for being user-friendly. Today, VAX refers to a family of computer systems. The VAX computer you work with may be a standalone VAX workstation or the powerful VAX 9000. It also is possible that the VAX you use is not one computer, but many VAX computers connected in a cooperative arrangement called a *VAXcluster*. Because VAX is an architecture, it doesn't matter which VAX you use; all VAX systems are nearly identical to the user.

What is VAX?

VAX is an acronym for Virtual Address eXtension. Virtual Address suggests that the VAX can use memory storage locations (addresses) that do not exist as true physical memory. Virtual memory is the illusion of a large amount of memory. Computers that use virtual memory process programs and data in segments called *pages*. The computer stores the memory pages being used in physical memory. The pages that do not fit in physical memory are stored on disk. The computer retrieves pages from disk as required, and returns other pages to disk to create room. The process of moving memory pages in and out of physical memory is called *paging*. The VAX computer architecture has special features that assist this memory management technique.

Although the acronym suggests that virtual memory is the premier feature of a VAX computer, there are other important attributes. For instance, the VAX architecture guarantees that software correctly developed on any VAX system will run on all VAX family members. This feature lets users upgrade to larger systems, as their needs increase, without having to rewrite software or convert data. Another VAX feature is its ability to support multiprocessing. Users running different programs can use a VAX simultaneously. Each user appears to have full control of the computer. In actuality, the VAX is processing pieces of each user's program one at a time.

Typical VAX Hardware Features

The typical VAX computer system has a central processing unit (CPU), memory, storage devices, and devices used to communicate with the computer and receive printed output. A minimum VAX configuration includes a CPU, one or more disk drives, and an operator console. A disk drive is a storage medium used to hold VMS, software, and the user's information. Most VAX systems have one or more magnetic tape drives for loading software products and backing up user information. Because VAX systems typically support many users, most VAX configurations include video display terminals and high-speed printers for hardcopy output.

A network is a common feature of VAX systems. A network connects computer systems for sharing information and resources, and for user communication. Digital Equipment's computer network is called *DECnet*, which is a combination of hardware and software products.

Some VAX systems use a team of VAX processors to create a larger processing capability. This is accomplished through a VMS software feature called *clustering*, which provides greater computing power, a higher degree of availability, and shared resources. VAX processors in a cluster work together to place the power and resources of two or more VAX systems at your fingertips.

For the technical user, VAX workstations bring the power of the VAX to the desktop. A VAX workstation provides impressive computer functions to a single user. Its 19-inch monochrome or color display and mouse (pointing device) allow the user to control multiple interactive jobs simultaneously. The VAX workstation user interface is a combination of the Digital Command Language (DCL) and DECwindows. DECwindows is graphically oriented.

What is VMS?

VMS is a computer operating system specific to VAX computers. *Operating system* defines a collection of software components that manages a computer's hardware resources. To the user, VMS is seen as a command language interpreter (CLI) and different software utilities. A CLI is the interface between the user and computer. Although it's possible to have more than one CLI on VMS, the one we'll discuss is the Digital Command Language (DCL).

VMS utilities are software programs that help users communicate with each other (such as electronic mail), or help manage the information processed and stored on the VAX. VMS does not include application software such as accounting or word processing. These software programs must be purchased separately and must be installed to work with VMS.

VMS^supports the VAX multiprocessing capability. VMS can run programs for and interact with a number of people or jobs at the same time. This usage is almost totally independent. VMS lets each user access system resources without regard for what other users are doing. For all practical purposes, VMS makes a VAX computer appear dedicated to each individual using it.

When you use VMS, you are known to the system as a *process*. A process is a hardware and software picture of your environment. All work is done in the context of this process. This process allows VMS to keep track of you and the work you're doing.

Your process is created when you log in and is deleted when you log out. It carries with it a process name, process identification, user identification code, and privileges. This information identifies you from other system users.

Chapter 1

Getting Started

This chapter has the information you need to begin using VMS. In it, you'll be introduced to many VAX features and the VMS operating system. You'll learn how to:

▼ Set up and use your terminal
▼ Log in to your VAX system
▼ Use the HELP command
▼ Log out

Computers cannot foretell what you want them to do or how you want it done. A VAX, like any other computer, needs precise instructions put in its own terms. We call these instructions commands.

The VMS operating system is interactive. When you use VMS, you and the VAX will conduct a dialogue. For example, you will enter commands and the VAX will respond; you will enter another command or respond to a query and the VAX will respond. The language you will use is DCL. When VMS is ready to accept a DCL command, it will prompt you with a dollar sign ($).

To communicate with your VAX, you will use a terminal. When you type at your keyboard, the characters, numbers and punctuation marks are collected in an area called a *buffer*. You can change the line you are typing until you press the <RETURN> key. DCL does not see your command until you press <RETURN>. When you press <RETURN>, the command you typed is interpreted by DCL. If DCL understands your command, it will do the work.

If DCL is unable to process your command, because of lack of information or misdirection, it will send a message to your terminal. Be sure to read all messages sent to your terminal. If you do not understand the message, write it down and call your system manager or help desk for assistance.

USING VT TERMINALS

A terminal is used for two-way communication between a computer and a user. Information you type at your keyboard appears on the display as you type. To show where you are typing on the screen, terminals use a cursor, which usually is a blinking block or underline.

A terminal communicates with a computer by sending and receiving characters one after another, in a serial fashion. In order for this information exchange to take place, the terminal and computer must communicate using a common protocol. The most important part of the protocol is the transmission rate, which is expressed in terms of bits per second (bps) or baud. Ten (10) baud is equivalent to one character per second. A terminal set to operate at 4800 baud can send (from the keyboard) or receive (on the display) 480 characters per second.

Most terminals connected to VAX systems operate at speeds of 4800, 9600 or 19,200 bps. The transmit and receive speeds must be set to the same value. If you do not know the appropriate setting for terminals at your site, you should check with your system manager or help desk. This is particularly important if you plan to call into the computer via a modem.

Although Digital Equipment manufactures many different terminals, we will discuss only the two most common: the VT200 and VT300. VT200 and VT300 terminals provide the same basic functions, so the following discussion applies to all models.

The Keyboard

All VT200 and VT300 terminals use the model LK201 keyboard (see Figure 1-1). This keyboard has four key areas. At the top of the keyboard are 20 function keys that can be used by application software and that can be programmed for special functions. The main keyboard is located below the function keys. It represents a standard typewriter keyboard layout. The editing keypad and numeric keypad are found to the right of the main keyboard. The editing keypad is used to move the cursor, and for special editing functions. The six keys above the arrow keys also are programmable. To the far right, the numeric keypad is used to enter numbers or for special functions by application programs such as electronic mail.

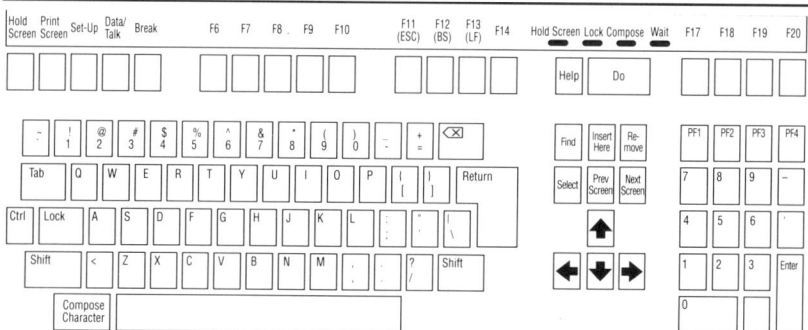

Figure 1-1. Model LK201 Keyboard

VT terminals incorporate a screen-saver feature that will blank the screen after 30 minutes of inactivity to prevent burning the screen phosphor. To restore the display, press any key on the keyboard. The <SHIFT> key is preferred because it will make the display come back on but will not send a character to the VAX.

Keyboard Indicator Lights

The LK201 keyboard has four red or green status lights:

▼ Hold Screen—This light indicates that the <HOLD

SCREEN> key was pressed. The <HOLD SCREEN> key is used to freeze the current display on the terminal screen.

▼ Lock—When this light is on, the keyboard is shifted into uppercase mode. In this mode, the keyboard generates uppercase letters. Press the <LOCK> key again to release the lock.

▼ Compose—This indicator light comes on after you press the <COMPOSE CHARACTER> key. The key is used to create a composite character, such as the copyright symbol (©).

▼ Wait—When this indicator light is on, your keyboard is locked. To unlock your keyboard, follow these steps:

1. Press the <SET-UP> key.

2. Select the CLEAR COMM function.

3. Press <ENTER>.

4. Select the EXIT function.

5. Press <ENTER>.

Using the Setup Function

When you press the <SET UP> key, a Setup Directory is displayed at the bottom of your screen. The directory provides access to seven setup screens.

Beneath each screen is a status line that indicates whether the terminal is in insert or replace mode, whether a printer is available or ready, and whether a modem is available or ready. Each screen displays information particular to the specific set-up function identified by the screen title. The seven set-up screens are:

1. Setup Directory

2. Display setup

3. General setup

4. Communications setup

5. Printer setup

6. Keyboard setup

7. Tab setup

The function of each screen is reflected by its name. For example, to set the transmit and receive rate for communicating with your VAX computer, select the Communications setup screen. To set the screen width or scrolling characteristics, use the Display setup screen. Each screen displays a number of named blocks called *fields*. While in setup mode, the terminal uses a field cursor to identify the currently selected field on a screen. The selected field is highlighted. Use the arrow keys to move from field to field.

To change a setup function, use the arrow keys to move the field cursor to the desired field, then press the <ENTER> key on the numeric keypad to change the value. If you make a mistake, press the <DELETE> key to restore the field to its original value. When you have made the changes you want, press the <SET-UP> key again. Your screen will return to its previous state.

Solving Common VT Terminal Problems

If you cannot log in to the computer, follow this check list:

▼ Are the computer and keyboard cables plugged in?
▼ Is the terminal On Line light on?
▼ Is the Hold Screen light on?
▼ Is the terminal set to operate at the same speed as the computer?

For more information on VT200 and VT300 terminals and the use of the setup function, refer to your Digital VT200 or VT300 *Owner's Manual*.

LOGGING IN

Before you can use the VAX, you must log in. Because there are many ways to connect terminals to VAX computer systems, several different login methods are possible. The most common terminal connection methods are by direct connection, network terminal server or modem. The following sections will explain these login methods. If you work at a high security site or your system uses special hardware, such as a terminal switch, private branch exchange (PBX) or a non-Digital network, consult your system manager for special instructions.

Direct Login

If your terminal is wired directly to a VAX, it is dedicated to that machine. In this case, there is little to do but turn the terminal on and begin. Follow these brief instructions:

1. Make sure the terminal's power is on.

2. Press the <RETURN> key. Sometimes you will have to press <RETURN> several times in rapid succession before the system will respond. The VAX will respond with a welcome message and a prompt requesting your system username:

```
Welcome to node Biff
Username:
```

3. At the Username: prompt, enter the account name your system manager has assigned, then press <RETURN>. Next, the VAX will prompt you for your password:

```
Password:
```

4. At the Password: prompt, enter your password, then press <RETURN>. Your password will not appear on your screen. If you have entered a correct username and password, the system log-on message will be displayed on the terminal:

```
Welcome to VAX/VMS V5.3

Last interactive login on Friday, 2-FEB-1990 13:47
Last non-interactive login on Monday, 28-JAN-1990 00:24
$
```

If you entered your account name or password incorrectly, you will receive this message:

```
User authorization failure
```

When this happens, press <RETURN> and the VAX will prompt you again for your username and password. If you're unable to log in after several attempts, ask your system manager for help.

When you have logged in successfully, the DCL dollar sign prompt ($) will be displayed. The dollar sign prompt indicates that the system is ready to accept commands. The prompt will appear after each command you issue to DCL processes.

Network Terminal Server Login

A common communication device used with VAX computers is the local area network (LAN) terminal server. A terminal server is an intelligent device that permits terminal users to connect to one or more VAX computers (see Figure 1-2). Terminal servers use a LAN to make the connection between your terminal and the host VAX computer.

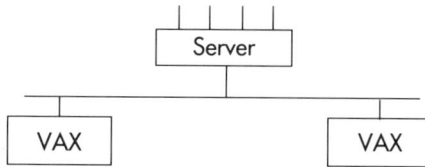

Figure 1-2. Terminal Server Connection

There are multiple situations that you can encounter when connected to a terminal server. The server port assigned to your terminal may automatically connect with a specific host. In this case, the terminal appears directly connected, and you can log in as explained under "Direct Login." If the server does not automatically connect to a host computer, you will need to enter CONNECT commands at a terminal server prompt. Terminal servers have two prompts: a *login prompt* and a *command prompt.* If you have not logged in to the terminal server, the server will prompt for your name:

```
Enter username>
```

The server is requesting a name that identifies you. Other server users need this name to identify those using the system. If you receive this prompt, enter your name and press <RETURN>. After you're logged in to the server port, or if you have already logged in, you will receive the local server prompt:

```
Local>
```

At this prompt, you can enter CONNECT commands. The CONNECT command creates a link between your terminal and the system you specify. For example, to connect to node Biff, you would enter the command CONNECT BIFF:

```
Local> CONNECT BIFF
```

When connected, you'll be prompted to log in to the VAX as explained under "Direct Login." When you log out of the VAX, you will return to the server prompt again. For more information about terminal servers, refer to the Digital Equipment *Terminal Server User's Guide* or consult your system manager.

DECnet Login
If the VAX system you work on is connected to a DECnet network, you can log in to other VAX systems on the network with the DCL command SET HOST. The SET HOST command makes your terminal appear directly connected to the remote VAX system.

To use the SET HOST command, you must be logged in to your account on your local VAX system. You also must have an account on the remote VAX system you wish to log in to. At the dollar sign prompt of your local system, enter the command

```
$ SET HOST node
```

where *node* is the DECnet node name of the remote VAX system. Once a connection is established, the remote VAX will prompt you for your username and password. Log in and you can use the VAX as if it were your local system.

Dial-Up Login

Many VAX systems can accept remote logins by telephone. In place of a local terminal, the VAX will have a modem connected to a telephone line (see Figure 1-3). To access the modem, you must have a compatible modem, phone line and terminal (or personal computer).

Most modems connect directly to a modular telephone jack and can dial the telephone. If you're using a terminal connected to the modem, you'll have to enter the modem dial command by hand. Many modems are compatible with the Hayes modem command set, developed by Hayes Microcomputer Products Inc. To make a Hayes-compatible modem dial the telephone, enter an attention command (AT), followed by the dial command (D)

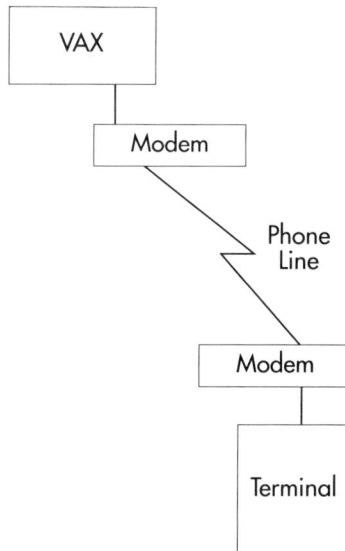

Figure 1-3. VAX-to-Modem Connection

and a letter that indicates the type of telephone line you have (T for tone or P for pulse). Follow the dialing command with the telephone number. For example, the following command dials 555-4567 on a touch-tone line:

ATDT 555-4567

When the modem has connected with the other system, you'll receive a connect message, such as:

```
CONNECT 2400
```

When you receive the connect message, start the login as usual by pressing <RETURN>. You may need to press <RETURN> several times before the VAX responds. If your modem cannot connect with the other modem, you will receive a message such as "NO CARRIER" or "BUSY."

If you're using a personal computer with VT terminal emulation software, the software probably will have a dialing function that maintains a list of numbers. Use this capability to dial the telephone number. Most terminal emulation packages detect the connection and switch to terminal mode. When you receive a connection message, begin the normal login steps.

Follow these steps to log in using a modem:

1. Turn on the equipment. If you are using a personal computer, be sure to load your VT terminal emulation software.

2. Dial the VAX modem number and wait for a carrier detect (CD) signal. A carrier is a tone presented by each modem. The data is modulated on the carrier for transmission between systems. When both modems detect each other's carrier, the carrier detect light comes on, and the connection is complete.

3. Press <RETURN> several times. If you do not get a response, wait several seconds, then try again. It may take a few seconds for the VAX to respond. Sometimes, you may need to hang up and start over.

If your attempts to dial in fail, ask your system manager for assistance.

Other Login Features

The three common methods of logging in can be tailored through the use of two special login features: /DISK and /COMMAND. When used after your username, the /DISK qualifier tells VMS to log you in to an alternate disk. Use the /COMMAND qualifier to specify an alternate login command procedure.

For example, when you log in, you can instruct VMS to execute the DATABASE.COM procedure instead of the default procedure called LOGIN.COM. Here's how:

```
Username: SMITH/COMMAND=DATABASE
Password:
```

THE VMS HELP UTILITY

Once you're logged in, help is as close as your keyboard because HELP is a DCL command. HELP is one of the most important commands available to new and experienced VMS users. With HELP, you have the equivalent of a VMS reference manual at your fingertips. The help facility includes information about every DCL command and many other programs and facilities.

You can use HELP in one of two ways. When you know the name of the command you need help with, use the direct mode. If you don't know the name of the command, use the query mode.

Query Mode

To use the query mode, enter HELP. You'll receive an alphabetical listing of all topics for which information is available. You'll then receive this prompt:

```
Topic?
```

Type the name of the topic you want help with, then press <RETURN>. The HELP information will include a discussion of what the command does and how to use it. You can exit HELP by pressing <RETURN>, <CTRL/C> or <CTRL/Z>.

Most topics have subtopics that provide additional information. All available subtopics will be listed alphabetically followed by the prompt:

```
COMMAND-NAME Subtopic?
```

From this prompt, you can enter the name of a subtopic to get more information, or press <RETURN> to return to the `Topic?` prompt. Here you can enter another command you want information about, or exit from HELP by pressing <RETURN>.

If you want to see a display of all the information in the HELP library for a given command, type HELP followed by the command name and an ellipsis (...) or the wildcard asterisk (*). For example, the command HELP SHOW... or HELP SHOW * will list information on all subtopics of the SHOW command.

Direct Mode

As you gain experience with DCL, you will begin to use the direct mode. To use HELP directly, enter HELP and the name of the topic you are interested in. This bypasses the listing of HELP topics and displays specific information immediately. In direct mode, you can enter a DCL command or a command and its qualifiers. For example, to find out about the SHOW TIME command, you would enter:

```
$ HELP SHOW TIME
```

Detailed information on most commands and topics covered by HELP can be found in Digital Equipment documentation. However, you will find that the HELP command generally provides you with all the information you need. For further information about the HELP command, log in to your account and enter the following commands:

```
$ HELP HINTS
$ HELP HELP/INSTRUCTIONS
```

LOGGING OUT

When you're finished using your terminal, you should log out. Until you've logged out, your account is open and your files and work are accessible to others. If you leave your terminal without logging out, another person will have direct access to your work. You can log out only from the DCL prompt. Use the LOGOUT command:

```
$ LOGOUT
```

If you used the SET HOST command to access a remote VAX, the LOGOUT command will return control to your local VAX system. In this case, to log out completely you must issue the LOGOUT command twice, once for each system you logged in to.

Remember, it is your responsibility to protect your account and the rest of the system, so log out!

WHERE TO GO FROM HERE

The next chapter, "Introduction to DECwindows," is meant for DECwindows users. If you'll be using a VAX workstation or an X Window System terminal, such as the DEC VT1000, this chapter will be of interest to you. If you're not a DECwindows user, move ahead to Chapter 3, "The Digital Command Language," where we'll discuss the language you'll use to communicate commands to VMS.

Chapter 2

Introduction to DECwindows

If you have access to a VAX workstation, such as a Digital Equipment VAXstation II, VAXstation 2000 or VAXstation 3100, this chapter is for you. In it you'll learn about:

- ▼ VAX workstation features
- ▼ Windowing terminology
- ▼ How to start a login session with DECwindows
- ▼ Windows and widgets
- ▼ The DECwindows session manager
- ▼ FileView
- ▼ How to log out from DECwindows

Unlike a VT terminal, a VAX workstation is an intelligent computing device. The workstation has four main components: the VAX processor, video display, keyboard, and a pointing device called a mouse.

Whereas other VAX systems, such as a MicroVAX or VAX 6000, service many users at the same time, the VAX workstation is for a single user.

The DECwindows software is another feature that differentiates a VAX workstation from a VT terminal. With DECwindows, a graphical user interface to the VMS operating system, you can divide your screen into one or more windows. Each window represents a utility program, such as VMS Mail, Calendar, Calculator or Notepad. Using DECwindows, you can create a working environment that suits your needs.

Application programs developed specifically for DECwindows are easy to use because DECwindows takes advantage of your workstation's graphics capability. Under DECwindows, you issue commands to the VAX by selecting objects and text on the screen with the mouse instead of by typing commands. Because DECwindows is an interface to VMS, you also have access to all VMS commands, utilities and application software. To access these VMS resources, DECwindows provides an application called *DECterm*. DECterm is a VT terminal emulator that pops up as a window on your workstation screen.

UNDERSTANDING WINDOWS

You can think of your workstation display as the top of your desk. At any given time it may be clear or cluttered with work. Just as you can manage and shuffle the work on your desk, you can shuffle the work on your workstation display. The windows you create are like pieces of paper. You can stack them, move them, bring one to the top of the screen, put another at the bottom of the screen, or move them aside. The arrangement of the windows is up to you.

To manage your windows and interact with the DECwindows software, you use a mouse. The mouse is logically connected to a pointer on your screen. When you move the mouse on a flat surface, the pointer on the screen moves with it.

At the top of your mouse (from left to right) there are three buttons called <MB1>, <MB2> and <MB3>. <MB1> (mouse button 1) is used primarily for selecting and moving screen objects. Most windows have a menu bar (e.g., File Edit Customize ...) below the top border. Each word in the menu bar represents a list of actions. To see or select an action, move the mouse pointer on top of a word in the menu bar, then press and hold <MB1>. This will open the pull-down menu for you to make a selection. Figure 2-1 shows a typical pull-down menu.

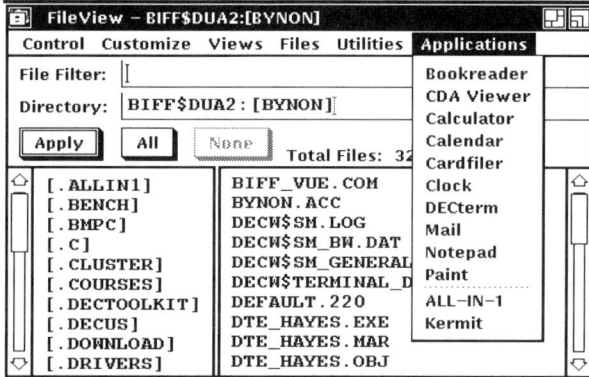

Figure 2-1. Typical Pull-Down Menu

Mouse Terms

In this book, the following terms will be used to describe a user action at the workstation:

Click — Many operations are initiated by pointing at an object on the screen, then pressing and quickly releasing <MB1>. The click is used most often to press buttons in a window or move the cursor to a new location.

Double click — Some objects may first be selected and then have other operations performed on them. A common example is selecting, then opening a mail message in the DECwindows Mail utility. The first click selects the message you point at, and the second click opens it for you to read. To double click, press and quickly release <MB1> twice in rapid succession.

Shift click — Many applications can perform operations on a list of items; deleting files is an example. To build a list, press and hold the <SHIFT> key and click on the item. This action will add the item to the list.

Drag — You "drag" by pointing to an item, pressing <MB1> and holding it down, moving the pointer, and releasing the button. Use this mouse action to invoke pull-down menus, change a window's size or location, and move sliders and other controls.

Press and hold — To perform a continuous operation, such as scrolling through a list of items using a scroll bar (located on the side of many windows), move your mouse pointer on top of the scroll bar arrow, press <MB1>, and hold. The operation will continue until you release the mouse button.

DECWINDOWS WIDGETS

Widgets are DECwindows user interfaces. Some widgets are operated by mouse input only, while others use both keyboard and mouse input. Common widgets you will encounter are *windows, pop-up menus, pull-down menus, scroll bars, dialog boxes* and *control panels.*

Controls

All widgets have controls. A control is an active screen object, comprising graphics, text or both. When you click on a control, it provides input to the application that presented the widget. Controls are labeled to indicate their purpose. There are four basic controls: *toggle buttons, radio buttons, push buttons* and *scales.*

Toggle buttons are square on/off switches you use to choose whether or not an option should be activated. If the small square next to the option is highlighted, the option is activated. If the small square next to the option is not highlighted, the option is not activated. To change the setting of a toggle button, move the mouse pointer to the square next to the option and click on it (see Figure 2-2).

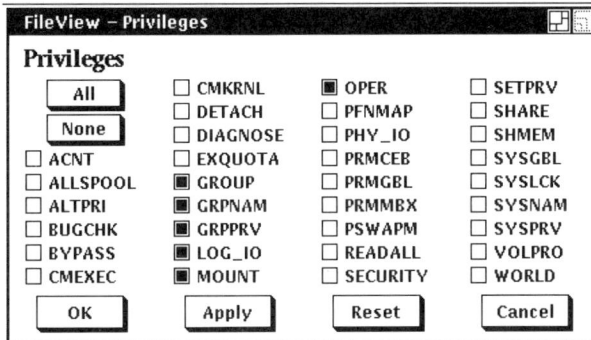

Figure 2-2. Window with Toggle Buttons

Radio buttons allow you to activate one option from a list of options. The radio button selected is a highlighted circle (see Figure 2-3). To change the activated button, move your pointer to the circle next to the option you want to activate, and click on it.

A push button is a word that appears in a dialog box within a rectangular frame, such as *OK* or *Cancel* (see Figure 2-4). To perform the action indicated by the push button, move the pointer to the push button and click on it.

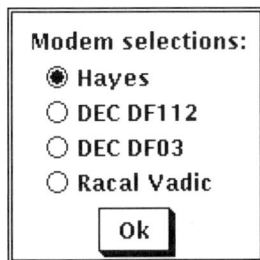

Figure 2-3. Radio Buttons

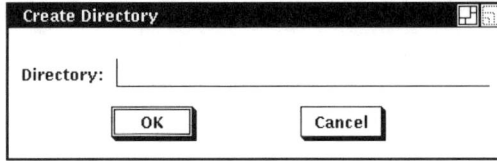

Figure 2-4. Push Buttons

Scales enable you to enter a value from a range of values by adjusting a pointer to the desired position along a line (see Figure 2-5). To operate a scale, place your mouse pointer on the arrow and drag it up and down (vertical scale) or back and forth (horizontal scale). Release <MB1> when you reach the scale position you want.

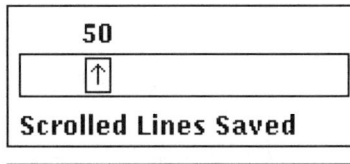

Figure 2-5. Window with Scale Widget

STARTING A WORKSTATION LOGIN SESSION

Because a workstation is a VAX, you must have an account to use it. When a VAX workstation has started correctly and is not in use by someone else, your screen will look like the screen in Figure 2-6, which shows the Start Session dialog box.

The Start Session dialog box window prompts you for your username and password. The box has two text entry fields, *Username* and *Password*, and two push buttons, *OK* and *Clear*.

To start a session, follow these steps:

1. If the Username field is not clear, click on the Clear button. This action also will move the cursor to the beginning of the Username field.

2. Type your username and press <RETURN>. The cursor will move down to the Password field.

3. Type your password (it will not be displayed as you type) and press <RETURN> or click on the OK button.

If you have not entered a valid username and password, a User Authorization Failure message box will pop up (see Figure 2-7). When this happens, click on the Acknowledge button (the OK button) and start over.

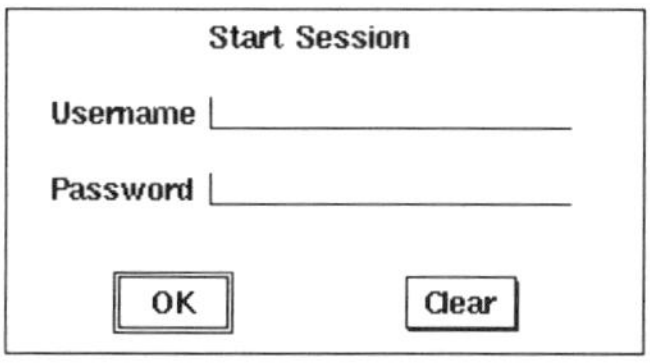

Figure 2-6. Start Session Dialog Box

If your username and password are correct, your DECwindows/ VMS session begins. After a few seconds, your screen will clear and the DECwindows Session Manager will appear. You will use the Session Manager to start applications, such as DECterm and FileView.

If your password has expired, DECwindows will display a password dialog box in which you must type a new password and verification. You will not be allowed to continue until your expired password is changed.

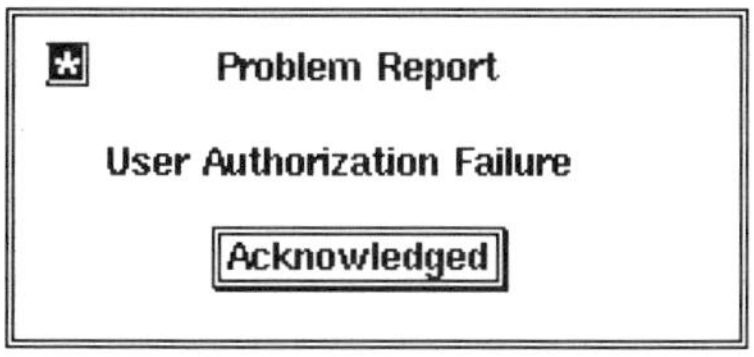

Figure 2-7. User Authorization Failure Message Box

THE DECWINDOWS SESSION MANAGER

When you log in to your workstation, a program called the *Session Manager* is run for you. The Session Manager is responsible for establishing your default environment. It starts the Window Manager, which you see on your screen as the Icon Box, sets up screen colors and default characteristics, then "auto-starts" applications for you. (You must specify which applications you want the Session Manager to "auto-start" for you.)

After you log in and are set up, the Session Manager performs five important functions:

▼ Session control (quitting and pausing)
▼ Starting applications
▼ Customizing the workstation to your preference
▼ Screen printing
▼ Displaying system messages

Each DECwindows application runs in its own window (a rectangular area on the screen). You access DECwindows applications through the Session Manager's Applications pull-down menu in the Session Manager window menu bar. By default, only DECwindows applications are accessible through this menu, but you can modify the menu to add any application.

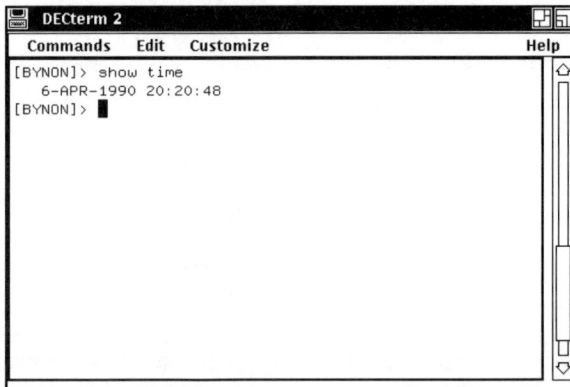

Figure 2-8. DECterm Window

CREATING A DECTERM WINDOW

DECterm is a DECwindows application that emulates VT100, VT200 and VT300 terminals. Using DECterm, you can communicate with your VAX computer as you would from a VT terminal.

To create a DECterm window, choose the DECterm menu item from the Session Manager's Applications menu. Once the DECterm window is displayed, give it input focus (so that it will control the keyboard) by moving the mouse pointer in the window and clicking. The title bar will be highlighted when the window has input focus (see Figure 2-8).

DECTERM SETUP

Below the top of a DECterm window, there is a menu bar with four pull-down menus: Commands, Edit, Customize and Help. The Customize menu lists several items that let you change DECterm characteristics.

You can change DECterm window features, such as the size of the window, by choosing Window... from the Customize menu. DECterm will then display a dialog box. The highlighted toggle buttons in the dialog box indicate the current settings. Click on a toggle button or its label to change the setting (on or off), then click on the OK button to apply your changes and close the dialog box. To quit without making changes, click on the cancel button.

You can select the type of terminal DECterm emulates by choosing General... from the Customize menu. A dialog box with toggle buttons will pop up on your screen. The highlighted buttons indicate the current setting. Click on the emulation type you need, then click on the OK button. To quit without making changes, click on the cancel button.

To change keyboard settings, such as the margin bell, choose Keyboard... from the Customize menu. Click on the appropriate buttons, then click on the OK button. To quit without making changes, click on the cancel button.

After modifying DECterm settings, you must save your changes to make them permanent. Once you save your changes, DECterm will use those settings each time you create a new DECterm window. If you change your mind and want to use the settings that came with your system, you can restore the original defaults.

To save your DECterm settings:

▼ Choose the Save Current Settings option from the DECterm Customize menu. This is for routine saving of customized features.

▼ Select the Save Current Settings As... option from the DECterm Customize menu when you want to save the current customized features under a different filename. DECterm displays a dialog box that prompts you for the file you want to use to save your customized features.

To restore customized settings:

▼ Choose the Use Last Saved Settings option from the DECterm Customize menu to restore a file.

▼ Select the Use System Defaults option from the DECterm Customize menu to restore the system defaults.

▼ Choose the Use Saved Settings From... option from the DECterm Customize menu to restore previously saved settings.

Closing a DECterm Window

To exit from DECterm and close the DECterm window, choose the Quit option from the DECterm Commands menu or type LOGOUT at the $ prompt.

MANAGING WINDOWS

A window is a rectangular area on the screen in which a DECwindows application runs. At the top of most windows there is a title bar, which contains the window's title and three square buttons. Many windows also have a menu bar located below the title bar, which lists the names of the available pull-down menus.

Your workstation screen can show many windows at one time, but only one window will have input focus. The window with input focus controls the keyboard. To select a window for input focus, move your pointer inside the window and click. The title bar of the window with input focus is highlighted, indicating that the window is active. Figure 2-9 shows a screen with overlapping windows.

You have control over where windows are located on your screen. To move a window to a different location, move your pointer to the window's title bar (not on a control button), then drag the window to its new location. An outline of the window appears as you drag. Remember, to drag, push and hold <MB1>. Release <MB1> when the window is where you want it.

You also can change the size of your windows when you only want to see part of what the window can display. To change a window's size, move your pointer to the sizing button in the title bar, then press and hold <MB1>. While holding <MB1>, move the

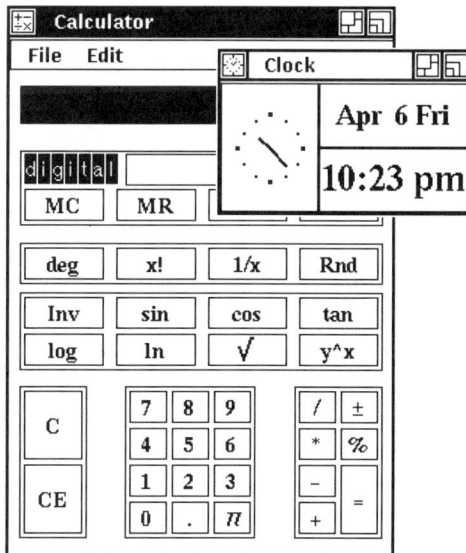

Figure 2-9. Overlapping Windows

pointer to the right of the window (outside of it) until a thin rubber-band line appears. Then, move your mouse to stretch or contract the window's size as needed. When the window is the size you want, release <MB1>.

After you have created a few windows, they will begin to overlap. You can change the stacking order of your windows by pushing windows to the back or pulling them to the front. By clicking on a window's push-to-back button, you can move the window to the bottom of the stack of windows. The push-to-back button does not change the input focus. To push the top window to the back and change the input focus to the new top window, click on the push-to-back button, then click inside the new top window. To pull a window to the top, click anywhere in the window, except on one of its controls.

To remove the windows you're not using, you can shrink them to icons. An icon is a rectangle that represents the window. Icons are held in a window called the *icon box*, which is located at the top of your screen. To shrink a window to an icon, click on the shrink-to-icon button. The window will disappear from the screen and reappear in the icon box. To expand an icon back to a window, click on the icon.

Scroll Bars

If a DECwindows window is associated with a file or a list of items, it will have a scroll bar. You use a scroll bar to display information not showing in the window.

A scroll bar is an elongated rectangle with stepping arrows at each end. The rectangular area between the stepping arrows is the scroll region. Within the scroll region is a control called a *slider*. The size of the slider indicates how much of the file or list is showing in the window. Figure 2-10 shows a window with a scroll bar.

There are several ways to use the scroll bar. The easiest way is to move your pointer to a stepping arrow and click on it. This

6	Calendar: BIFF$DUA2:[BYNON]DECW$CALENDAR_FILE.DWC;1		

File	Edit	View	Customize				Help

April, 1990

Wk	Sun	Mon	Tue	Wed	Thu	Fri	Sat
14	1	2	3	4	5	**6**	7
15	8	9	10	11	12	13	14
16	15	16	17	18	19	20	21
17	22	23	24	25	26	27	28
18	29	30					
''			1	2	3	4	5

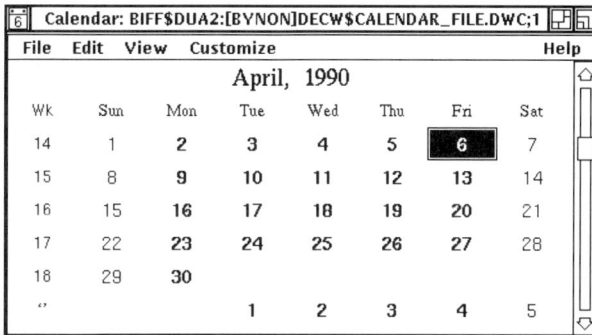

Figure 2-10. Window with Scroll Bar

will move the window one line or column in the direction of the stepping arrow. If you find this method too slow, click on the stepping arrow with <MB1> and hold.

Use the slider when you want to move quickly through the information in the window. Move your pointer to the slider, then drag the slider through the scrolling region. When you release <MB1>, the information relative to the slider position will be displayed.

DECwindows Menus

DECwindows has two basic menu types: pull-down and pop-up. Pull-down menus are the most common and are the only menus with titles. The titles of pull-down menus appear in the window's menu bar (see Figure 2-11).

To choose an item from a pull-down menu, position your pointer on the menu title and drag to the menu item you want. The menu will appear with a rectangular outline around the menu item you are selecting. When the rectangle is on the choice you want, release <MB1>. If you decide not to choose a menu item, simply move your pointer outside the menu and release <MB1>.

Some pull-down menus have submenus, indicated by a submenu icon (an arrow pointing to the right). To display a submenu, drag to the menu item you want, then drag right to the submenu

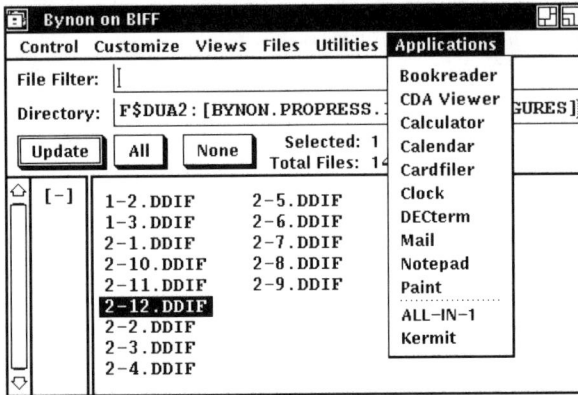

Figure 2-11. Window with Pull-Down Menu

icon. To choose a submenu item, release <MB1> when the rectangle is on the desired item.

Pop-up menus differ from pull-down menus in that they allow you to keep the pointer in the area where you're working. This eliminates the need to move the pointer back to the menu bar so frequently. The contents of a pop-up menu change in response to the location of your pointer and the current selection. Generally speaking, pop-up menus are invoked through pull-down menus or by the application itself.

The DECwindows Dialog Box

A dialog box is a window DECwindows uses to request input from the user. It contains various controls that you can manipulate. Most often, a dialog box is displayed in response to some action, such as clicking on a menu item. Dialog boxes may contain various controls, such as push buttons, option menus and list boxes. All dialog boxes will contain at least one push button for acknowledgment. There are six push buttons, as explained in Table 2-1. The FileView window, shown in Figure 2-12, is an example of a complex dialog box.
presented in a dialog box.

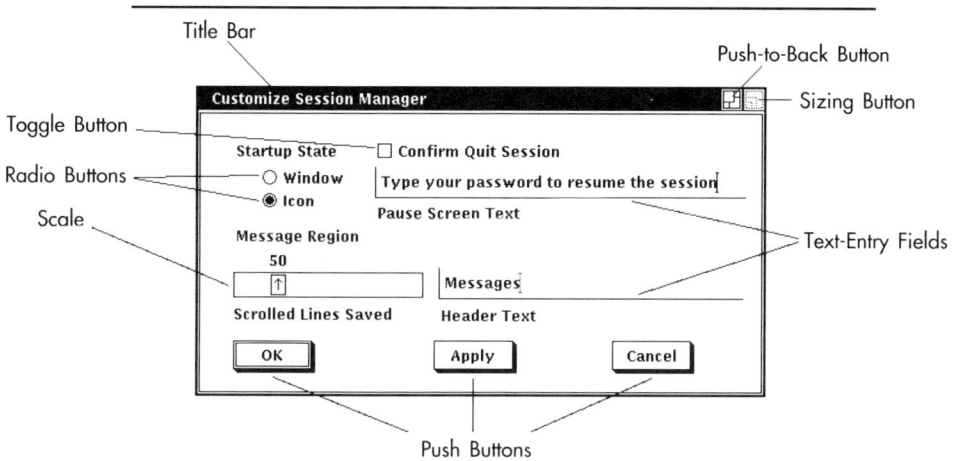

Figure 2-12. Session Manager's Customize Dialog Box

Table 2-1. Dialog Push Buttons

Button Name	Button Action
Apply	Supplies the current dialog box information and settings to the application program. You may continue to alter the settings until you are satisfied.
Cancel	Removes the dialog box without applying any changes you have made.
Dismiss	Same as Cancel.
No	Supplies a "no" answer to a question presented in a dialog box.
OK	Supplies the current settings and information in the dialog box to the application program and removes the dialog box.
Reset	Returns the dialog box settings to their original state before the dialog box was displayed.
Yes	Supplies a "yes" answer to a question presented in a dialog box.

Most dialog boxes will have a default push button assigned to them. A default push button provides you with the least destructive response. You can activate it by pressing <RETURN> or <ENTER>, or by clicking on it. A default push button is easily recognized by its bold (double-line) border.

Some dialog boxes include text entry fields, where you enter text. You can change the text in a text entry field by deleting the text with the <DELETE> key and typing new text. If a dialog box has more than one text entry field, the cursor will be located in the first text entry field when the dialog box appears on the screen. To move the cursor to the next text entry field, press the <TAB> key or move the pointer to the next text entry field and click on it.

Dialog boxes also can have option menus. An option menu is a type of pop-up menu. To make an option menu appear, move your pointer to the active area or item and press <MB2>. This action is specific to each application.

ENDING YOUR DECWINDOWS SESSION

Unless you're in a private office or your home, you should be concerned about leaving your workstation session unattended. If you want to leave the workstation for a short time, put your current session on hold by selecting the pause function from the Session menu in the Session Manager menu bar. The pause function will clear the screen and open a password dialog box. To resume your session, simply enter your VMS password.

If you plan to be away from your workstation for a long time, you should end your session. When you end a session, DECwindows stops all applications you have running, clears the screen, and returns the Start Session dialog box to the screen. To end your session, choose the Quit option from the Session menu.

WHERE TO GO FROM HERE

DECwindows and DECterm are fully documented in the *VMS DECwindows User's Guide*, which is part of Digital Equipment's VMS documentation set. In this book, you will find additional information on DECwindows in Chapter 7.

Chapter 3

The Digital Command Language

In order for a computer to work for you, there must be a common language that you and the computer understand. For VMS systems, the language is called the Digital Command Language (DCL). In this chapter we'll explore:

- ▼ The structure of a DCL command
- ▼ The use of default values with commands
- ▼ Command line editing and recall

UNDERSTANDING DCL

DCL is a command line interpreter. It lets you conduct a human-to-machine dialogue with your VAX by interpreting the commands you enter for the VAX to process.

DCL is built on a foundation of more than 200 commands called verbs. Each DCL verb acts on a parameter or an assumed parameter. The action of these verbs and the scope of their parameters can be modified with qualifiers. As software is added to your VAX system, the number of verbs will expand.

DCL is an interpretive computer language. There are rules governing the proper use of its commands, parameters and qualifiers. These rules are similar to the rules of grammar in the

English language. Commands, parameters and qualifiers must be used in a specific order and combination.

The rules of DCL's grammar are called its syntax. If you do not follow the rules, the VAX will display a DCL syntax error message on your screen. This indicates that the VAX does not understand your command.

DCL COMMAND STRUCTURE

Even though there are many DCL commands, DCL is easy to learn and use. The names used as DCL command verbs tell you exactly what each command will do. For example, if you want to get a printed copy of a letter called MY_LETTER, you would enter the command PRINT MY_LETTER. As in the English language, PRINT is a verb and MY_LETTER is the object of the verb. The subject of the command sentence (the VMS operating system) is always understood.

Command Line Components

Figure 3-1 shows the format of a DCL command. Only the command verb is required. All other components are optional.

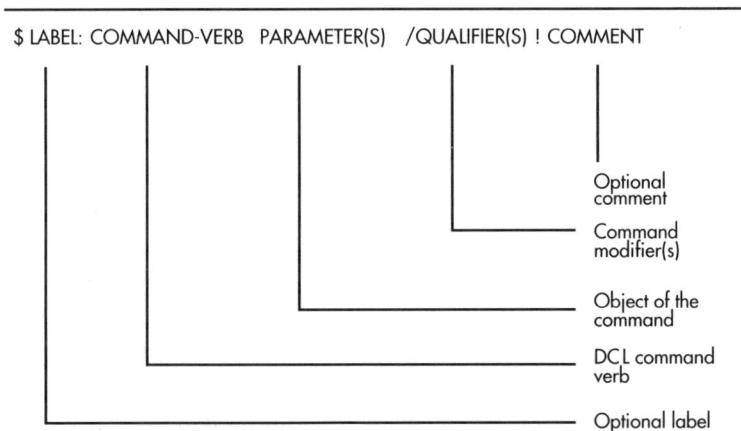

$ LABEL: COMMAND-VERB PARAMETER(S) /QUALIFIER(S) ! COMMENT

Optional comment

Command modifier(s)

Object of the command

DCL command verb

Optional label

Figure 3-1. DCL Command Structure

A *label* is an optional, user-specified string with a maximum length of 255 characters. Labels are used in command procedures, which are discussed in Chapter 9. When used, the label precedes the DCL command verb and is separated from it by a colon (:).

A DCL *command verb* defines the action the VMS operating system will take when the command line is interpreted. When commands are entered from the keyboard, the verb is always the first component of the command.

Parameters specify the object or list of objects the command verb will act on. You can specify multiple parameters on a single DCL command line, but the parameters must be separated from the command verb, qualifiers or other parameters by a space, multiple spaces or a tab.

Qualifiers further define or modify the function a DCL command will perform. They consist of a keyword, or a keyword followed by a value or list of values. The qualifier keyword must be preceded by a slash (/). There are three classes of qualifiers: parameter qualifiers, positional qualifiers and command qualifiers. You can specify more than one qualifier as long as each qualifier is preceded with a slash. Qualifiers are usually not required.

A *comment* is an optional, user-specified comment about the command. You will use comments in command procedures to document a command for future reference.

Command Case

You can enter DCL commands in uppercase, lowercase or both. DCL converts all commands to uppercase characters before interpreting them. You also can use multiple spaces or tabs where a single space or tab is allowed. DCL discards excess spaces and tabs.

Abbreviating Your Commands

Although most DCL command verbs have more than four or five letters, you can abbreviate them to their shortest unique length. For example, the DIRECTORY command has nine letters, but you can abbreviate the command to three letters: DIR. This saves key strokes.

In no case will you have to enter more than the first four characters of any DCL command, but the command you enter must be unique. In the next example, you will see what happens when only the first two characters of the DIRECTORY command are entered:

```
$ DI
%DCL-W-ADVERB, ambiguous command verb-supply more characters
$
```

The problem with this command is that DCL does not understand what you want because the characters "DI" are the first two letters in the commands DIRECTORY, DIFFERENCES, DISCONNECT and DISMOUNT. The command line interpreter has no way of knowing which command you wanted.

DCL Defaults

A default is a device, directory, filename or value automatically used by DCL when you do not supply a value yourself. In other words, a default value is a value assumed by VMS. For example, the TYPE command, used to display the contents of a file at your terminal, assumes a default file type of .LIS. If you have a file called APPOINTMENTS.LIS that you want to display on your screen, enter:

```
$ TYPE APPOINTMENTS
```

Remember that the file type must be .LIS for the default to work. If your file was named APPOINTMENTS.TXT, you would have to enter the full name. Otherwise, DCL would return an error message saying it cannot find the file. Default values are different for each command.

Command Parameters

Most DCL commands accept or require parameters. Parameters must be positioned in a specified order within the command, but you do not need to memorize them. If you enter a command that requires a parameter but omit the parameter, the command will prompt you for it.

For example, the COPY command requires you to enter the name of the file you are copying and the location you are copying it to. If you do not specify these two parameters, you will be prompted as follows:

```
$ COPY
$_From: (Enter your source file here.)
$_To: (Enter your destination file here.)
```

The same COPY command can be entered to DCL on a single line:

```
$ COPY MEMO.TXT MEMO_JUL27.TXT
```

This command instructs VMS to create a new file, MEMO_JUL27.TXT, and to copy the file MEMO.TXT into the new file.

You also can specify a list of parameters to be acted on. For example, if you have three chapters of a book you want to print, you would not enter three separate PRINT commands. Instead, you would specify a list of the files you want printed:

```
$ PRINT CHAPTER1.TXT,CHAPTER2.TXT,CHAPTER3.TXT
```

Parameters in a parameter list must be separated by commas. Remember that not all DCL commands accept parameter lists. These commands will respond with an error message.

Command Qualifiers

Qualifiers enable you to control specific attributes of DCL commands. Most DCL commands have qualifiers, although the qualifiers are never required to execute the basic command. For this reason, prompts are not presented, as they are with parameters, if you do not enter a qualifier.

Qualifiers are command-, position-, or parameter-oriented. A command qualifier applies to the whole command, and is placed at the end of the command. The following command demonstrates the use of a command qualifier acting on two parameters. The command displays a listing of two directories, using the /SIZE qualifier of the DIRECTORY command:

```
$ DIRECTORY [BYNON],[BYNON.PROCEDURES]/SIZE
Directory BIFF$DUA2:[BYNON]
LOGIN.COM;29 2
PROCEDURE.DIR;1          1
Total of 2 files, 3 blocks.

Directory BIFF$DUA2:[BYNON.PROCEDURES]
BANNER.COM;1 18
REMCOPY.COM;1    1
Total of 2 files, 19 blocks.
Grand total of 2 directories, 4 files, 22 blocks.
```

A positional qualifier takes on a different meaning depending on where it is located in the command. If a positional qualifier is placed after the command verb but before the first parameter, the qualifier will affect the entire command. If the same positional parameter is placed after a parameter, only that parameter will be affected. Consider, for example, the following PRINT commands:

```
$ PRINT/COPIES=3 MEMO1.TXT,MEMO2.TXT
$ PRINT MEMO1.TXT/COPIES=2,MEMO2.TXT
```

The first PRINT command requests that three copies of each file be printed. The second PRINT command requests that two copies of the first file but only one copy of the second file be printed.

A parameter qualifier affects only the parameter it follows. In the following example, MEMO1.TXT is sent to queue LASER and MEMO2.TXT is sent to queue LINEPRINT:

```
$ PRINT MEMO1.TXT/QUEUE=LASER,MEMO2.TXT/QUEUE=LINEPRINT
```

Qualifiers also can take the format of value qualifiers, positive/negative qualifiers, qualifier lists and default qualifiers. A value qualifier is one that accepts a value. You specify a value qualifier by appending an equal sign and a value to the qualifier name, as shown in this example:

```
$ PURGE *.*/KEEP=2
```

The PURGE command deletes old versions of a file. The /KEEP=2 qualifier tells the PURGE command to keep the two most recent file versions.

Positive/negative qualifiers take on a true or false value. You specify this by naming the qualifier or prefixing it with NO. In the first of the following examples, the broadcast feature of your terminal would be turned on and in the second it would be turned off:

```
$ SET TERMINAL/BROADCAST
$ SET TERMINAL/NOBROADCAST
```

Qualifier lists apply only to value qualifiers that can accept a list of values. You must enclose the values inside parentheses and separate them with commas, as demonstrated in this example, which removes jobs 28 and 31 from the SYS$BATCH queue:

```
$ DELETE/QUEUE/ENTRY=(28,31) SYS$BATCH
```

Default qualifiers are qualifiers used by default, even if you do not specify them. For example, the following DIRECTORY commands are the same because the /BRIEF qualifier is the DIRECTORY command default:

```
$ DIRECTORY *.*
$ DIRECTORY *.*/BRIEF
```

COMMAND LINE EDITING

A convenient feature of DCL is its ability to let you recall and edit command input lines. DCL stores the last 20 commands you have entered.

To recall a previous command line press the <UP ARROW> key. To display all commands in the DCL command buffer, enter the command:

```
$ RECALL /ALL
```

The resulting display will be similar to the following:

```
1 DIR
2 COPY CHAZ::DUB1:[BYNON]LOGIN.COM LOGIN.COM;1
3 EDIT LOGIN.COM
$
```

To recall a specific command from the command buffer, use the RECALL command with a command line number as the parameter, as in this example:

```
$ RECALL 2
$ COPY CHAZ::DUB1:[BYNON]LOGIN.COM LOGIN.COM;1
```

You also can recall a command by telling the RECALL command what you're looking for, as in this example:

```
$ RECALL ED
$ EDIT LOGIN.COM
```

In the example, the RECALL command recalls the first command in the command buffer with the characters "ED."

When you recall a command line, as in the examples, you can use the arrow keys and other editing keys to modify the command line. (See Appendix C for a list of editing keys.) The DCL command line editing and recall feature is useful when you are editing long command lines that contain typographical errors, or when you simply want to repeat a command.

THE TYPE-AHEAD BUFFER

One VMS feature that you will want to become familiar with is the type-ahead buffer, which enables you to type commands into your terminal while the VAX is processing another command. Commands are stored in the type-ahead buffer until the operating system is ready to accept them.

For instance, if you have directed the computer to list the users who are logged in to the system and to display this list at your terminal, you can enter additional commands before the computer finishes displaying the list. These commands will not be displayed or echoed on your screen as you enter them. They are loaded directly into the type-ahead buffer in sequential order.

As soon as the listing is complete, VMS will scan the type-ahead buffer and read the first command stored there. This command will appear on your screen when it is input to the command line interpreter for processing. When the system has finished processing this command, it scans the type-ahead buffer for additional commands, which it will read and process sequentially.

The type-ahead buffer lets you enter a series of commands or program responses as rapidly as you wish, even though the VAX may not be ready to act on them. You should exercise caution when using this feature, especially when buffered commands will affect previously entered commands that have not executed properly.

Table 3-1. Control Keys and Their Functions

Key	Function
<CTRL/A>	Allows you to insert, rather than overstrike, characters on a DCL command line.
<CTRL/C>	Interrupts the command being processed or the program being executed.
<CTRL/E>	Positions the cursor at the end of the line.
<CTRL/H>	Positions the cursors at the beginning of the line.
<CTRL/Q>	Enables (toggles on) output to the display after <CTRL/S> has been pressed. Use of the <HOLD SCREEN> key is preferred.
<CTRL/R>	Retypes the current input line and repositions the cursor at the end of the retyped line.
<CTRL/S>	Disables (toggles off) output to the display until <CTRL/Q> is pressed. Use of the <HOLD SCREEN> key is preferred.
<CTRL/U>	Discards the current input line and inserts a carriage return.
<CTRL/W>	Refreshes the screen.
<CTRL/X>	Flushes the type-ahead buffer.
<CTRL/Y>	Interrupts command or program execution and returns control to DCL.
<CTRL/Z>	Indicates the end of the file for data entered from the terminal, causing most commands and utilities to terminate.

DCL CONTROL KEY COMMANDS

DCL supports a number of control key functions. These functions are invoked by pressing the <CTRL> key and a specific alphabetic key simultaneously. Using the <CTRL/*letter*> combinations, you can perform special functions and issue or modify commands. Some common <CTRL/*letter*> functions recognized by DCL are listed and described in Table 3-1.

For a complete list of DCL control keys, refer to Appendix C.

INFORMATIONAL AND ERROR MESSAGES

VMS responds to some DCL commands with an informational message. This message tells you what the operating system has done in response to your command. For example, when you direct the system to print a file with the PRINT command, it responds with information about your request, as shown below:

```
$ PRINT LOGIN.COM
Job LOGIN (queue SYS$LASER, entry 316) started on HP$LASER
$
```

The information includes the name of your job (LOGIN), the job identification number (316), the print queue on which the job has been entered (SYS$LASER), and the name of the line printer on which it will be printed (HP$LASER).

Most DCL commands do not provide informational messages the way that PRINT does. In general, the only notification you will receive when a DCL command executes successfully is the DCL dollar sign prompt.

If you make a mistake when entering a DCL command or if the system cannot process the command, it will return an error

%FACILITY-L-IDENT, TEXT

Explanation of the error message

Abbreviated message text, for reference

Error severity (see codes below)

VAX/VMS facility or component (error source)

Message number: "%" = first, "-" = subsequent

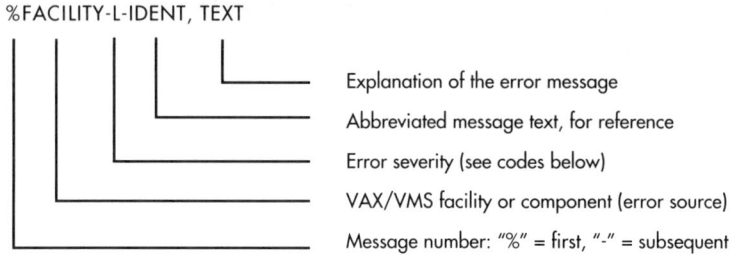

Figure 3-2. Error Message Format

message. If, at this point, you try to log out of the system by typing GOODBYE, the system will respond with a message such as this:

```
$ GOODBYE
%DCL-W-IVVERB, unrecognized command verb—check validity and spelling
\GOODBYE\
$
```

Error messages and informational messages conform to a standard format. The error message facility will report the source of the error or message, its severity, a mnemonic abbreviation of the error or message, and an explanation of the error or message. Figure 3-2 shows the format of an error message.

A percent sign (%) identifies the first message a facility issues for a given error. Subsequent messages issued for the same error begin with a hyphen (-).

The facility indicates the source of the error. The source may be the DCL command line interpreter, a VMS utility, or an application software package, such as a word processor.

The severity level indicator (L) will have one of the following values:

S — Successful completion
I — Information
W— Warning
E — Error
F — Fatal or severe error

Success and information messages let you know that the system has completed the function you requested. Warning messages indicate that some, but not all, the functions requested by your command have been performed. Error messages tell you that the output of your command or program is incorrect. Fatal messages indicate that your command or request has failed and the system cannot continue to process the command or request.

The *ident* is an abbreviation of the error message text. It can be used to look up the error and possible recovery procedures in the Digital Equipment *VAX/VMS System Messages* manual. In most cases, the ident and text will provide you with enough information to correct the error.

The text offers an explanation of the error message. For example, "file not found" is displayed when you try to do something to a file that does not exist.

When you encounter an error message that is not self-explanatory, turn to the *VAX/VMS System Messages* manual, where you will find all idents listed alphabetically.

ERROR RECOVERY PROCEDURES

The most common causes of errors are improper specification of a DCL command, improper use of a utility, or improper syntax. The following sections describe common errors and recovery procedures you should follow.

DCL Command Errors

If you have specified a command incorrectly, re-enter the command. Make sure you spell the command correctly and specify valid parameters or qualifiers. Be sure that your punctuation is correct. Check your use of asterisks, brackets, colons, commas, equal signs, parentheses and quotation marks. Use the <UP ARROW> key to recall and edit the commands.

You may receive error messages during the execution of an otherwise valid DCL command if the system cannot perform the functions called for by the command. For example, you might enter the TYPE command to display a nonexistent file. In this case, you will receive an error message stating that the file cannot be found.

File Specification Errors

Make sure that the file specification you have entered is complete and correct. If you are referencing a file in your default directory on your default disk, the filename and file type should be adequate for a file specification. More information is required if you are specifying a file located in another directory, on another disk, or on another network node. In these cases you must specify the directory, device name, and, if applicable, the network node name. This information is covered in detail in Chapter 4.

Utility Errors

If the error message returned by a utility does not provide enough information to correct the error, refer to the *VAX/VMS System Messages* manual for further information.

Programming Errors

If a program you are compiling or running "blows up" or finishes abnormally, check your program code for calls that it makes to external procedures or system services. Then, check the program logic. Make sure you have assigned logical names properly to files or peripheral devices used by the program.

System Errors

You will receive an error message if a peripheral device you attempt to use is unavailable, offline, or allocated to another user. Ready the device, place it online, or wait until you can allocate it for use. Fatal system software or hardware errors should be reported to your system manager.

WHERE TO GO FROM HERE

Several sources of information are available to assist you in learning more about DCL. The *VAX/VMS Digital Command Language Dictionary* provides a complete explanation of all DCL commands and the rules for their use. For a list of most DCL commands and their parameters, turn to Appendix A. Finally, don't forget the HELP command, which provides information on all DCL commands and VMS utilities.

In the next chapter, "Files and Directories," you will learn to use DCL to manage files and directories. After reading Chapter 4, you will be able to create, copy, modify and delete files using the most common DCL commands. DECwindows users should be interested to know that FileView, a DECwindows utility, makes file and directory management a snap. For an in-depth discussion of FileView, see Chapter 7.

Files and Directories

VMS offers a productive environment for storing, manipulating and organizing files. In this chapter, we'll explore:

- ▼ VMS files and their relationship to directories
- ▼ Components of a VMS file specification
- ▼ The use of wildcard characters to specify files and directories
- ▼ Common commands used to create and work with files
- ▼ Directories and the importance of logical names

WHAT IS A FILE?

A file is a collection of records (such as a line of text) stored on media such as a magnetic disk, optical disk, tape or cassette. Like a folder stored in a file cabinet, a computer file holds information. A file can contain a letter, computer program, mailing list, graphics image, or chapter of a book. Anything that can be represented by alphanumeric characters or numeric values can form a file.

To organize related files, VMS supports a special file called a directory. A directory holds the names and locations of files stored within it, in the same way a file cabinet holds individual documents. Directories are structured in a treelike manner, as shown in Figure 4-1.

```
                              [BYNON]
                    /            |            \
         [PROGRAMMING]           |         [WORD PROCESSING]
            /      \        LOGIN.COM          /        \
    [FORTRAN]    [MACRO]                   [BOOK]      [MEMOS]
        |           |                         |           |
  WINDOWS.FOR   DYRDRIVE.MAR             CHAP1.TXT     BOSS.TXT
  BROWSE.FOR    WHO.MAR                  CHAP2.TXT
                                         CHAP3.TXT
                                         CHAP4.TXT
```

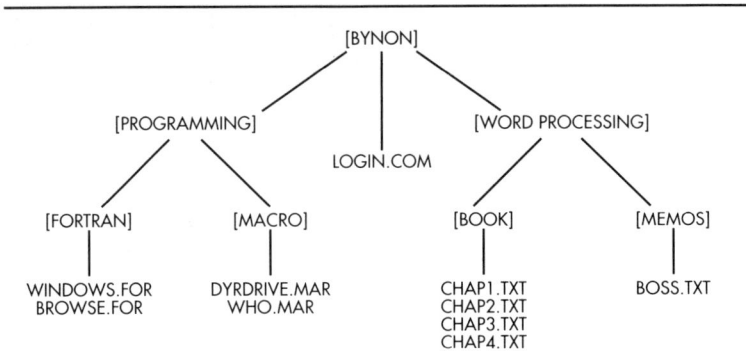

Figure 4-1. Directory Structure

The names in brackets represent directories and subdirectories. The other names are files stored within the directory above. Note that files and directories may reside in the same directory.

Files and directories are created by the computer user and the computer itself. Each time you use an editor to write a memo or letter, you are creating or modifying a file. The computer system creates and updates files in response to events, such as logins.

A VAX computer can manage thousands of files and directories, so there must be a way for you and the VAX to distinguish between them. This task is managed by both you and VMS. You give names to the files you create, and VMS assigns a unique identifier to each file. A file's identification number ensures that your memorandum to the boss doesn't get confused with another memorandum. The name you give a file is called its *file specification*.

THE VMS FILE SPECIFICATION

A file's specification describes its exact location and name. A complete file specification has a node name, device name, directory name, filename, file type and file version number. With this information, you can specify the location of any file on a single VAX system or on a network of VAX systems. Fortunately, you'll rarely have to use more than the filename and file type to locate a file.

VMS takes advantage of default values for the node name, device name, directory name and version number if you do not supply them. Figure 4-2 shows an example of a full file specification.

BIFF: :DUAØ: [BYNON.PROGRAMMING.FORTRAN]WINDOWS.FOR;3

node   device   directory   filename   type
                                                     version

Figure 4-2. Example of a Full File Specification

The following list briefly defines each component of the full file specification shown above.

Node name—Identifies a computer system in a DECnet network. A computer network is two or more computers connected together for the purpose of sharing information and resources. Each system in the network is called a node and is identified by a unique name. A DECnet node name is one to six characters in length and ends with a double colon (::). If your system is not part of a network, it does not have a node name.

Device name—The name of the storage device on which the file is stored. A device name can have up to 15 alphanumeric characters and ends with a colon (:). If you omit the device name in a file specification, your default device is assumed.

Directory—The name of the directory that holds the file. Directory names are hierarchical, separated by periods, and they must be enclosed in brackets [] or angle brackets. If you omit the directory name from a file specification, your default directory is assumed.

Filename—A name that identifies a file. Filenames should be as descriptive as possible.

File type—A code that indicates the type of information stored in the file. You can supply a file type of your choice, but most VMS utilities and commands rely on default file types. Refer to Appendix D for a list of the most common VMS file types.

Version number—An integer that the system assigns to a file. When a file is created, VMS assigns it a version number of 1. Each time the file is edited or another version of it is created, the version number is automatically incremented by 1. Alternatively, you can specify a version number of your choice.

File Specification Defaults

In most cases it isn't necessary to enter an entire file specification. If BIFF:: is your default node, or if your system is not considered a node in a network, you can omit the node name from your file specifications. If DUA1: is your default disk, you can omit the disk name when you reference files on that disk. For example, to see the contents of the file NOTES.TXT in your default directory, enter the following:

```
$ TYPE NOTES.TXT
```

This is easier than entering the full file specification, such as:

```
$ TYPE BIFF::DUA1:[SMITH]NOTES.TXT;8
```

If version eight of the NOTES.TXT file is the only version of NOTES.TXT, or if it's the highest version, you do not need to specify a version number. If you omit the version number, the highest version of the file you specify is selected.

There are two methods of identifying a specific version of a file. You can enter the exact version number that you want, or you can enter a negative version number. For example, if your directory contains the files NOTES.TXT;6, NOTES.TXT;7, and NOTES.TXT;8, you can display the contents of NOTES.TXT;6 at your terminal by entering:

```
$ TYPE NOTES.TXT;6
```

or

```
$ TYPE NOTES.TXT;-2
```

When you indicate a negative version number, the system counts back that number of versions from the highest version number. In the example, -2 instructs VMS to select the file that is two versions older than the highest version.

Rules for Assigning File Specifications

File specifications must be unique. No two files can have identical file specifications. You can have several hundred NOTES.TXT files in a directory, but you can never have more than one file named NOTES.TXT;8.

If you observe a few simple rules when creating and using VMS filenames, you'll avoid invalid file specification errors. The rules you should know are listed below.

Punctuation—The components of a file specification must be separated with punctuation characters recognized by VMS. The components and punctuation separators that must follow the components are:

node name	double colon (::)
device name	single colon (:)
directory name	left and right brackets ([...])
filename	period (.)
file type	semicolon (;)

Blank spaces—No blank spaces are permitted within a file specification. You can use an underscore (_), hyphen (-), or dollar sign ($) to simulate a blank space or separator as necessary.

Valid names—You can use alphanumeric names within a file specification. However, each element of a file specification may not exceed the maximum allowable length.

Maximum name lengths—Each portion of a file specification has a maximum allowable length, as follows:

node name	six characters
device name	four characters
directory name	39 characters
subdirectory name	39 characters
filename	39 characters
file type	39 characters
version number	Five decimal digits with a value between 1 and 32,767

FILENAME AND DIRECTORY WILDCARDS

VMS supports the use of wildcard characters in place of directory names, filenames, file types and file version numbers. A wildcard character is a character used to represent all or part of a filename when the filename is unknown or when the command is to be performed on more than one file. The use of wildcards saves you time and keystrokes.

WARNING: Always use wildcard characters in conjunction with the DELETE command with extreme care. The potential exists to delete many files with a single command.

File-Matching Wildcards

VMS recognizes two file-matching wildcard characters: the asterisk (*) and the percent sign (%). Use the asterisk as a substitute for the filename, file type or version number parts of a file specification. To match a single character within a filename or file type, use the percent sign.

The Asterisk Wildcard

To see how the asterisk wildcard works, assume that you need to print the files in a directory called [AUTOMOBILES.SEDANS]. Rather than entering the PRINT command for each file in the directory, enter the following:

```
$ PRINT [AUTOMOBILES.SEDANS]*.*
```

All files in the directory will be printed because the asterisk wildcard character is a valid substitute for the filename and file type. Even if your directory contains dozens of files, this single command will print all the files.

More examples that demonstrate the asterisk wildcard follow:

```
$ TYPE *.TXT
```

displays all files in the default directory with the file type .TXT.

```
$ DIRECTORY 1990.*
```

displays a directory listing of all files with the filename 1990.

```
$ DELETE *.TXT;*
```

deletes all versions of any file with the file type .TXT in the default directory.

The Percent Wildcard

The percent wildcard enables you to be even more selective when specifying files. Use the percent wildcard to identify all files that contain a single character in a given position. The percent sign identifies that position.

The following example demonstrates the selectivity of the percent sign wildcard. Assume that in addition to the 1990.TXT file, your directory also contains sequential files named 1975.TXT through 1989.TXT. If you want to print the files named 1980.TXT through 1989.TXT but suppress the printing of 1974.TXT through 1979.TXT, use the percent wildcard in the following manner:

```
$ PRINT 198%.TXT
```

This command prints any file that contains one character directly after the 8 in 198. However, it will not print the files 1974.TXT through 1979.TXT.

The percent wildcard permits you to be very selective specifying files with similar names. As you gain experience with VMS, wildcarding will save you time and keystrokes whenever you use a DCL command to work with more than one file.

The percent sign also is a valid wildcard character in a directory specification.

Directory Wildcards

In addition to filename wildcards, DCL recognizes two directory wildcards: the ellipsis [...] and the hyphen [-]. The ellipsis wildcard permits you to search down the hierarchy of a directory, as demonstrated in the following examples:

```
$ DIRECTORY [AUTOMOBILES...]1989.TXT
```

displays a directory listing of all files named 1989.TXT in the directory [AUTOMOBILES] and all subdirectories under [AUTOMOBILES].

```
$ TYPE [...SPORTS_CARS]1990.TXT
```

displays all files named 1990.TXT from the default directory to the [.SPORTS_CARS] subdirectory.

```
$ DELETE [...]1984.TXT;*
```

deletes all files in your default directory and all subdirectories under your default directory with the filename 1984.TXT.

```
$ COPY [*...]MODELS.TXT []
```

copies all files with the filename MODELS.TXT, in all directories on the default device, to your default directory.

The second directory wildcard, the hyphen, lets you search upward through a directory hierarchy. Each hyphen represents the next highest directory. Using the hyphen, you can move up a directory and then back down another path. For the following examples, assume a default directory of [AUTOMOBILES.COUPES]:

```
$ DIR [-]
```

displays a directory of all files in directory [AUTOMOBILES].

```
$ TYPE [-.SPORTS_CARS]*.*
```

displays all files in the directory [AUTOMOBILES.SPORTS_CARS].

You also can use the hyphen and ellipsis together, such as in this example:

```
$ COPY [-.SEDANS...] []
```

This combination copies all files in the directory [AUTOMOBILE.SEDANS] and all subdirectories under [AUTOMOBILE.SEDANS] to your default directory.

FILE OPERATIONS

Now that you know how to use file specifications and reference individual files or groups of files, you can learn some DCL commands used to create, move, modify or delete files.

Creating Files

The most versatile way to create or modify a file is with a text editor, but there are many other methods as well. This section discusses a few DCL commands that create files.

The CREATE command, although not often used, produces a file from text entered at the keyboard. We'll use CREATE as an example because we need a tool to create a file to use with other commands. The CREATE command requires a filename as a parameter. CREATE prompts you with a blank line to enter your text. When you have finished entering text, press <CTRL/Z>. For example:

```
$ CREATE ITALIAN_EXOTICS.TXT
Ferrari 246 Dino
Lamborghini Miura
Maserati 5000 GT
Ferrari 512 Boxer
Lancia Fulvia
Ferrari 348s
Lamborghini Countach
Testarossa
<CTRL/Z>
```

Press <RETURN> at the end of each line. Note that you cannot modify a line after you have pressed <RETURN>. If necessary, you can cancel the CREATE command by pressing <CTRL/C>. Pressing <CTRL/Z> tells the CREATE command that you're finished entering information and that you're ready for it to be saved. The CREATE command will write the text you entered to your new file and your DCL prompt will return.

Renaming Files

The RENAME command changes the name of a file and optionally relocates it to a different directory. The following example renames the file ITALIAN_EXOTICS.TXT to EXOTICS.TXT:

```
$ RENAME ITALIAN_EXOTICS.TXT EXOTICS.TXT
```

The next example renames the file and copies it to a new directory. After being renamed, the file EXOTICS.TXT no longer exists in the default directory:

```
$ RENAME EXOTICS.TXT [AUTOMOBILES.SPORTS_CARS]SPORTSCARS.TXT
```

NOTE: A file cannot be renamed to another device (e.g., RE-NAME DUA0:EXOTICS.TXT DUA6:[SPORTS_CARS]EXOTICS.TXT is not a valid command).

Copying Files

The COPY command creates a new file from the contents of one or more current files. In this example, the file ITALIAN_EXOTICS.TXT is copied to EXOTICS.TXT in the default directory:

```
$ COPY ITALIAN_EXOTICS.TXT EXOTICS.TXT
```

You also can use the COPY command to copy two or more files into a single new file:

```
$ COPY EXOTICS.TXT,PORSCHE.TXT,CORVETTE.TXT FAST.TXT
```

In this example, the three files separated by commas are combined to create a new file, FAST.TXT.

Appending Files

The APPEND command enables you to string files together. In the following example, the APPEND command appends a copy of the file PORSCHE.TXT to the end of EXOTICS.TXT:

```
$ APPEND PORSCHE.TXT EXOTICS.TXT
```

Unlike the COPY command, APPEND does not create a new file. The first file is appended to the end of the second file.

Deleting Files

To erase a file from the system, use the DELETE command. You must supply a filename, file type and version number. There are two exceptions to this rule: you can use the asterisk wildcard instead of the version number or file type, or you can delete the most recent version of a file by specifying a semicolon instead of the version number. Any of the following commands will delete the file named CORVETTE.TXT;1:

```
$ DELETE CORVETTE.TXT;1
$ DELETE CORVETTE.*;*
$ DELETE CORVETTE.TXT;*
```

When using wildcard characters to delete files, consider using the /CONFIRM qualifier to confirm each deletion, as in the following example:

```
$ DELETE *.TXT;* /CONFIRM
DUA1:[AUTOMOBILES.SPORTS_CARS]CORVETTE.TXT;3 delete? [N]:
DUA1:[AUTOMOBILES.SPORTS_CARS]PORSCHE.TXT;21 delete? [N]:
DUA1:[AUTOMOBILES.SPORTS_CARS]ITALIAN_EXOTICS.TXT;1 delete? [N]:
```

If you work at a site with special security requirements, you should use the /ERASE qualifier when deleting files. The DELETE command without /ERASE does not erase the file's data from the disk; it only makes the space available. The /ERASE qualifier instructs DELETE to overwrite the file with a predefined data pattern. Check with your system manager for more information.

Purging Files

Use the PURGE command to erase obsolete versions of your files. By default, the PURGE command erases all but the most recent version. In this first example, all obsolete files are purged:

```
$ PURGE
```

When you provide a file specification, you cannot specify a version number. This PURGE example will purge all files with the file type .TXT:

```
$ PURGE *.TXT
```

If you want to retain the most recent versions of a file, use the /KEEP qualifier:

```
$ PURGE /KEEP=2
```

With this command, the two highest versions of all files are retained.

Displaying Files

In previous examples, you used TYPE to display files at your terminal. If the file you want to display is lengthy, you can use the /PAGE qualifier to send the file to your screen one page at a time. After sending a page of the file to your screen, TYPE will wait until you press <RETURN> before continuing with the next page. For example:

```
$ TYPE /PAGE COUPES.TXT
```

An alternative is to use the EDT editor. To make sure that you do not modify the file, use the /READ_ONLY qualifier:

```
$ EDIT/EDT/READ_ONLY SEDANS.TXT
Pontiac 6ØØØ SE
BMW 325e
Ford LTD
Honda Accord
Nissan Maxima
[EOB]
*QUIT
$
```

When you're finished reading the file, press <CTRL/Z>, then enter QUIT. For more information about the EDT text editor, see Chapter 6.

Listing a File Directory

VMS files are organized in directories, which catalog groups of files. To list the files in a directory, use the DIRECTORY command:

```
$ DIRECTORY


Directory DUA1:[AUTOMOBILES.SEDANS]

1979.TXT;4
1980.TXT;2
1981.TXT;4
1982.TXT;1
1983.TXT;2
1984.TXT;1
1985.TXT;3
1986.TXT;1
1987.TXT;1
1988.TXT;1
1989.TXT;9
1990.TXT;3


Total of 12 files.
```

The DIRECTORY command has several qualifiers that control additional information listed with the directory output. For example, if you want to know the size (in blocks) of your files, use the /SIZE qualifier. The /PROTECTION qualifier will tell you the access protection of your files. The /FULL qualifier provides all information about a file, such as size, protection, creation date, and the date the file was last modified.

Printing Files

To produce a printed copy of a file, use the PRINT command. Under the control of VMS, files are not sent directly to a printing device (as they are on a PC). Instead, files are routed to a print queue, which holds files until the printer is free to print them.

When you submit a file to a print queue, the system displays an information message indicating the name of the file (the job name), the name of the queue to which it has been submitted, and the queue entry number assigned to your print job. A typical PRINT message is shown in this example:

```
$ PRINT SEDANS.TXT
 Job SEDANS (queue SYS$PRINT, entry 252) started on $LASER
```

The PRINT command has several qualifiers. The most common are /QUEUE and /COPIES. The /QUEUE qualifier tells the PRINT command where you want your file printed. Each print device is assigned its own queue. The default queue is called SYS$PRINT. In the following example, the file PORSCHE.TXT is printed by the SYS$COLOR queue:

```
$ PRINT PORSCHE.TXT /QUEUE=SYS$COLOR
 Job PORSCHE (queue SYS$COLOR, entry 253) started on $COLOR
```

If you want to print more than one copy of your file, use the /COPIES qualifier:

```
$ PRINT SEDANS.TXT /COPIES=3
 Job SEDANS (queue SYS$PRINT, entry 254) started on $LASER
```

DIRECTORY OPERATIONS

When your system manager created your account, he or she created a top-level (root) directory for you. The name of this directory and the name of the disk on which it resides are stored in a system database called the *System Authorization File*. This file tells VMS the location of your default disk and directory (i.e., your account). VMS uses this information each time you log in.

Creating Directories and Subdirectories

Within your default directory, you can create as many as seven levels of subdirectories. Each subdirectory can contain as many subdirectories as you wish, within the capacity of the disk. The ability to create and use subdirectories allows you to set up as many work spaces in your account as you need.

For each subdirectory you create, there is a corresponding directory file in the directory one level above it. A directory file is identified by the file type .DIR. The operating system uses the directory file to catalog the contents of the directory. You cannot store data in a directory file yourself. In general, all you can do with directory files is create them, rename them and delete them.

For the following example, assume that you have a root directory named [JONES] and want to create a subdirectory called BUDGET for your budget planning files. The command would be:

```
$ CREATE/DIRECTORY [JONES.BUDGET]
```

Directories are enclosed in brackets and subdirectory names are preceded with a period. If [JONES] is your default directory when you issue the CREATE/DIRECTORY command, the command can be shortened to:

```
$ CREATE/DIRECTORY [.BUDGET]
```

When you are in the root directory [JONES] and issue the DIRECTORY command, the BUDGET subdirectory will appear in the directory listing as BUDGET.DIR;1. None of the files contained in the BUDGET directory will be listed by the DIRECTORY command.

Setting a New Default Directory

When you log in, VMS establishes your login directory as the default directory. You can change your default directory to any directory or subdirectory that belongs to you or to which you have access.

Use the SET DEFAULT command to specify a new default working directory. If you will be working with files in a subdirectory, for example [.BUDGET], it makes sense to set your default directory to [.BUDGET] so you do not have to add a directory specification with each filename. The command is as follows:

```
$ SET DEFAULT [JONES.BUDGET]
```

If your current default directory is [JONES], you can shorten the command to:

```
$ SET DEFAULT [.BUDGET]
```

To return to the main directory [JONES], you can use these commands:

```
$ SET DEFAULT [JONES]
```

or

```
$ SET DEFAULT [-]
```

Deleting Directories and Subdirectories

You can delete a directory when you no longer need it. For the following example, assume that your default directory is [JONES.BUDGET] and you decide that you no longer need the [.BUDGET] subdirectory. To delete the BUDGET subdirectory, you would take the following steps:

1. Make sure that your default directory is one level above the subdirectory you plan to delete. Then, delete all the files in the subdirectory, or copy them to another subdirectory:

```
$ SET DEFAULT [JONES]
$ DELETE [JONES.BUDGET]*.*;*
```

2. The file protection of the subdirectory you're deleting must permit you to delete it:

```
$ SET PROTECTION=(O:D) BUDGET.DIR;1
```

3. Use the DELETE command to delete the subdirectory file:

```
$ DELETE BUDGET.DIR;1
```

You must reset the protection code on the subdirectory because by default, a subdirectory is protected against inadvertent deletion by its owner. You'll find more information on file protection codes in Chapter 5, "The VMS User Environment."

LOGICAL NAMES

A logical name is a substitute name for a file specification, a portion of a file specification, or another logical name. Logical names have two primary functions: file and device independence, and file specification shorthand.

File and Device Independence

File and device independence means that you are not constrained by a physical device name, such as DUA0: (a disk) or LCA0: (a printer). VMS allows you to achieve this independence through logical names that your system manager defines for systemwide use, or logical names that you define for files, directories and devices that you use.

To illustrate why device independence is so important, let's assume that you have a large database in the [DATABASES] directory called PARTS.DAT. The [DATABASES] directory is on a removable disk, which is normally mounted in drive DJA2:. All the programs you use to update the database reside in your default account on DUA1:. Because your programs and database are located in different directories and on different devices, you must use full file specifications in your programs.

Now, what happens if the physical disk drive DJA2: goes down? Will you wait until the drive is repaired before you access your database again? Or will you move the disk pack to another drive and modify your programs for the new file specification?

By using logical names, this problem is easily avoided. Using logical names, if your programs or data move to another physical device, all that's required is a simple command that redefines your logical name.

File Specification Shorthand

A byproduct of the logical name is a shorter file specification. If you commonly use files nested deep into subdirectories, with long names, or on devices other than your default, you can define a meaningful logical name equivalent to the filename. Such names are faster to type and easier to remember than the full file specification.

Defining Logical Names

To create a logical name, use the DEFINE command. The following example creates a logical name called PARTS$DATA that is equivalent to the filename DJA2:[DATABASES]PARTS.TXT:

```
$ DEFINE PARTS$DATA DJA2:[DATABASES]PARTS.TXT
```

You now can use the name PARTS$DATA anywhere you would reference the full file specification.

If the logical name represents a device, such as a tape drive, disk drive or terminal port, you must indicate this by terminating the equivalent name with a colon. For example:

```
$ DEFINE MY$MODEM TXA7:
```

Note that if you define a partial file specification, it must be the first part (left side), and it must be separated from the rest of the file specification with a colon. For example:

```
$ DEFINE COM USER$DISK:[FRED]*.COM
```

A logical name can be used with the DIRECTORY command (e.g., DIRECTORY COM) to list all .COM files in the directory USER$DISK:[FRED].

Displaying Logical Names

To display the definition of a logical name, use the SHOW LOGICAL command:

```
$ SHOW LOGICAL PARTS$DATA
"PARTS$DATA" = "DJA2:[DATABASES]PARTS.TXT" (LNM$PROCESS_TABLE)
```

In the example above, LNM$PROCESS_TABLE indicates that this logical name resides in your process logical name table (as opposed to the system logical name table or a group logical name table).

Deassigning Logical Names

If you must deassign a logical name (remove its definition from the system), use the DEASSIGN command, as in this example:

```
$ DEASSIGN PARTS$DATA
```

VMS deletes the logical names defined in your process logical name table when you log out.

System Default Logical Names

The VMS operating system defines a number of logical names when the system comes up. DCL uses these logical names to locate your login directory, default input device (the keyboard), and default output device (the screen).

A system default logical name is identified by the SYS$ prefix. You can use system logical names with interactive commands and within command procedures to handle input/output functions. (See Chapter 9, "Command Procedures," for more information.) Table 4-1 lists the most common system default logical names.

Logical Name Tables

Logical names are stored in system areas called logical name tables. VMS uses several types of logical name tables to separate system information from personal information. Some logical name tables are available to your process and its subprocesses, whereas others are available to all system users. The following four logical name tables are the most commonly used:

Group table—Contains the logical names available to all users in your user identification code (UIC) group.

Job table—Contains the logical names available to your process and any subprocesses it creates.

Process table—Contains the logical names available only to your process.

System table—Contains the logical names that may be used by all system users.

Table 4-1. System Default Logical Names

Logical Name	Equivalence Name
SYS$COMMAND	The initial file, or input stream, from which the DCL command line interprcter reads input data. The logical name SYS$COMMAND is equated to your terminal for interactive processes.
SYS$DISK	Your default login disk.
SYS$ERROR	The device on which the system displays all error and informational messages. By default, SYS$ERROR is assigned to your terminal for interactive processes. When your process runs in batch mode, SYS$ERROR is assigned to the batch job log file.
SYS$INPUT	The default file or input stream from which data and commands are read by either the DCL command line interpreter or programs executing in your account. By default, SYS$INPUT is equated with your terminal for interactive processes and with the batch job stream (or command procedure) for batch processes.

Table 4-1. System Default Logical Names (continued)

Logical Name	Equivalence Name
SYS$OUTPUT	The default file or output stream to which the DCL command line interpreter or a program executing in your account writes command responses or program output. By default, SYS$OUTPUT is equated with your terminal for interactive processes and with the batch job log file for batch processes.

WHERE TO GO FROM HERE

Only a handful of DCL file and directory commands was presented in this chapter. For more information, refer to the Digital Equipment *DCL Dictionary*, or turn to Appendix A in the back of this book.

Learning to manage your files and directories is an important step in becoming a productive VMS user. To learn more about the VMS user environment and VMS utilities, turn to the next chapter.

Chapter 5

The VMS User Environment

The VMS user environment is robust, secure, flexible and friendly. As a VMS user, you have an amazing amount of control over your environment. This chapter is designed to give you a better understanding of your account and working environment. In this chapter, you'll learn about:

▼ Your VMS account
▼ Processes and VMS resources
▼ Tailoring your account to suit your needs
▼ File protection and account security

USER ACCOUNTS

When authorized, your VAX system manager or other designated person will set up an account for you. Your account is identified to VMS by your username. In order to run a program, use a DCL command, or interact with the VAX in any other manner, you must be logged in to your account.

When you log in, VMS creates a process that represents you to the system. A process is the basic user entity known to the system. All work is done within the context of your process.

Later in this chapter, we'll show you how to view and change your process.

The User Authorization File

VMS allocates resources and privileges to you (your account) based on the information stored in the System User Authorization File (SYSUAF). The SYSUAF is controlled and modified by the system manager. It provides information used by VMS to control your account and environment. A record for each user is stored in the SYSUAF.

Your Account Name and Password

When you are issued an account, you are given a username that identifies you to the system and a password that verifies your access to the account. In most cases you will have control of your password and will be able to change it whenever you wish. Some sites with strict security requirements manage passwords through a security administrator.

User Identification Code

A user identification code (UIC) is an identifier VMS uses to identify users and groups of users. The UIC is the means by which VMS protects disks, directories, files and other objects. To VMS security, you are a subject of the system. Your files and directories are objects. By associating your account UIC with your files and directories, VMS knows that you have the right to access them. VMS prevents other users from accessing your files and directories because their UICs do not match yours.

A UIC may be specified as numeric or alphanumeric. A numeric UIC has two parts, a group and a member, specified in this format:

[group,member]

For example, UIC [130,103] identifies group 130, member 103. The group number is an octal number between 1 and 37776, and the member number is an octal number between 0 and 177776.

An alphanumeric UIC contains a member name and, optionally, a group name in the format:

[*member*] or [*group,member*]

For example, UIC [CONSULTANTS,WILLIS] identifies the group CONSULTANTS and the member WILLIS. The group and member names in an alphanumeric UIC may contain from 1 to 31 alphanumeric characters. Valid characters are A to Z, 0 to 9, underscore and the dollar sign.

PRIVILEGES, RESTRICTIONS AND RESOURCES

Depending on your particular requirements, the system manager will assign privileges and impose restrictions on your account in the SYSUAF, as explained below.

Resources and Quotas

Each system user is limited in his or her consumption of system resources, such as memory, CPU and input/output (I/O). These limits control the amount or rate at which your process, or any subprocesses you create, can consume a resource; for example, the number of files you can have open at one time, the number of subprocesses you can create, the amount of physical memory (working set) you can use, and the rate at which you may perform I/O.

Of the above resources, the memory working set is the most important because it determines the realistic job size you can process. Your working set defines the amount of available system memory your process can consume. VMS dynamically adjusts your working set size, between the parameters set in the SYSUAF, as the needs of the system and your process change.

Process Priority

As a multiuser system, VMS juggles many user processes and system processes to make sure that each process gets its work done. To keep this activity in balance, all processes have a priority that tells VMS the processing importance.

There are 32 levels of priority; 0 is the lowest and 31 the highest. The priorities are divided into two ranges: timesharing (0 to 15) and realtime (16 to 31). The default user priority is 4.

VMS operates on a highest-priority, first-served basis. Depending on what your process has been doing, VMS can raise your processing priority above the default value. This is typically the case if your process has been tied up doing disk I/O. VMS raises your priority because your process had to wait for the disk and therefore did not get the CPU time it would have otherwise.

Privileges

Privileges restrict the performance of select system activities to certain users. These restrictions protect the operating system's integrity and the integrity of the services it provides. The system manager grants privileges on the basis of need and the user's experience in using the privilege without disrupting other users.

There are 35 VMS privileges. They fall into seven categories classified by the amount of damage they can cause to the system:

- ▼ None—No privileges
- ▼ Normal—The minimum privilege needed to use the system effectively
- ▼ Group—The ability to affect members of the same UIC group
- ▼ Devour—The potential to consume noncritical systemwide resources
- ▼ System—The ability to interfere with normal system operation
- ▼ File—The potential to bypass file protection security
- ▼ All—The ability to take over or control the system

Access Restrictions

Access restrictions specify the hours and days you will be permitted to access the system locally, remotely, via a dial-up line, or via DECnet, and the hours permitted for batch jobs (see Figure 5-1). The system manager institutes the restrictions primarily for security or resource control.

Proxy Access

If you will be working in a DECnet network environment, the system manager or network manager can assign you proxy access privileges on the remote systems. Proxy access allows you to do remote file access or task-to-task communication without supplying your username and password in the command line. The difference is illustrated by the following commands:

```
$ DIRECTORY LIZ"WILLIS GANORMPH"::$DISK2:[WILLIS]*.DAT (without proxy)
$ DIRECTORY LIZ::$DISK2:[WILLIS]*.DAT      (with proxy)
```

Without proxy access to a remote DECnet node (computer), you must supply your username and password in the command. Not only does this make your command longer, but it also is a security risk if someone else can see your screen. Be sure to ask your system manager if proxy access is set up for you on the remote systems you need to access.

System Accounting

VMS systems keep a record of overall computer system usage (by account holder) in a system file called ACCOUNTING.DAT. The system manager and security manager use this file to produce reports with the Accounting utility. The Accounting utility indicates how the system is being used, how it performs, and, in some cases, how a particular user is using the system. The Accounting utility also may be used as a means of billing users for system usage.

```
Username:     T_BYNON          Owner:   TAMELA BYNON
Account:      T_BYNON          UIC:     [101,1]([T_BYNON])
CLI:          DCL              Tables:  DCLTABLES
Default:      USER$DISK2:[T_BYNON]
LGICMD:       LOGIN.COM
Login Flags:
Primary days: Mon Tue Wed Thu Fri
Secondary days:                 Sat Sun
Primary   00000000000111111111112222  Secondary 00000000000111111111112222
Day Hours 012345678901234567890123    Day Hours 012345678901234567890123
Network:  -----  No access  -----        -----  No access  -----
Batch:    -----  No access  -----        #####  Full access  ######
Local:    ##### Full access ######       #####  Full access  ######
Dialup:   ##### Full access ######       #####  Full access  ######
Remote:   -----  No access  -----        -----  No access  -----
Expiration:      (none)  Pwdminimum: 8  Login Fails:   0
Pwdlifetime:   60:00:00  Pwdchange: 19-JAN-1990 08:51
Last Login: 8-FEB-1990 16:48 (interactive), (none) (noninteractive)
Maxjobs:       0    Fillm:      60  Bytlm:         13408
Maxacctjobs:   0    Shrfillm:    0  Pbytlm:            0
Maxdetach:     0    BIOlm:      50  JTquota:        1024
Prclm:         2    DIOlm:      50  WSdef:           512
Prio:          4    ASTlm:      45  WSquo:          1024
Queprio:       0    TQElm:       0  WSextent:       2048
CPU: (none)        Enqlm:      200  Pgflquo:       10000
Authorized Privileges:
 TMPMBX NETMBX
Default Privileges:
 TMPMBX NETMBX
```

Figure 5-1. Sample SYSUAF Record

Disk Quotas

Every computer system has a limited information storage capability. To control this limited resource, VAX system managers impose disk quotas. Your disk quota is the maximum amount of disk space you can use.

If you exceed your disk quota, you will receive an error message and will be unable to create new files or edit existing files. If this occurs, you have three options: purge or delete obsolete files, copy or back up files to magnetic tape for future use, or ask the system manager to increase your disk quota.

To avoid exceeding your disk quota, it is a good idea to purge files regularly and to delete them when they are no longer valuable. Disk storage space is almost always at a premium. It takes the operating system longer to run programs, respond to commands, and process other users' requests as disks fill up with data because of system overhead—the amount of time the operating system must devote to managing disks and the files they contain.

In some instances, you may be required to share a quota and files with other users in your department or with other users working on the same project. In this case, each person has a unique username and password, and all project members have access to the same files.

LOGIN Command Procedure

One of the most useful tools of your VMS account is the LOGIN command procedure. A LOGIN command procedure is a file containing certain DCL commands. When you log in, VMS executes the commands in your LOGIN command procedure. You can use this file to customize your account to suit your needs. To view the commands in your LOGIN command procedure, enter the command:

```
$ TYPE/PAGE LOGIN.COM
```

Chapter 9 describes how to create and use command procedures.

EXPLORING THE USER ENVIRONMENT

There is a variety of information about your VMS environment, or process, that you can view or change using the SHOW, SET and DEFINE commands. In this section, we'll explore the VMS user environment and some commands you can use to obtain information about your process and working environment.

Who's on the System with Me?

Unless you are using a VAXstation, you are likely to be using the system at the same time as other users. It is often useful or necessary to see who else is logged in with you. This information is easily obtained with the SHOW USERS command:

```
$ SHOW USERS

   VAX/VMS User Processes at 21-FEB-1990 20:40:04.35
   Total number of users = 4, number of processes = 9


Username           Interactive         Subprocess        Batch
  BYNON                 3                   2
  SHIPMAN               1
  WILLIS                1                                   1
  T_BYNON               1
```

What Time Is It?

The VAX keeps an accurate clock that you can access through the SHOW TIME command:

```
$ SHOW TIME
21-FEB-1990 20:47:08
```

Displaying Terminal Characteristics

At times it will be necessary to change one or more characteristics of your terminal. For instance, you can change the number of characters per line from 80 to 132, or you can change line editing mode from overstrike to insert. To see the characteristics VMS has associated with your terminal, use the SHOW TERMINAL command. A display similar to Figure 5-2 will appear.

```
$ SHOW TERMINAL
Terminal: LTA17: Device_Type: VT300_Series Owner: LTA17: Username: BYNON

Input:     9600   LFfill: Ø   Width:  80   Parity: None
Output:    9600   CRfill: Ø   Page:   24


Terminal Characteristics:
Interactive        Echo                Type_ahead       No Escape
Hostsync           TTsync              Lowercase        Tab
Wrap               Scope               No Remote        Eightbit
Broadcast          No Readsync         No Form          Fulldup
No Modem           No Local_echo       No Autobaud      Hangup
No Brdcstmbx       No DMA              No Altypeahd     Set_speed
Line Editing       Insert Editing      No Fallback      No Dialup
No Secure Server   No Disconnect       No Pasthru       No Syspassword
SIXEL Graphics     No Soft Characters  Printer Port     Numeric Keypad
ANSI_CRT           Regis               No Block_mode    Advanced_video
Edit_mode          DEC_CRT             DEC_CRT2         DEC_CRT3
$
```

Figure 5-2. SHOW TERMINAL Display

From the output of this SHOW TERMINAL command, we can tell
that the terminal is not on a dial-up line (No Modem), the terminal has a printer port (Printer Port), and that the terminal is
a graphics terminal (SIXEL and Regis). We also can see that
the baud rate is set at 9600 and the width is set to 80 columns.

NOTE: For an explanation of each characteristic, use the Help
utility.

The SET TERMINAL command qualifiers correspond to the SHOW
TERMINAL display. You will use the SET TERMINAL command to
modify the characteristics of your terminal to suit your needs.

Changing Your Terminal's Line Width

You can set the number of characters or columns that appear on each line displayed by your VT200 or VT300 terminal to any value between 0 and 132 by using the command SET TERMINAL/WIDTH=n. If you specify /WIDTH=40, each line of text will have a maximum of 40 standard-size characters, and the line will take up half the screen's width. If the value you specify is greater than 80, your screen will display narrow characters.

For example, if you log in and enter SET TERMINAL/WIDTH=132, your terminal will display lines with up to 132 narrow characters. A 132-column display is compatible with the output of most line printers, and is useful when you want to see an on-screen preview of a document or text file before you send it to the line printer.

By default, lines that are output to your screen and are longer than the width characteristic will wrap. With wrapping enabled, your terminal automatically will perform a carriage return and a line feed when the number of characters on a line exceeds the value specified by the /WIDTH qualifier. You can disable wrapping with the SET TERMINAL/NOWRAP command. If you disable wrapping, characters will continue to be output at the last position on the same line even when they exceed the width of the screen.

Setting Your Terminal's Broadcast Mode

Using the VMS Mail and Phone utilities (discussed in Chapter 7), it is easy to communicate with other VAX users. When someone sends you new mail or tries to phone you at your terminal, your terminal bell rings.

If you are working on something important, and you do not wish to be disturbed by new mail or by other users phoning you, you can turn off terminal broadcasting. To do so, use the following SET TERMINAL command:

```
$ SET TERMINAL/NOBROADCAST
```

NOTE: This command also will suppress system-generated messages, such as shutdown notification.

You can turn the broadcast feature back on with the command:

```
$ SET TERMINAL/BROADCAST
```

A better way to shut out messages is with the command SET BROADCAST. SET BROADCAST lets you receive or shut off messages selectively. For example, if you want to shut off new mail and phone calls, but want other messages to reach you, issue this command:

```
$ SET BROADCAST=(NOMAIL,NOPHONE)
```

Other message class parameters are available for the SET BROADCAST command. Use HELP for a full listing:

```
$ HELP SET BROADCAST PARAMETERS
```

The Alternate Type-Ahead Buffer

On most VMS systems, the system manager defines a large buffer size for the alternate type-ahead buffer. If you find yourself overrunning the default type-ahead buffer, you should select the alternate:

```
$ SET TERMINAL/ALTYPEHD
```

Using the alternate type-ahead buffer also may solve buffer overflow problems when you are connecting to remote systems using the SET HOST/DTE command.

Terminal Line Editing Modes

As you become proficient in DCL, you'll discover that one of the most useful features is the ability to recall and edit your commands. Two line-editing modes are available—insert and overstrike. In insert mode, characters to the right of the cursor are pushed right as you type. In overstrike mode, characters

under the cursor are deleted and replaced by the characters you
type. The default mode is overstrike. To switch to insert mode
use the command:

```
$ SET TERMINAL/INSERT
```

From insert mode, you can change to overstrike mode with this
command:

```
$ SET TERMINAL/OVERSTRIKE
```

Regardless of which mode you choose as your default, you can
always select the other by pressing <CTRL/A>.

Defining Key Assignments

Using Digital Equipment VT200 and VT300 terminals and most
terminals that emulate them, you can define function keys and
keypad keys to represent certain commands. In this way, you
can invoke the commands you use most frequently with a single
keystroke. For example, if you regularly set your default to a
specific directory, or if you often use the PURGE command, you
can define function keys to execute these commands.

To define a function key, use the DEFINE/KEY command. The
DEFINE/KEY command takes the form

```
$ DEFINE/KEY key "dcl command"
```

where *key* is the name of the function key and *"dcl command"* is the
command string. In the following example, keys <PF1> and <PF2>
are defined to set a default and purge some files, respectively:

```
$ DEFINE/KEY PF1 "SET DEFAULT DUA3:[INVENTORY.SUPPLIES]"
%DCL-I-DEFKEY, DEFAULT key PF1 has been defined
$ DEFINE/KEY PF2 "PURGE DUA1:[DATABASES]*.RPT"
%DCL-I-DEFKEY, DEFAULT key PF2 has been defined
$
```

User-definable keys include <HELP>, <DO>, <F15> to <F18>, <E1> to <E6>, and <PF1> to <PF4>.

Key definitions made during a terminal session are deleted when you log out. To make these definitions permanent, include them in your LOGIN.COM file (see Chapter 9).

Displaying Key Assignments

To display the key assignments you have made, use the SHOW KEY command. This command works for all or individual keys you have defined:

```
$ SHOW KEY PF1
DEFAULT keypad definitions:
    PF1 = "SET DEFAULT DUA3:[INVENTORY.SUPPLIES]"
$
```

or

```
$ SHOW KEY/ALL
DEFAULT keypad definitions:
    PF1 = "SET DEFAULT DUA3:[INVENTORY.SUPPLIES]"
    PF2 = "PURGE DUA1:[DATABASES]*.RPT"
$
```

DEFINE/KEY Qualifiers

There are several DEFINE/KEY qualifiers that make key definitions more useful. Consider trying the following:

/NOECO   Suppresses displaying the key command when pressed.

/TERMINATE   Automatically terminates the key when pressed, as if you pressed the <RETURN> key.

/NOLOG   Suppresses the messages when the key is defined.

Consider this command:

```
$ DEFINE/KEY/TERMINATE/NOECHO/NOLOG PF1 "LOGOUT/BRIEF"
```

When this key is defined, the usual message "%DCL-I-DEFKEY, DEFAULT key PF1 has been defined" is not displayed, and when you press the key, you will be logged out immediately.

Deleting Key Assignments

You can delete your key definitions singly or as a group with the DCL DELETE/KEY command. This command removes the definition from the <PF2> key:

```
$ DELETE/KEY PF2
%DCL-I-DELKEY, DEFAULT key PF2 has been deleted
$
```

This command deletes all key definitions:

```
$ DELETE/KEY/ALL
%DCL-I-DELKEY, DEFAULT key PF1 has been deleted %DCL-I-DELKEY,
DEFAULT key PF2 has been deleted
$
```

Changing Your VMS Prompt

If you prefer a DCL prompt other than the default dollar sign, use the SET PROMPT command to define a prompt of your choice. For example, to change your system prompt to *What now?*, enter the following command:

```
$ SET PROMPT = "What now?"
What now?
```

As with key definitions, a personalized prompt will remain in effect only until you change it with another SET PROMPT

command or until you log out. To make your prompt text permanent, include the SET PROMPT command in your LOGIN.COM
file (see Chapter 9).

Displaying Information About Your Process

The SHOW PROCESS command provides a wide range of information about your process. Without qualifiers, the SHOW
PROCESS command gives a brief overview of process information:

```
$ SHOW PROCESS


11-FEB-1990 10:57:34.28                    User: BYNON
Pid: 00000042     Proc. name: BYNON_11   UIC: [BYNON]
Priority: 4       Default file spec: $DISK2:[BYNON.ALLIN1]
$
```

In this example, the SHOW PROCESS command displays the process identification number (PID), process name, priority, UIC
and default file specification. When you require more specific
information, use one of the SHOW PROCESS qualifiers, as in these
examples:

```
$ SHOW PROCESS/MEMORY


11-FEB-1990 10:57:47.76                     User: BYNON
 Process Dynamic Memory Area
 Current Size (bytes)   25600   Current Total Size (pages)   50
 Free Space (bytes)     21496   Space in Use (bytes)        4104
 Size of Largest Block  21424   Size of Smallest Block         8
 Number of Free Blocks      4   Free Blocks LEQU 32 Bytes      2
$
```

```
$ SHOW PROCESS/PRIVILEGES

11-FEB-1990 10:58:15.39                    User: BYNON
Process privileges:
 SYSNAM        may insert in system logical name table
 LOG_IO        may do logical I/O
 TMPMBX        may create temporary mailbox
 OPER          operator privilege
 NETMBX        may create network device

Process rights identifiers:
 INTERACTIVE
 LOCAL
$
```

```
$ SHOW PROCESS/ACCOUNTING

11-FEB-1990 11:16:30.93                    User: BYNON
 Accounting information:
 Buffered I/O count:    418   Peak working set size:   704
 Direct I/O count:      141   Peak virtual size:      3645
 Page faults:          1252   Mounted volumes:           0
 Images activated:       15
 Elapsed CPU time:  0 00:00:17.42
 Connect time:      0 01:02:37.78
$
```

```
$ SHOW PROCESS/QUOTA

11-FEB-1990 11:16:10.08                    User: BYNON
 Process Quotas:
 Account name: BYNON
 CPU limit:                     Infinite  Direct I/O limit:       50
 Buffered I/O byte count quota:     7824  Buffered I/O limit:     50
 Timer queue entry quota:             29  Open file quota:        35
 Paging file quota:                 6868  Subprocess quota:        4
 Default page fault cluster:          16  AST limit:              44
 Enqueue quota:                      160  Shared file limit:      30
 Max detached processes:               0  Max active jobs:         0
$
```

Modifying Your Process

Just as you can look at your process characteristics, you also can modify them to a limited extent. For example, if you have special privileges, in addition to the default VMS privileges, you can assign them to your process. The following examples illustrate some of the things you can do with the SET PROCESS command:

```
$ SET PROCESS/NAME="Valerie"
```

This command redefines your process name to the string you supply. Any utilities or DCL commands that display process names will reflect this change.

```
$ SET PROCESS/PRIVILEGES=OPER
```

As previously mentioned, if you have special privileges, you can assign them to your process. The SET PROCESS/PRIVILEGES command provides this service. To grant yourself more than one privilege, enclose the privilege names in parentheses, separating each name with a comma.

```
$ SET PROCESS/PRIORITY=3
```

In this example, the default processing priority is lowered from the default (4). You can always lower your process priority, but raising it requires the privilege to do so.

Displaying Device Information

VMS keeps a watchful eye on every device connected to the VAX. VMS knows who is using each device and the characteristics of each device. To see this information, use the SHOW DEVICES command.

The SHOW DEVICES command produces a list of all peripheral devices associated with your VMS system. You also can direct it to list the characteristics of a single device. To show a specific system device, enter the SHOW DEVICES command followed by the device name. The examples below illustrate the use of the SHOW DEVICES command and the related SHOW MAGTAPE and SHOW PRINTER commands.

The following example shows the output of the SHOW DEVICES command for all disk drives with a DU controller type:

```
$ SHOW DEVICE DU

Device          Device     Error     Volume    Free   Trans  Mnt
  Name          Status     Count     Label    Blocks  Count  Cnt
BIFF$DUA0:      Mounted      0      BIFF$V5    184113   221    1
BIFF$DUA1:      Mounted      0      BIFF$USER1 317265    14    1
BIFF$DUB2:      Mounted      0      BIFF$USER2 194913    21    1
BIFF$DUB3:      Mounted      0      BIFF$USER3 617265    14    1
```

This listing indicates the device names, labels, error count, free blocks and mount status.

To view the characteristics of a magnetic tape drive, use the SHOW MAGTAPE command. The listing below is for a tape drive called MUA0:

```
$ SHOW MAGTAPE MUA0:

Magtape BIFF$MUA0:, device type TK50, is online, file-oriented
device, available to cluster, error logging is enabled.
Error count              0     Operations completed             0
Owner process           ""     Owner UIC              ·        [0,0]
Owner process ID   00000000     Dev Prot S:RWED,O:RWED,G:RWED,W:RWED
Reference count          0     Default buffer size           2048
Density               1600     Format                   Normal-11

Volume status: no-unload on dismount, odd parity.
```

You can show the characteristics of a line printer with the SHOW PRINTER command. This listing is for a spooled line printer called LPA0:

```
$ SHOW PRINTER LPA0:
 LPA0: LP11, WIDTH=132, PAGE=64, NOCR, FF, UPPERCASE
       NOPASSALL, NOWRAP, NOPRINTALL
 Device spooled to BIFF$DUA0:
 $
```

Information and instructions for working with these and other physical devices are available in the *DCL Dictionary*, the *Guide to VMS Disk and Tape Operations*, and other Digital Equipment VMS reference manuals.

ACCOUNT AND FILE SECURITY

Security is one of the most important computer issues today. VMS offers users several ways to increase the security and integrity of their accounts. Users can increase the level of protection on their account or specific files; users also can set the protection on their entire account, specific directories or subdirectories, and specific files within directories or subdirectories.

UIC-Based Protection

The main element of VMS file protection is the user identification code. Although users with related tasks may share group numbers, their member numbers always remain unique. The system manager can permit or deny access to accounts based on the UIC structure that the system manager establishes for the system, and on the basis of access privileges assigned to individual accounts in the User Authorization File (UAF).

UIC Protection Codes

UIC-based protection permits access to be granted or denied based on protection codes that reflect four user categories: System, Owner, World and Group.

System — The system manager
Owner — The account owner
Group — Users in the same UIC group
World — All system users regardless of the UIC

Four types of file access can be granted or denied to members of the categories mentioned above:

Read (R) — The ability to read the contents of a file
Write (W) — The ability to create or modify a file
Execute (E) — The ability to run a program
Delete (D) — The ability to delete a file

In general, any category of user can be granted or denied file access with this protection scheme. There are two exceptions: Execute access and the System category. First, you can read a file in a subdirectory, with Execute access, if you know its filename and file type. Second, because System privileges include the ability to bypass all file protection, anyone within the System category can read a file.

Control access, or the ability to change the protection and ownership of a volume, is never specified in the UIC-based protection code. This is a fifth type of access that can be specified in an access control list. It is automatically granted to two user categories when VMS examines UIC-based protection. Because Control access grants the accessor of a file or device all privileges of the rightful owner of that object, users in the System and Owner categories receive Control access by default. The Group and World categories are denied Control access by default.

Default File Protection

When you create a file, it is protected by default values as follows:

System: RWED
Owner: RWED
Group: RE
World: NO ACCESS

Alternatively, file protection may be inherited from the directory in which the file is created, or from a previous version of the file. Note that each access type must be abbreviated to its first letter.

This default protection allows the system and account owner full access to the file. Members of the same UIC group can read files and execute programs, and users in the World category are denied any form of access.

At some installations, the system manager may change the default file protection values to increase security. To determine a file's level of protection, use the SHOW PROTECTION command. The default protection in the previous example would appear as follows:

```
$ SHOW PROTECTION
 SYSTEM=RWED, OWNER=RWED, GROUP=RE, WORLD=NO ACCESS
$
```

If you want to examine the protection of all files in a directory, use the DIRECTORY/PROTECTION command.

Modifying File Protection

The SET PROTECTION command increases security by allowing you to permit or deny account or file access to members of the four user categories.

To change the protection of a file, use the SET PROTECTION command:

```
$ SET PROTECTION=(O:RWE,G,W) LOGIN.COM
$ DIRECTORY /PROTECTION LOGIN.COM

Directory DUB1:[BYNON]

LOGIN.COM;2 (RWED,RWE,,)

Total of 1 file.
$
```

In this example, the account owner has Read, Write and Execute access to his or her LOGIN.COM file. The Group and World categories have no access, and System access remains unchanged.

Rules for specifying protection codes:

1. Access types must be abbreviated to one letter: R, W, E or D.

2. User categories may be spelled out or abbreviated.

3. Each user category must be separated from its access types with a colon.

4. If you specify multiple user categories, separate each with a comma and enclose the entire code in parentheses.

5. User categories and access types may be specified in any order.

6. If you include a user category but do not specify an access type for that category, access is automatically denied.

7. If you omit a user category, protection for that category remains unchanged.

If you reset a file's protection to grant other users access to it, remember that VMS evaluates directory protection before it interprets the protection codes applied to files within the directory. For example, you could grant World:R protection to a file, but a user in the World category could not read that file unless the directory containing the file also had World:R access.

You should not set your file protection to deny System access. This protection can be bypassed. However, if you do deny System access, your files will not be copied and saved by the Backup utility when it is run. So if your files become corrupted or unreadable, you will have no way to restore them.

The SET PROTECTION command can be very useful in another way. By removing Delete access from the Owner category, you can protect your important files from accidental erasure. This is easily done and can save you the time and effort involved in recreating a file deleted by mistake. However, restricting your own Delete access may complicate editing.

In summary, take the following actions when invoking file and directory protection in your account:

1. Deny World access to all directories and files containing personal or sensitive data.

2. After you edit a file with the EDT editor, invoke the SET PROTECTION command to restore the original protection assigned to the file. (EDT assigns your default protection to the files that it creates.)

3. To permit another user to run an executable image (.EXE file) but not copy it into another account, grant Execute access but deny Read access to the file.

4. To let another user access files in a directory or subdirectory by explicit filename and type but deny wildcard access to the files, assign Execute access and deny Read access to the files.

PASSWORD PROTECTION

The password is the first line of defense against unauthorized system use. At most VAX sites, you can use the SET PASSWORD command to change your account password whenever you want. However, there are exceptions to this rule, as well as restrictions that may be imposed on password selection and use at high security sites.

Changing Your Password

When you enter the SET PASSWORD command, VMS will prompt you for your old password, the new password and a verification of the new password to guard against unseen typing errors. If you mistype either the new password or the verification, your old password will remain unchanged. An example of this command is shown below. Note that none of your password entries is displayed or echoed as you type them at your terminal:

```
$ SET PASSWORD

 Old password: (Type in your current password.)
 New password: (Type in your new password.)
 Verification: (Type the new password again.)

$
```

Your password may consist of six to 31 alphanumeric characters. No blank spaces are allowed, but you can use the underscore character (_) to simulate a blank space. Some system managers will request that you choose a password longer than six characters. If you are not sure about the policy at your site, ask your system manager.

Selecting a Password

It is a good idea to select an obscure or random password of at least seven or eight characters and to change it frequently. Never use obvious passwords, such as a spouse's name, your license plate number, zip code, telephone number or birth date. Passwords such as these are too easily guessed by someone trying to break in to your account.

If you have trouble thinking of obscure passwords, VMS can help you with its password generator. The VMS password generator will produce, at random, five passwords from which you can choose. For example:

```
$ SET PASSWORD /GENERATE
Old password:


labiumlu          la-bi-um-lu
jeynzil           jeyn-zil
ilumyoo           i-lu-myoo
olhyzi            ol-hy-zi
locejpue          lo-cej-pue


Choose a new password from this list, or press RETURN.


New password:
Verification:
$
```

TERMINAL SECURITY

When you are finished using the system or you need to leave your terminal unattended for any length of time, make sure you log out. After typing the LOGOUT command, wait for the LOGOUT confirmation before you turn your terminal off or walk away. If you fail to log out, someone else can use your account and privileges. Remember, turning your terminal off does not log you out of your account.

If you are using a Digital Equipment VT terminal and somebody seems to be taking too much interest in what is on your screen, press the <SET-UP> key to clear the screen. Your display will return intact when you press the <SET-UP> key again.

If you notice anything unusual during your login and terminal session, notify your system manager immediately. An example might be the display of the "User authorization failure" message when you are certain you entered your password correctly. Another example might be an unexpected program crash that appears to log out your account and reprompt you for your username and password. Programs known as "password grabbers" trick you into thinking you are logging in; they take your username and password then disappear.

Depending on the degree of security at your installation, you may have to remove the paper from the console of a hardcopy terminal and dispose of it properly. The logout confirmation message includes your username. Because your username is currently valid on the system, knowledge of it would simplify the task of anyone attempting to break in to the system.

WHERE TO GO FROM HERE

This chapter covered most of what you'll need to know about your account, security, the user environment, and how to modify the environment to suit your needs. For more information on computer security, including a description of extra security measures that may be in use at your installation, refer to the Digital Equipment *VMS Guide to System Security*.

In the next chapter, you'll learn how to use EDT and EVE, two VMS text editors. If you are more interested in learning about electronic mail and other utilities, turn to Chapter 7.

Chapter 6

VMS Text Editors

To add to or modify a text file, you must use a text editor. A text editor is a program that is similar to a word processor. With a text editor you can insert, delete and rearrange text on your screen.

In this chapter, you'll learn about two VMS text editors: EDT and Extensible VAX Editor (EVE). Specifically, you will:

▼ Explore the text editor that is best for you
▼ Learn keypad editing commands
▼ Learn to tailor your text editor

Text editors are used for many tasks. Programmers use text editors to write source code, electronic mail users use a text editor to write mail messages, and writers use a text editor for text processing. You also can use a text editor to enter a series of DCL commands, called a command procedure, that you then can execute with a single command.

The two VMS text editors, EDT and EVE, have the same basic capabilities. You should choose the text editor you will use based on your experience and preference. If you have previous experience with VMS, you've probably been introduced to EDT.

The EDT editor is the original general-purpose VMS text editor. With EDT, you use the editing keypad and the numeric keypad to edit your text files. Using an EDT start-up file, you can easily define special keys and other EDT features.

EVE is a newer VMS text editor. It has the same basic functions as EDT, but you can easily adapt it to your editing needs. EVE is a Text Processing Utility (TPU) program. If you are familiar with the TPU language, you can modify EVE. This feature makes EVE a powerful tool for programmers and other computer professionals.

BASIC TEXT EDITING

As text editors, EDT and EVE share common functions, as described in the following sections.

Starting an Edit Session

Text editing refers to adding and modifying text in a file. The file's name and directory are managed by you. Unlike word processing files, text files do not have special formatting such as bold or underlining. A text file can be typed to your screen, and can be used for special applications such as command procedures or program source code.

To create a text file, use the EDIT command and an edit style qualifier: /EDT or /TPU. The /EDT qualifier invokes EDT and the /TPU qualifier invokes EVE. You must specify a filename parameter when you issue the command, as shown in this example:

```
$ EDIT/EDT MYFILE.TXT
```

or

```
$ EDIT/TPU MYFILE.TXT
```

When you issue either command, an editing session starts with the file you have named. Your screen will clear and you can begin typing. In the examples above, if MYFILE.TXT was an existing text file, the editor would load the file's contents into a workspace for you to edit.

The Editing Keypad

Both EDT and EVE make extensive use of the editing keypad (see Figure 6-1). The editing keypad has 12 keys clustered together. The keys are arranged in the order in which they are most frequently used.

The <HELP> key provides editor-specific help. When you press <HELP>, a screen is displayed that tells you to press the key or enter the command that you want information about.

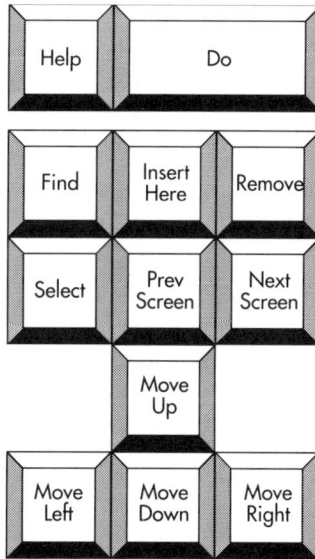

Figure 6-1. Editing Keypad

Moving Your Cursor

The arrow keys are located at the bottom of the editing keypad. Each key moves the cursor in the direction indicated by the arrow: left, right, up or down. Left and right cursor movement is character by character, while up and down movement is line by line. You cannot move the cursor where text has not been typed. In other words, the last line in your file is the last line to which you can move your cursor.

The <NEXT SCREEN> and <PREV SCREEN> keys move your cursor from one page to the next. The <NEXT SCREEN> key advances your cursor 20 lines. The <PREV SCREEN> key takes your cursor back 20 lines. Using these two keys is the fastest way to navigate between pages in your file.

Another easy method of moving your cursor through text is to use the <FIND> key. The <FIND> key invokes the editor's search function to search for a string of characters you specify. When you press <FIND>, you will be prompted to enter the search string. EDT prompts with *Search for*: and EVE prompts with *Forward Find*:. Enter the text string you want to find, then press <ENTER> (using EVE, you also can press <RETURN>). If the editor finds the search string, it will put your cursor on the first character.

Deleting Text

There are several ways to delete text with EDT and EVE. The fastest way to delete one or more characters is to use the delete key, marked <WORD CHAR> on the main keyboard (to the right of the plus sign). This key deletes characters to the left of the cursor.

If you want to delete a word, line or page of text, use the <SELECT> and <REMOVE> keys. First, move your cursor to the first character you want to delete, then press . Next, use the arrow keys (or other cursor movement keys) to move your cursor to the last character you want to delete. The editor will highlight the selected text as you move the cursor. Finally, press the <REMOVE> key to delet the text you have selected.

The select-and-remove method is the safest method of deleting text because your text is saved in a buffer. The buffer, called a cut buffer, will hold the text you have deleted until you delete text again, or until you leave the editor. If you need to restore (paste) the text, you can do so with a simple command.

To paste the text in your cut buffer with EDT, position your cursor to where you want the text, then press <PF1><KP6> (<KP6>

is the 6 key on the numeric keypad). The text you cut will be pasted back into your file.

To paste the text in your cut buffer with EVE, position your cursor to where you want your text, press <DO>, then enter PASTE and press <RETURN>. The text you cut then will be restored.

Saving Your Text File

When you have completed your editing session, you can save your work and return to the DCL prompt by exiting. This procedure is similar for both editors.

To exit from an EDT session, press <CTRL/Z>. When you press <CTRL/Z>, EDT will present an asterisk, its line mode prompt. At the line mode prompt, enter EXIT and press <RETURN>. EDT will save your work and return your DCL prompt.

To exit from an EVE editing session, press <CTRL/Z>. EVE will save your work and your DCL prompt will return.

Error Recovery

Whenever you are editing a file, the editor maintains a journal file. The journal file stores all the editing commands and text you have typed during the editing session. When you exit an editing session, your new file is saved and the journal file is deleted.

The journal file is used for recovery when your file is inadvertently lost because of a system failure or crash, because you have interrupted your session by pressing <CTRL/Y> or if you exceed your disk quota while editing. To recover an editing session using the journal file, enter the command:

```
$ EDIT/EDT/RECOVER file_spec
```

or

```
$ EDIT/TPU/RECOVER file_spec
```

The editor uses the journal file to reedit your file in the same way you did before the problem, showing a high-speed replay of your editing session on your screen. Do not touch the keyboard until the file is restored. You can type <CTRL/O> to suppress the video display during the recovery procedure, which will speed the file recovery process.

EDT COMMAND REFERENCE

EDT has three edit modes: *line, keypad* and *nokeypad*. The three modes often are used in combination with one another. Line mode is typically used only on hardcopy terminals. In line mode, you can work with a range of one or more lines of text. In nokeypad mode, keyboard commands are used to manipulate text on screen. In keypad mode, you use simple keystrokes to manipulate text on the screen. Only the keypad and line modes will be discussed in this chapter.

EDT enables you to redefine keys to suit your needs. To define keys permanently, enter the EDT commands in a file called an EDT start-up file. An EDT start-up file lets you set the specific editing characteristics you want before starting an editing session.

Starting an EDT Edit Session

To start an EDT edit session, use the following command:

```
$ EDIT/EDT filename
```

EDT will establish a working space for your file called a main buffer. A journal file buffer also is opened at this time. Both buffers typically require 80 blocks of disk space, so you must have a minimum of 160 free blocks in your account to use EDT effectively. A smaller buffer, called the paste buffer, is opened if the appropriate commands are issued, and you can create additional buffers to store segments of text.

If you are using EDT to create a new file, the editor will respond with:

```
Input file does not exist
[EOB]

*
```

The first line of this display informs you that no text was copied to the main buffer. The [EOB] symbol indicates the last line of the file. The asterisk, on the third line, is the EDT line mode prompt. To move from line mode to keypad mode, type CHANGE and press <RETURN>. Many system managers set up a default EDT start-up file called EDTINI.EDT, which enters the CHANGE command for you. If this is the case at your site, you do not have to enter CHANGE. (The asterisk will not appear on the third line.)

If you are editing an existing file, it is not changed by EDT. A copy of the file will be created and loaded into the main buffer, where text manipulation takes place. The copy in the main buffer does not become an actual file until you end your editing session with the EDT EXIT command.

EDT Keypad Mode Editing

Keypad mode EDT enables you to insert, delete, copy, substitute and rearrange text at a number of entity levels, including character, word, line, sentence, paragraph, page and buffer. Keypad mode editing often is referred to as screen-mode editing, because it enables you to edit text anywhere on the terminal screen, not just on a specific line of text.

When you use EDT's keypad mode, text is entered directly into EDT's main buffer as you type. The cursor on the terminal screen indicates exactly where characters will be placed, and the display is constantly updated as text is inserted or deleted.

You can move the cursor around the screen using the keyboard arrow keys, or by using the keypad commands TOP, BOTTOM, CHARACTER, WORD, LINE, EOL (end of line) and PAGE. More information on file manipulation in EDT is presented later in this chapter.

To enter EDT's keypad mode, invoke the editor and type CHANGE or C at the asterisk prompt. On a Digital Equipment VT terminal, the first 22 lines of text will be displayed. If you are creating a new file, the [EOB] symbol will appear in the upper left-hand corner of the screen.

Occasionally, you may receive this prompt:

```
C*
```

This is EDT's way of telling you that the terminal you are using is not compatible with a VT terminal, or that it is not configured correctly. If you are using a DEC VT terminal or a true compatible, you solve this problem by entering one of the following DCL commands:

```
$SET TERMINAL/INQUIRE
```

or

```
$SET TERMINAL VT100
```

You now can begin inserting text by typing it at the keyboard. Each time you press <RETURN> you create a new line. As your screen fills, the lines automatically scroll upward. To modify or manipulate text in keypad mode, use the numeric keypad to the far right of the main keyboard.

If the system sends (broadcasts) a message to your terminal screen during an editing session, the message will not be included in your text file. This informational message displayed on your screen will write over a portion of the text you are editing. You can erase these messages by pressing <CTRL/W> to refresh the screen.

If you want to switch from keypad mode to line mode EDT (to enter a series of line mode commands), press <CTRL/Z> . You will receive the line mode asterisk prompt.

VMS TEXT EDITORS 6-9

The EDT Keypad

The EDT keypad consists of the numeric keypad, arrow keys and the editing pad above the arrow keys. Different functions are assigned to each key when you are using the EDT editor. Figure 6-2 displays the layout and function names of the EDT keypad for VT200 and VT300 keyboards.

Each key (except the <GOLD> key and <HELP> key) has two functions. To select the "gold" function (or lower function) for a key, press the <GOLD> key, then press the desired function key.

Keypad Mode Commands and Functions

The EDT keypad mode commands are listed below. Refer to Figure 6-2 for the location of the keys you must press to invoke each command. Key names followed by (G) indicate a <GOLD> key sequence. To use these keypad commands, you must press the <GOLD> key before pressing the keypad key (e.g., press <GOLD><BOTTOM> to advance to the bottom of the file).

ADVANCE sets the cursor in its default mode. When EDT is in the ADVANCE mode the cursor moves forward by a character,

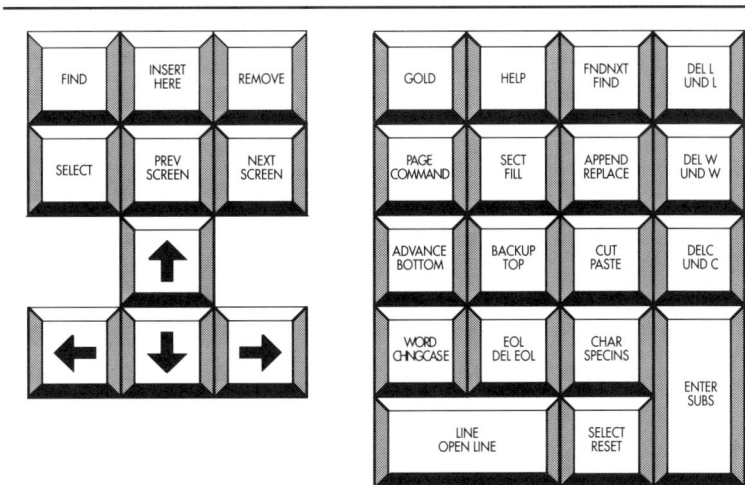

**Figure 6-2. EDT Keypad for VT200
and VT300 Terminals**

word, line or other entity. ADVANCE is the default mode; BACKUP is the alternate mode.

APPEND enables you to append the selected range of text to the end of the paste buffer. To use APPEND, select each passage or text entity (using the <SELECT> key), then press <APPEND>.

BACKUP sets cursor movement in a backward direction. This is useful if you are at the bottom of a file and want to search for a phrase without first returning to the top of the file.

BOTTOM (G) moves the cursor to the end of the file.

CHAR moves the cursor one character position in the current direction (set by ADVANCE or BACKUP).

CHANGE CASE changes the case (uppercase or lowercase) of the character or selected range of characters.

COMMAND (G) lets you enter a line mode EDT command while you are in keypad mode. The *Command*: prompt will appear at the bottom left of the screen. At the prompt, enter a valid line mode command, then press <ENTER> (not <RETURN>).

CUT and **PASTE** enable you to rearrange text within a file rapidly and easily. The **CUT** command removes a portion of text previously selected with the **SELECT** command and deposits it into the paste buffer.

DELETE CHARACTER deletes the character directly under the cursor.

DELETE LINE deletes the line to the right of the cursor.

DELETE WORD deletes the word to the right of the cursor.

ENTER terminates *Command*:, *Search for*:, and line mode commands.

EOL (end of line) moves the cursor to the end of the line on which it is positioned.

DELETE EOL (G) deletes the text between the cursor and the end of the line.

FILL (G) formats the selected range of text by filling lines with as many whole words as possible. This may be necessary after changing the line width with the SET WRAP command.

FIND (G) is used to locate text strings. At the bottom of the screen, the *Search for*: prompt appears. Type in the word or character string you want to find, then press <ENTER> (not <RETURN>).

FIND NEXT finds the next occurrence of a string specified with the FIND command.

GOLD invokes the gold function of the next key that is pressed.

HELP gives you access to EDT's online Help facility.

LINE moves the cursor to the beginning of the next line.

OPEN LINE (G) terminates the line at the current cursor position.

PASTE (G) places the contents of the paste buffer into your text file, starting at the cursor position. The contents of the paste buffer are not affected by the PASTE command. The contents of the paste buffer will be altered by subsequent CUT or APPEND commands.

REPLACE (G) deletes a selected range of text and replaces it with the contents of the paste buffer.

RESET (G) cancels the action of a <GOLD> key function, or any other key sequence, and sets EDT to the default cursor movement direction (ADVANCE). It also is useful for canceling or deselecting a range of selected text.

SECTION advances the cursor to the next section (screen) of the file. The direction of the cursor is affected by the current mode (ADVANCE or BACKUP).

SELECT is used by many keypad mode commands to perform their work on a range of text. To use SELECT, position the cursor at the beginning of the text to be selected, then press SELECT. Then move the cursor through the text you wish to select, using <ARROW>, <CHARACTER>, <WORD>, <EOL> or <LINE> keys. The selected text will be highlighted in reverse video. Enter the command that you wish to apply to the selected text.

SPECIAL INSERT (G) allows you to enter special characters, such as <ESC>, into your text file. To enter a special character into a file, first determine its ASCII equivalent (e.g., <ESC> = 27), then enter the following command string: <GOLD>27<GOLD> <SPECINS>.

SUBSTITUTE (G) replaces a range of selected text, or a text string found using <FIND> or <FIND NEXT>, with the contents of the paste buffer.

TOP (G) moves the cursor to the top of the file you are editing.

WORD moves the cursor one word forward or backward, depending on the current mode (ADVANCE or BACKUP).

UNDELETE CHARACTER (G) restores the last character deleted with the <DEL C> key at the current cursor location.

UNDELETE LINE (G) restores the last line deleted with the <DEL L> key at the current cursor location.

UNDELETE WORD (G) restores the last word deleted with the <DEL W> key at the current cursor location.

EDT also recognizes several keyboard keys and control keys as described in Table 6-1.

Table 6-1. EDT Keyboard and Control Keys

Key or Keys	Function
<F12>	Moves the cursor to the beginning of the current line.
<F13>	Deletes all characters from the cursor to the beginning of the word.
<RETURN>	Inserts a line terminator at the current cursor position.
<TAB>	Moves the cursor to the next tab stop (inserts a a horizontal tab character).
<CTRL/A>	Resets the indentation level count.
<CTRL/C>	Aborts the current EDT command.
<CTRL/E>	Increments the tab indentation count by one.
<CTRL/H>	Same as <F12>.
<CTRL/I>	Same as <TAB>.
<CTRL/J>	Same as <F13>.
<CTRL/L>	Inserts a form feed character.
<CTRL/U>	Deletes text from the cursor to the beginning of the line.
<CTRL/W>	Refreshes the display.
<CTRL/Z>	Changes the EDT mode from keypad to line mode.

Line Mode EDT

When you invoke EDT, you automatically enter line mode unless an EDTINI.EDT file is set up to do otherwise. Line mode is indicated by the EDT asterisk prompt. All line mode commands are issued at the asterisk prompt and are terminated by pressing <RETURN>. Lines that you input are sequentially numbered by the editor, and you can reference a line or group of lines based on these numbers.

Because EDT is generally used in the keypad mode, only a brief introduction to EDT's line mode commands will be made. Table 6-2 lists common line mode EDT commands and their functions. Each command may be abbreviated to the character or characters shown within the parentheses.

Exiting from an EDT Edit Session

To exit from an EDT editing session (to terminate keypad EDT), press <CTRL/Z>. This will put you into line mode. At the line mode asterisk prompt, type EXIT and press <RETURN>. EDT will terminate after writing a new output file containing the results of your editing session.

If you finish your editing session with the QUIT command or by typing <CTRL/Y>, the main buffer will be deleted and you will be left with the original file. This file will not reflect any changes made to it during the editing session.

Customizing EDT

You can customize your EDT editing environment by writing a start-up command file, which can contain any valid line mode commands. The editor reads the file at the beginning of each editing session. By including the appropriate commands in the file, you can direct EDT to automatically set tab stops, word wrapping, and edit mode for you, as well as define special function keys.

Some system managers will consider defining a systemwide EDT start-up command file for all users. Otherwise, the EDT editor

Table 6-2. EDT Line Mode Commands

EDT Command	Function
CHANGE (C)	Switches EDT from line to keypad mode.
COPY (CO)	Allows you to copy a line or group of lines from one part of a text file to another. If you enter the command CO 5 to 10, line 5 will be copied to the line immediately preceding line 10. The command CO 5:10 to 20 would copy the contents of lines 5 through 10 into the area immediately preceding line 20.
DELETE (D)	Enables you to delete a line or group of lines from a text file. The command D13 would delete line 13 from your text file, while the command D 13:30 would delete lines 13 through 30.
EXIT (EX)	Terminates your EDT editing session, saving all the changes made to your file during that session. EXIT also creates a new version of the file you have been editing.
HELP (H)	Provides online help for all EDT line mode commands. The help messages will not be included in the file that you are editing. HELP will give you more detailed information on the commands discussed in this section as well as the commands that were omitted, i.e., CLEAR, DEFINE, FILL and JOURNAL.
INCLUDE (INC)	Enables you to copy text from an external file into the file you are editing. This command is valuable if you frequently include stock or boilerplate text in your

Table 6-2. EDT Line Mode Commands (continued)

EDT Command	Function
INCLUDE (INC) (cont.)	files. When you enter the EDT command INCLUDE FILENAME.TYPE during an editing session, FILENAME.TYPE is copied into the file you are editing.
INSERT (I)	Inserts the text you specify directly before the current position in the file. While you are inserting text (either directly from the keyboard or by referencing another file), you will not receive the EDT * prompt. Press <CTRL/Z> to return to the * prompt when you have finished inserting text.
MOVE (M)	You cannot cut and paste with a line-oriented editor. However, EDT's line mode MOVE command allows you to move one or more lines of text. Text will be moved to the area immediately preceding a specified line. For example, the command M 10:15 to 50 would move lines 10 through 15 to the area immediately preceding line 50.
QUIT (QUIT)	Lets you exit EDT without saving the changes made during the editing session. No new version of the file is created, and the file remains as it was before the editing session. If you use the QUIT command on a file that you created during the current editing session, the file will be lost. If you exit EDT with the command QUIT/SAVE, a journal file will be provided. Using this journal file, you can re-create the changes that you made to a file. You also can restore a file that was created by an editing session.

Table 6-2. EDT Line Mode Commands (continued)

EDT Command	Function
REPLACE (R)	Deletes a specified line or group of lines, then enters the insert mode so you can add text in that space. The command R 5:10 would delete lines 5 through 10 and switch to the insert mode so that you can enter new text. To exit the replace mode and receive the *prompt, press <CTRL/Z>.
RESEQUENCE (RES)	Renumbers in increments of one all lines in the file that you are editing. This is useful because text insertion, movement or deletion causes the file to lose decimal numeric sequence. For example, 5 lines inserted before line 50 would be numbered 49.01, 49.02, 49.03, 49.04 and 49.05. Resequencing eliminates the confusion that can result from these numbering changes.
SUBSTITUTE (S)	Enables you to substitute a new text element for an old one, in the format S/old text/new text/range. The old and new text elements must be separated by slashes (/) and the range must be specified.
WRITE (WR)	Allows you to write a given range of text to a new file. For example, the command WR HISTORY.TXT 50:100 would cause lines 50 through 100 of the file that you are editing to be written into a new file called HISTORY.TXT. This command has no effect on the file you are editing. The command will only replicate the stated range of lines in an external file.

will search your default directory for your personal EDT start-up file (named EDTINI.EDT by default). If EDT finds a start-up file, it will execute the commands it contains.

Although a start-up command file can contain any commands available in line mode EDT, your file probably will consist of the DEFINE KEY and SET commands. The following EDT start-up command file demonstrates some of the things you can do:

```
! EDTINI.EDT
!
! Function Key Definitions
!
! Exit and quit commands
!
DEFINE KEY GOLD E AS "EXT EXIT."
DEFINE KEY GOLD Q AS "EXT QUIT."
!
! Replace command
!
DEFINE KEY GOLD S AS "EXT S/?*´REPLACE: ´/?*´ WITH:
´/WHOLE."
!
! Write and include commands
!
DEFINE KEY GOLD W AS "EXT WRITE ?*´WRITE TO FILE: ´."
DEFINE KEY GOLD X AS "EXT INCLUDE ?*´INCLUDE FILE: ´."
!
SET QUIET
!
! Define entity delimiters
!
SET ENTITY WORD ´ .,?!;:[]()*-+=/\´
SET ENTITY SENTENCE ´. ?!´
!
! Set line wrap
SET WRAP 72
SET MODE CHANGE
```

This is a very simple example of a start-up command file. To create a more sophisticated EDT initiator, refer to Digital Equipment's documentation for the EDT editor.

EVE COMMAND REFERENCE

EVE is a TPU program, which makes it a powerful tool for programmers and other computer professionals because it allows them to modify the editor to meet their needs.

Starting an EVE Edit Session

To start an EVE editing session, enter the EDIT/TPU command. You must include the name of the file you want to edit or create. For example, if you want to edit the site-specific start-up file, enter the command:

```
$ EDIT/TPU LOGIN.COM
```

This command loads the file and displays the following status lines at the bottom of the screen:

```
Buffer LOGIN.COM                    Insert
Forward


%TPU-S-FILEIN, 77 lines read from file LOGIN.COM;13
```

When you edit a file, EVE stores it in a work area called a buffer. The buffer name (in our example LOGIN.COM) and your current editing modes are displayed in a highlighted status line.

The contents of a buffer are displayed in an area of your screen called a buffer window. All editing on the contents of the buffer is performed through the buffer windows. When you finish editing, you instruct EVE to save or throw away the edited buffer contents.

```
┌──────────┐ ┌──────────┐ ┌──────────┐ ┌──────────┐
│   F11    │ │   F12    │ │   F13    │ │   F14    │
│ FORWARD  │ │ MOVE BY  │ │  ERASE   │ │  INSERT  │
│ REVERSE  │ │  LINE    │ │  WORD    │ │ OVERSTR  │
└──────────┘ └──────────┘ └──────────┘ └──────────┘

┌──────────┐ ┌─────────────────────────┐
│   HELP   │ │           DO            │
└──────────┘ └─────────────────────────┘

┌──────────┐ ┌──────────┐ ┌──────────┐
│   FIND   │ │  INSERT  │ │  REMOVE  │
│          │ │   HERE   │ │          │
└──────────┘ └──────────┘ └──────────┘
┌──────────┐ ┌──────────┐ ┌──────────┐
│  SELECT  │ │   PREV   │ │   NEXT   │
│          │ │  SCREEN  │ │  SCREEN  │
└──────────┘ └──────────┘ └──────────┘

              ┌────────┐
              │   ↑    │
              └────────┘
     ┌────────┐┌────────┐┌────────┐
     │   ←    ││   ↓    ││   →    │
     └────────┘└────────┘└────────┘
```

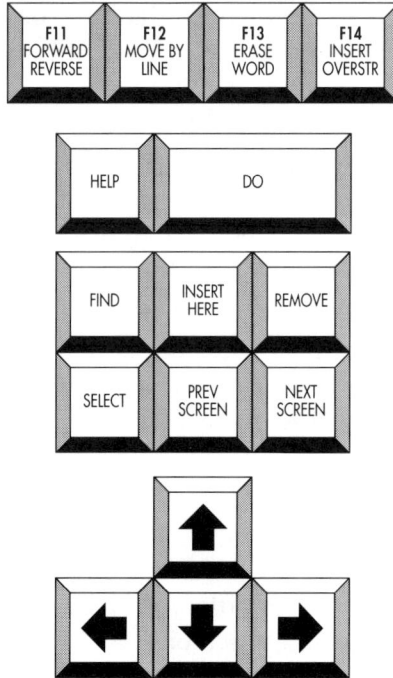

Figure 6-3. EVE Editing Keys

Using the EVE Keypad

Once you are in an EVE session, you can press EVE keypad keys and enter EVE commands to manipulate your text. Figure 6-3 shows the location of the EVE editing keys.

Table 6-3 lists the function of each EVE editing key.

Table 6-3. EVE Editing Key Functions

Command	Function
<EXIT>	Stores the contents of the current buffer in a new file.
<FORWARD/REVERSE>	Toggles between forward and reverse mode.
<MOVE BY LINE>	Moves the cursor to the next line. In the forward direction, the cursor moves to the end of the next line. In the reverse direction, the cursor moves to the beginning of the previous line.
<ERASE WORD>	Erases the word beneath the cursor or, if the cursor is not on a word, erases the next word.
<INSERT/OVERSTRIKE>	Toggles between text insert and text overstrike modes.
<HELP>	Displays a keypad help screen.
<DO>	Enables you to enter an EVE command. Press <DO> and then type the command at the *Command*: prompt. End the command by pressing <RETURN>.
<FIND>	Searches for a particular string of text. <FIND> will prompt you for the search string. When you are finished entering the string specified, press <RETURN>. To search for the last string specified, press <FIND> twice. <FIND> is not case-sensitive.

Table 6-3. EVE Editing Key Functions (continued)

Command	Function
<INSERT HERE>	Used to move and copy text. To copy text press <INSERT HERE> immediately after pressing <REMOVE>. This will put the text back in its original position. Then move the cursor to where you want to insert the text, and press <INSERT HERE> again to make another copy. To move a block of text, press <INSERT HERE> only after you have moved the cursor to the new position.
<REMOVE>	Cuts the text in the currently selected range.
<SELECT>	Selected range is a block of text on which various operations, such as <REMOVE>, can be performed. To create a selected range, put the cursor on the first character to be selected, press <SELECT>, then move the cursor to the last character to be selected.
<PREV SCREEN>	Moves the cursor vertically through the file, one screen of text at a time. The cursor moves backward, filling your screen with the previously entered lines of text.
<NEXT SCREEN>	Moves the cursor vertically through the file, one screen of text at a time. The cursor moves forward, filling your screen with the following lines of text.

EVE Commands

You can enter EVE commands at the EVE Command: prompt, which you invoke by pressing <DO>. After typing your EVE command, press <RETURN> or <DO>.

Like DCL, EVE allows you to abbreviate and recall commands. EVE will store your last 20 commands and will accept any command that is not ambiguous. If you make a typing mistake, you can use the DCL editing keys to correct it (i.e., <CTRL/U> to erase the line, <CTRL/A> to toggle insert/overstrike mode, and so on). Tables 6-4, 6-5 and 6-6 list the most common EVE commands.

Exiting from EVE

You can use either the EXIT or QUIT command to exit from an EVE editing session. When you use the EXIT command, EVE saves your editing session in a new version of the file. The QUIT command discards all your editing changes for the session you are ending.

NOTE: Once you exit an editing session using the QUIT command, there is no way for you to retrieve your previous editing changes.

To save your editing changes using the EXIT command, press <DO>, type EXIT at the *Command*: prompt, then press <RETURN>. Alternately, you may press <F10> or <CTRL/Z>, which duplicates the EXIT command. If you have made editing changes, EXIT will create a new version of the file with your modifications. For example:

```
<DO>
Command: EXIT <RETURN>
$
```

To exit from an editing session without saving the changes, press <DO>, type QUIT at the *Command*: prompt, then press <RETURN>. EVE will prompt you for confirmation:

```
<DO>
Command: QUIT <RETURN>
Buffer modifications will not be saved, continue (Y or N)?


Press <Y> then <RETURN>.
```

WHERE TO GO FROM HERE

For more detailed information on EDT and EVE, refer to Digital Equipment's *VMS General User's Manual*. In upcoming chapters, you will have a chance to test and sharpen your editing skills. In the next chapter, you'll learn to use electronic mail, an interoffice communication tool. You have the option of using either EDT or EVE to create your electronic messages.

Table 6-4. EVE Text Delete and Restore Commands

Command	Function
ERASE CHARACTER	Deletes the character under the cursor.
ERASE LINE	Deletes the line.
ERASE PREVIOUS WORD	Deletes the word to the left of the cursor.
ERASE START OF LINE	Deletes all characters left of the cursor to the beginning of the line.
ERASE WORD	Erases the word below the cursor or the next word.
RESTORE	Restores, at the current cursor location, the character, word, line or sentence most recently deleted with an ERASE command or an editing key.
RESTORE CHARACTER	Restores, at the current cursor position, the last character deleted by a command or an editing key.
RESTORE LINE	Restores, at the current cursor position, the last line deleted by a command or an editing key.
RESTORE WORD	Restores, at the current cursor position, the last word erased by a command or an editing key.

Table 6-5. EVE Cursor Commands

Command	Function
BOTTOM	Moves the cursor to the end of the buffer.
BUFFER	Puts the specified buffer in the current window and moves the cursor to the end of the new buffer.
END OF LINE	Moves the cursor to the end of the line.
LINE	Moves the cursor to the beginning of a line that you specify by its number.
MOVE BY LINE	Moves the cursor to the beginning or end of a line, depending on the direction specified.
MOVE BY PAGE	Moves the cursor to the next page break.
MOVE BY WORD	Moves the cursor one word forward or backward, depending on the direction specified.
NEXT SCREEN	Scrolls the next screen of text into the window. The cursor remains at the same position on the screen.
NEXT WINDOW	Moves the cursor to the next window on your screen (if another exists).
PREVIOUS WINDOW	Moves the cursor to the previous window you were editing (if one exists).
START OF LINE	Moves the cursor to the beginning of the line.
TOP	Puts the cursor at the top of the file.

Table 6-6. EVE Text Formatting Commands

Command	Function
CAPITALIZE WORD	Capitalizes a word or selected range of text highlighted by the <FIND> or <SELECT> function keys.
CENTER LINE	Centers the current line of text.
FILL	Reformats the current paragraph or selected range of text according to the margins set for the buffer.
FILL PARAGRAPH	Reformats the current paragraph according to the margins set for the buffer.
INSERT PAGE BREAK	Inserts a form feed character.
SET LEFT MARGIN	Establishes a new left margin for the current buffer.
SET RIGHT MARGIN	Establishes a new right margin for the current buffer. The right margin must be greater than the left margin.
SET TABS AT	Sets tab stops at the locations you specify.
SET TABS EVERY	Sets tabs at the specified interval.
SET TABS VISIBLE	Displays tabs as characters on the screen.
SET TABS INVISIBLE	Prevents tabs from appearing on the screen.
SET WIDTH	Establishes the width of lines displayed on the screen (e.g., 80 or 132 columns).
SET WRAP	Enables word wrapping at the location specified.
SET NOWRAP	Disables word wrap.

Chapter 7

VMS Mail, Phone and DECwindows FileView

This chapter introduces the VMS Mail and Phone utilities and the DECwindows FileView application. In this chapter, you'll learn how to:

   ▼ Use VMS Mail to send electronic messages. You're likely to use this utility almost every day.
   ▼ Use the Phone utility to communicate with other VAX users.
   ▼ Use FileView as a DECwindows interface to DCL.

VMS MAIL

VMS Mail is a utility you use to exchange messages with other VAX users. Using Mail, you conveniently can send, receive and store electronic messages and files at your terminal.

If another VAX user sends you electronic mail, VMS will notify you in several ways. If you are logged in, a message will appear on your terminal screen. For example:

```
New mail on node BIFF from BIFF::BYNON
```

If you are not logged in, you will be notified the next time you log in. If messages have been sent to you since the last time you logged in, you will receive a message when you log in. For example:

```
You have 3 new messages.
```

The best way to begin exploring Mail capabilities is to send mail to yourself. The next section explains how to do this.

Sending Mail

You can send mail interactively or directly. With the interactive method, you use Mail in a conversational fashion. You would use the direct method if you wanted to send a file as mail.

The interactive method is the most common method. To start Mail, enter the MAIL command:

```
$ MAIL
MAIL>
```

At the MAIL prompt, enter the SEND command. Mail will prompt you for the name of the user to whom you want to send your message and for the subject of the message. After you enter the addressee and subject information, Mail will give you instructions to complete or abort the message. For example:

```
MAIL> SEND
To:   WILLIS
Subj: Trip to Florida
Enter your message below. Press CTRL/Z when complete, or CTRL/C
to quit:
Lee,
Let's take the early flight on Saturday. We can be on the beach
by noon!

David <CTRL/Z>
```

The message is completed when you press <CTRL/Z>, at which time it will be sent.

To send the same message to multiple users, supply a list of names at the To: prompt:

```
MAIL> SEND
To: WILLIS,SHIPMAN . . .
```

To send a message to a user on another system, specify the node name, then the user's name. For example:

```
MAIL> SEND
To: CHAZ::SMITH . . .
```

If you are creating a long message, you can use the Mail SEND command with the /EDIT qualifier. When you use SEND/EDIT, your default editor will start. To send the message after you have typed it, exit normally from the edit session. (For more information about exiting, refer to Chapter 6.) If you use the QUIT command to end the edit session, the message will be aborted and you will be returned to the MAIL prompt.

Sending a File as Mail

The second way to send mail is to use the MAIL command at your DCL prompt with two parameters: a filename and a username. For example:

```
$ MAIL LOGIN.COM WILLIS /SUBJECT="My LOGIN procedure"
$ MAIL SCHEDULE.TXT LIZ::SHIPMAN /SUBJECT="Schedule"
```

The first example sends the file LOGIN.COM to user Willis, and the second sends SCHEDULE.TXT to user Shipman on VAX node LIZ. The /SUBJECT qualifier is optional.

You also can send a file as mail from the MAIL prompt. To do so, simply enter the filename after the SEND command. Using the

SEND/EDIT command, you can edit the file before it is sent. The following example demonstrates:

```
MAIL> SEND LOGIN.COM
To:   WILLIS
Subj: My LOGIN procedure

MAIL>
```

After the file is sent to the addressee, the MAIL prompt returns.

Reading Your Mail

When you start Mail, you will be informed if you have new mail waiting to be read:

```
$ MAIL


You have 1 new message.
```

To read your new mail, use the READ command. READ, the default Mail command, displays your messages on the screen one page at a time. For example:

```
MAIL> READ
#1              24-FEB-1990 15:45:29.93              NEWMAIL
From: BIFF::BYNON              "David Bynon"
To:   WILLIS
CC:
Subj: Trip to Florida


Lee,


Let's take the early flight on Saturday. We can be on the beach
by noon!


David


MAIL>
```

Pressing <RETURN> is the same as entering the READ command. So to read new mail, simply press <RETURN>. The message will appear on your screen. If the message is longer than one screen, Mail will put the message "Press RETURN for more..." at the bottom of the screen. To continue reading the message, press <RETURN> again. If you want, you can enter a new Mail command at the prompt. You do not have to finish reading the message before entering the next command.

When you receive more than one new message, you can choose the first message you want to read by entering its number. To see a listing of your new messages, use the DIRECTORY command:

```
MAIL> DIRECTORY                                          NEWMAIL
    # From              Date                Subject

    1 BIFF::BYNON       24-FEB-1990         Trip to Florida
    2 BIFF::SHIPMAN     24-FEB-1990         When are you going?

MAIL> READ 2
.
.
.
```

In the above example, the DIRECTORY command lists the new messages. The READ command tells Mail to display message number 2.

Finally, to read messages you receive while you are in Mail, use the READ/NEW command. This command is equivalent to entering the SELECT command to select new messages and the READ command.

Replying and Forwarding

At times, you will receive a message that requires a response, or you will get a message that also should have been sent to someone else. For these situations, Mail has the REPLY and FORWARD commands.

Use the REPLY command to reply to the message you have just read. This command works like the SEND command, except that Mail does not prompt you for an addressee or subject. Instead, it takes this information from the message to which you are replying:

```
MAIL> REPLY
To:      BIFF::BYNON
Subj:    RE: Trip to Florida
Enter your message below. Press CTRL/Z when complete, or CTRL/C
to quit:

David: Sounds good...let's do it! Are you sure you don't want to
ride the bikes down?
Lee
```

Use the /EDIT qualifier with REPLY to invoke your default editor.

The FORWARD command sends a copy of the message you have just read to one or more users. Mail will prompt you for the usernames with the To: prompt. You can cancel the FORWARD command by pressing <CTRL /C>.

Mail Folders

VMS Mail uses folders to store and organize your messages. There are three default folders — Newmail, Mail and Wastebasket — but you can create as many folders as you like. The Newmail folder stores your new mail messages until you read them. Once you have read a new message, Mail automatically moves it to the Mail folder, which is your default folder. The Wastebasket folder is a temporary folder that stores messages you have deleted. The deleted messages remain in this folder until you exit from Mail. At that time, the Wastebasket folder is emptied.

Creating Your Own Folders

You can create folders in which to store and organize your messages. To create a folder, use the FILE command. If you want to

place a message into a folder, you first must select the message
by reading it, then enter the FILE command and a folder name.
If you try to move a message to a nonexistent folder, VMS Mail
will inform you that the folder does not exist and will ask you if
you want to create it. Respond by entering Y or YES, and Mail
will create the new folder.

The following example demonstrates how to create a new folder
in which to store message number 1:

```
MAIL> READ 1
  •

  •

  •
MAIL> FILE PERSONAL

Folder PERSONAL does not exist.
Do you want to create it (Y/N, default is N)? Y
MAIL-I-NEWFOLDER, folder PERSONAL created
MAIL>
```

Moving Between Folders

Use the SELECT command to move from one folder to another.
For example, if you type SELECT PERSONAL at the MAIL prompt,
then your default folder becomes PERSONAL. Mail will respond
with a message that lists the number of messages contained in
the folder you have selected. For example:

```
MAIL> SELECT PERSONAL
  MAIL-I-SELECTED, 1 message selected
MAIL>
```

To list the names of your folders, use the DIRECTORY/FOLDER command, as illustrated in the next example:

```
MAIL> DIRECTORY/FOLDERS
Listing of folders in SKIP$DUB1:[BYNON.MAIL]MAIL.MAI;1
     Press CTRL/C to cancel listing
IMPORTANT_STUFF
MAIL
MEMOS
PERSONAL
WASTEBASKET
MAIL>
```

Deleting Old Messages and Folders

If a message is not important, you should delete it after you have read it. Doing so reduces wasted disk space and makes important messages easier to find.

Use the DELETE command to delete unwanted messages. The DELETE command accepts a message number as a parameter or, optionally, deletes the current message.

When you delete a message, it is moved to your Wastebasket folder. If you accidentally delete a message, you can retrieve it by selecting the Wastebasket folder and refiling the message with the FILE command. When you exit from Mail, the Wastebasket folder is emptied.

To delete a folder, simply delete all messages in that folder. The easiest way to do this is with the DELETE/ALL command. In the next example, the Memos folder is deleted:

```
MAIL> SELECT MEMOS
%MAIL-I-SELECTED, 1 message selected

MAIL> DELETE/ALL
```

Printing Messages

The PRINT command adds a copy of the current message to an output file for printing. The output file is not sent to the designated printer until you exit from Mail, unless you specify /NOW. For example:

```
MAIL> PRINT/QUEUE=SYS$LASER/COPIES=1
```

If you do not specify an output queue, the default print queue, SYS$PRINT, is assumed. The most commonly used qualifiers of the DCL PRINT command, such as /AFTER, /COPIES, /FORM, /FEED, /QUEUE and /NOTIFY, are available with the Mail PRINT command.

Creating a File from a Message

Often, you will find it necessary to create a file from an electronic message. The EXTRACT command is available for this purpose. In the next example, message number 1 is selected and extracted:

```
MAIL> 1
MAIL> EXTRACT/NOHEADER FLORIDA.TXT
```

Use the EXTRACT qualifier /NOHEADER to delete the message header information (i.e., From, To, Subj) added by Mail.

Customizing Mail

VMS Mail has a number of features that you can customize using the SET commands. Corresponding SHOW commands let you see the current settings.

Setting Your Personal Name

A popular item to customize is your personal name. With the SET PERSONAL_NAME command, you can append a text string to the end of the From: field of outgoing mail. You can fill this field with a nickname, your full name, or any other information you want. For example:

```
MAIL> SET PERSONAL_NAME "David"
MAIL> SHOW PERSONAL_NAME
Your personal name is "David".
```

System managers and privileged users can list the personal name of another user with the command SHOW PERSONAL_NAME/ USER=user_name.

Changing Your Default Editor

The default Mail editor is EDT. To change the default to TPU, use the SET EDITOR command:

```
MAIL> SET EDITOR TPU
MAIL> SHOW EDITOR
Your editor is TPU
```

If you use EVE as your default editor, TPU is the correct choice.

Getting Copies of Everything You Send

If you would like to receive a copy of everything you send via the Mail utility, use the SET COPY_SELF command. Parameters for this command are [NO]SEND, [NO]REPLY and [NO]FORWARD. For example:

```
MAIL> SET COPY_SELF SEND REPLY NOFORWARD
MAIL> SHOW COPY_SELF
Automatic copy to yourself on SEND,REPLY.
```

Sending Carbon Copies

The carbon copy feature lets you send a carbon copy of your messages to users other than the primary addressee. This is not a default feature; you must turn it on with the SET CC_PROMPT command:

```
MAIL> SET CC_PROMPT
```

When carbon copy is on, you are prompted for carbon copy addressees after the primary addressee:

```
MAIL> SEND
To: TOM
CC: DICK,HARRY
Subject: . . .
```

To turn the carbon copy feature off, use SET NOCC_PROMPT.

Mail Distribution Lists

If you frequently send messages to the same group of people, you can save time by creating a distribution list. A distribution list is a text file with the names of users you want to receive your messages.

Each username in the list must be on a separate line. You can include names of other distribution lists by preceding the name of the list with the at sign (@). You can include comments by preceding them with an exclamation point. For example:

```
! THE_GANG.DIS
!
WILLIS
T_BYNON
BYNON
SHIPMAN
```

To send a message to the users on a distribution list, enter the following at the SEND command To: prompt:

```
@file_spec
```

Each user listed in the distribution file will receive a copy of your message. For example:

```
MAIL> SEND
To: @THE_GANG
MAIL>
```

You can create as many distribution list files as you like for different groups of users. The default file type for a MAIL distribution list is .DIS.

Using The Mail Keypad

VMS Mail recognizes keypad keys as commands. Figure 7-1 shows the commands mapped to the keypad. The second (or lower) command of each key (except <PF1>) is a <GOLD> key command. To invoke these commands, first press the <GOLD> key (do not hold), then press the desired key.

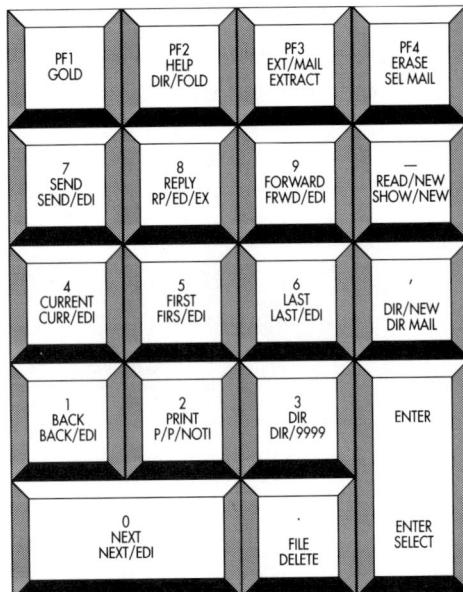

Figure 7-1. The Mail Keypad

VMS PHONE

The VMS Phone utility allows you to "talk" with other users on your VAX system through your terminal. It simulates the functions and features of a real telephone system, including call holding, conference calls and telephone directories.

Placing a Call

To place a call using the Phone utility, enter

```
$ PHONE username
```

where *username* is the VMS name of the person you want to communicate with. Your terminal screen will split horizontally into two sections. The screen will indicate that the Phone utility is ringing the other party. Your part of the conversation will be displayed in the top half of the screen, while the other party's responses will appear in the lower half.

The Phone utility, like Mail, also can be used interactively. At the DCL command level, enter:

```
$ PHONE
```

Your terminal will enter split screen mode (see Figure 7-2), and

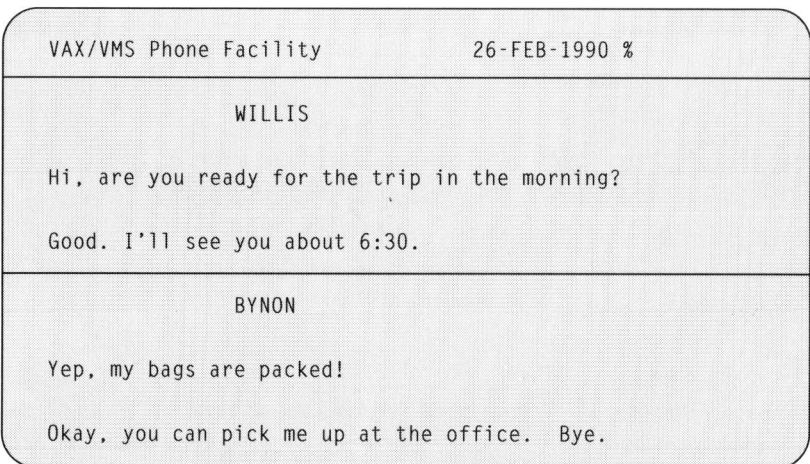

```
VAX/VMS Phone Facility              26-FEB-1990 %

                   WILLIS

Hi, are you ready for the trip in the morning?

Good. I'll see you about 6:30.

                   BYNON

Yep, my bags are packed!

Okay, you can pick me up at the office.  Bye.
```

Figure 7-2. The Phone Screen

you will be placed at the PHONE prompt (%). You then can enter Phone commands. For example, if you enter DIRECTORY, the Phone utility will display a directory of users available to Phone.

Figure 7-2 depicts a phone call from user Willis to user Bynon. If you are having a conversation with another user, you can return to the PHONE command prompt by entering the percent sign. You must do this, in any case, to exit the Phone utility with the EXIT command.

Answering a Call

To answer an incoming call, you must be at the DCL command prompt or at the PHONE prompt. At the DCL prompt, use this command:

```
$ PHONE ANSWER
```

At the PHONE prompt enter:

```
% ANSWER
```

You and the caller will be linked and can carry on the conversation.

INTRODUCTION TO DECWINDOWS FILEVIEW

As a VAX workstation or VT1000 (X Window terminal) user, you have the choice of entering commands at the DCL prompt, through a DECterm window, or of using DECwindows FileView.

FileView allows you to access DCL commands and other DECwindows applications. You can use FileView to copy, compile, edit, print, search and display files, and to create directories to organize your work. You will find that you have access to most DCL commands through FileView's pull-down menus.

To start FileView, select FileView from the session manager's Applications menu. Depending on the way you have set up your session manager, FileView will appear on your workstation display as a window or an icon. Change the icon into a window by clicking on it. The FileView window has three components:

▼ Modifiable menu bar
▼ Default directory and file filter dialog box
▼ File and directory list box

A typical FileView window is shown in Figure 7-3.

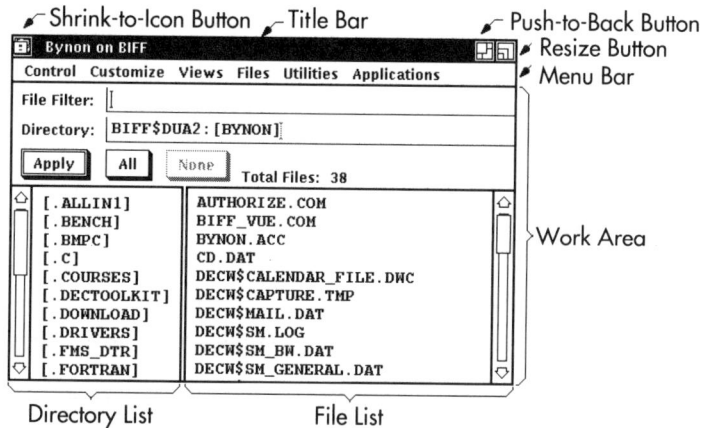

Figure 7-3. FileView Window

Using FileView to Enhance DCL

FileView makes working with files and getting around in directories a snap. With a single click on <MB1>, you can change
your default directory or read a file. Some FileView menu commands require keyboard input, but many do not.

In this section, we'll discuss FileView's Files menu and the con-
cept of a view. The Files menu contains most DCL commands
you're likely to use on a daily basis.

When you use a DCL command from the FileView window, you
receive DECwindows assistance with the command. We can use
FileView's Files menu to demonstrate. To use a DCL command on
the Files menu, pull down the Files menu by dragging it open.
Hold the <MB1> button down until the rectangle is on the command you want, then let go. DECwindows assistance then begins.

When a DCL command requires parameters or has qualifiers, FileView will open a dialog box with widgets that control the command's parameters and qualifiers. A good example is the PRINT command. When you select Print from the Files menu, FileView opens a dialog box titled "FileView - Print." This dialog box (shown in Figure 7-4) prompts for the filename and lets you request additional queue options by clicking on a toggle button. When you have completed this dialog box, click on OK to continue. If you clicked on the "Show Queue Options" toggle button, a second dialog box, called "FileView - Queue Options" will appear (see Figure 7-5). With this dialog box you can select the number of copies you want printed, the printer, and the document orientation. As you can see, FileView's assistance is extensive.

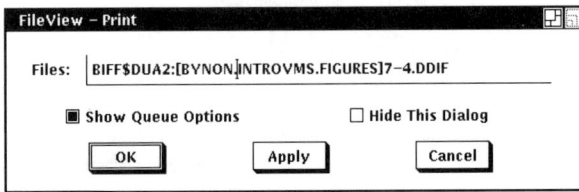

Figure 7-4. FileView Print Dialog Box

Changing Your View

A view is a list of files displayed in FileView's list box (see Figure 7-3). It is a "window" into your default directory. You specify your View directory in FileView's Directory field. A view is not necessarily the full set of files in the default directory. You can specify a file filter so that only files with a specific name or type show in the list. By default, all files within the View directory are displayed. A view enables you to work with as many or as few files as you need.

Use the Directory field and File Filter field to choose the files that will show in the file list. For example, you can choose to see only command procedures by entering *.COM in the File Filter field.

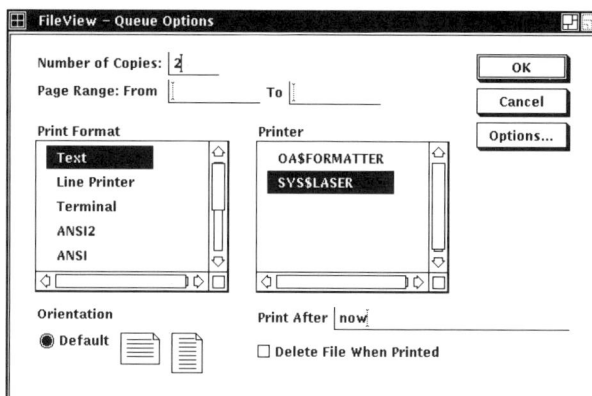

Figure 7-5. FileView Queue Options Dialog Box

To change files listed in the file list:

1. Point the mouse at the File Filter field and click. This will activate the field so you can type in it.

2. Enter a valid file specification. You can use the asterisk or percent wildcard characters as defined in Chapter 4. For example, to list all files that begin with D, enter:

`D*.*`

3. Click on Apply or press <RETURN>. FileView will update the file list.

To change the View directory:

1. Click on a subdirectory name displayed in the subdirectory list. The directory list and file list will be updated with the new directory information.

2. If your destination directory is nested several subdirectories deep, you will have to move to the new directory by clicking on each subdirectory name in its path. For example, if your current directory is [SMITH] and you want to be at [SMITH.REMINDERS. MARCH], you would click on [.REMINDERS], then on [.MARCH].

When you move from a top-level directory to a subdirectory, you will notice the [-] at the top of the subdirectory list. This represents the directory above. Click on [-] to move up one directory level.

If the view you want is not a subdirectory of your login directory or disk, you must specify a full directory path. To enter one directory path:

1. Click on the Directory field to make it active.

2. Press <CTRL/U> to clear the Directory field, then enter the full directory pathname. If the directory is not on your default disk, specify the disk name before the directory pathname.

3. Click on Apply or press <RETURN>. FileView will update the directory list and the file list.

If the view you want is a directory on another computer in your network, follow these steps:

1. Click on the Directory field, then press <CTRL/U> to clear the field.

2. Click on the File Filter field.

3. Edit the File Filter field to include the full file specification of the view you want. For example, if the view you want is the directory [GAMES] on disk DUA3: on node BIFF, enter:

```
BIFF::DUA3:[GAMES]
```

4. Click on Apply or press <RETURN>.

Selecting Files and Using DCL Commands

When you click on a filename in the file list, it is selected. FileView highlights selected files. When you select a file, you can use a DCL command from FileView's Files menu, such as EDIT, DELETE or COPY, that acts on the selected file.

You can select more than one file at a time. To select adjacent files:

1. Point to the first file in the range.

2. Drag the pointer through the files you want to select. FileView highlights the files as you drag through them. The number of selected files is reported by FileView.

3. After selecting the last file, release <MB1>.

To select scattered files:

1. Select the first file by clicking on it.

2. Select each additional file by pressing and holding the <SHIFT> key, then click on the other files.

3. After selecting the last file, release <SHIFT>.

To select all files, click on FileView's All button.

FileView's Files menu lists the DCL commands commonly used to work with files. When you select a command from the Files menu, FileView displays a command dialog box that you'll use to tailor the DCL file operation. For example, you can request that the DELETE command request confirmation before deleting all files (see Figure 7-6).

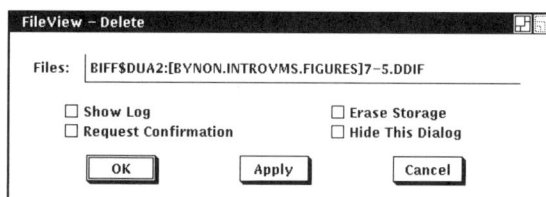

Figure 7-6. FileView DELETE Command Dialog Box

If you selected one or more files, the selected files will be entered in the Files: field of the command dialog box (see Figure 7-7). Commands that require two parameters (e.g., the COPY and RENAME commands) will have a From: field and a To: field. In this case, selected files will be listed for you in the From: field.

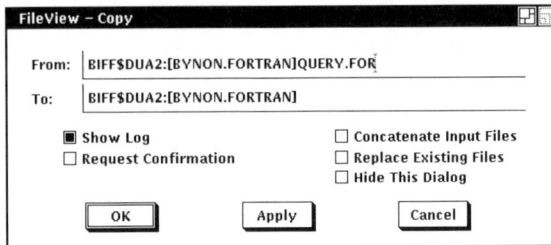

Figure 7-7. FileView COPY Dialog Box

When you have completed the dialog box for a DCL command, click on the OK button or press <RETURN>. FileView will start the command and display an output window to show the command's progress. If you make a mistake or change your mind, click on the Cancel button. The Apply button activates the command (like the OK button), but the command's dialog remains open. This is useful if you need to use the command again.

Using Pop-Up Menus to Work with Files

With most file types, you'll often use a small set of DCL commands. For example, if you program in FORTRAN, you edit, compile and link a program's source file. To speed access to often-used commands, FileView has file-type pop-up menus. Each file type (e.g., TXT, COM, FOR, C, DDIF) has a unique pop-up menu.

To use a file-type menu:

1. Point the mouse at the file you want to work with, then press and hold <MB2>. The file-type menu will pop up.

2. Choose the command you want to execute by dragging the pointer to it. When the rectangle is on the command you want, release <MB2>. To cancel the pop-up menu, move the pointer outside the menu and release <MB2>.

FileView will remember the last command you used. The next time you display the same menu, the command you last used will appear under the pointer.

Using FileView to Create a Directory

To create a directory using FileView:

1. Choose the Create Directory option from the Utilities menu. FileView displays the Create Directory dialog box.

2. Type the name of the directory you want to create, following the directory-naming rules defined earlier in this book. For example, to create a subdirectory called MEMOS in the top-level directory SMITH, enter [SMITH.MEMOS].

3. Click on OK or press <RETURN>.

FileView will create the new directory, and no further information will be displayed. You then should update FileView's directory list by clicking on Apply or by pressing <RETURN>. (Apply is FileView's default function.)

Using FileView to Define Logical Names

To define or change a logical name with FileView:

1. Choose the Logical Names... option from the Utilities menu. FileView displays the Logical Names dialog box.

2. Type the name of the logical name you are defining or changing in the Name field, then press <RETURN>.

3. Click on the Definition field, then type the definition you want assigned to the logical name.

4. If you want to conceal logical name translation (which is typically the case when creating a logical name for a disk or directory), click on the Conceal Translation toggle button (which appears on the dialog box).

5. Click on Define. The logical name is added to your job logical name table. If you have the appropriate privilege, you can add the logical name to other tables.

6. Click on Dismiss to put the dialog box away.

The Logical Names... choice also is useful if you need to see the definition of a logical name. To display a logical name without changing it, follow steps 1, 2 and 6 above.

```
┌─────────────────────────────────┐
│ Customize                       │
│  Layout...                      │
│  Menu Bar...                    │
│  Privileges...                  │
│  Window...                      │
│ ................................│
│  Exclude Files...               │
│  Filter by Size...              │
│  Filter by Date...              │
│  Filter by Owner...             │
│ ................................│
│  Save Startup View              │
│  Save View...                   │
│  Unsave View...                 │
│  Verbs and Menus...             │
│  File Types...                  │
└─────────────────────────────────┘
```

Figure 7-8. FileView Customize Menu

To delete a logical name, follow steps 1 and 2 above, then click on Deassign. FileView removes the logical name definition. Click on Dismiss to put the dialog box away.

Customizing FileView

FileView is very flexible. You can even change the way it looks and works. Through FileView's Customize menu, you have full control of your FileView layout, window, icon name, menu bar and the options in each menu (see Figure 7-8).

Use the Layout... option on the Customize menu to describe the filename fields you want listed with each file in your FileView's file list. Typically, only the file type is listed, but you have the option to see the file attributes, such as the associated device, protection and size. With the Layout... option, you also can select the order in which your files will be listed. When you are satisfied with your new layout, be sure to click on OK.

The Menu Bar... option lets you select the pull-down menus for your FileView menu bar. The Menu Bar dialog box has two list boxes (see Figure 7-9). The list box on the left is the list of menus that has not been selected to be in your menu bar. The list box on the right shows the menus that have been selected

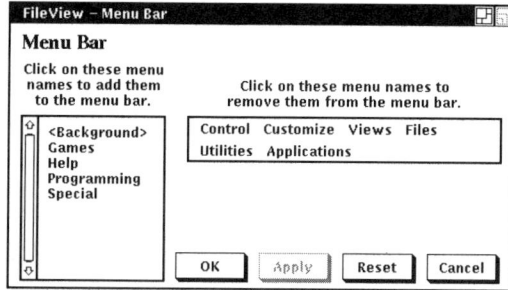

Figure 7-9. FileView Menu Bar

for your menu bar. To move a menu from one list to the other, click on it.

To change the name in the title bar or the icon of your FileView, use the Window... option. The Window... option pops up a dialog box you use to specify a name for your FileView title bar and icon. Within this dialog box, you also can indicate the initial state of your FileView — window or icon. You can change these items to suit your preference.

Each FileView option (verb) is linked to a DCL command or a command file. When you select a FileView option from a pull-down menu, FileView executes the command or command procedure for you, just as if you had typed the command at the DCL prompt. You can add options to your FileView menus (Utilities, Applications, Files and others) by defining new verbs using the Verbs and Menus... option, which uses the Verbs and Menus dialog box, shown in Figure 7-10.

You can add a new verb to your FileView in a few simple steps:

1. Enter the new verb name in the Verb Names entry field. When you begin typing, the Enter button will become active. To add the new verb name you have typed, press <RETURN> or click on the Enter button.

2. Enter a valid DCL command for your new verb in the DCL Command for Selected Verb entry field. Once you have entered the command, your verb will execute.

3. Select the menu you want to add the verb to from the Menu Names list by clicking on it. That menu's verbs will appear in the Verbs in Menu box.

4. Click on the Add button. To make the verb permanent, click on the OK button.

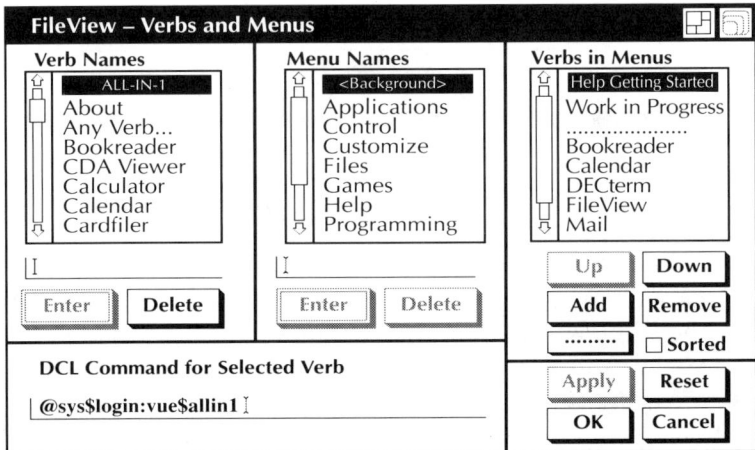

Figure 7-10. Verbs and Menus Dialog Box

WHERE TO GO FROM HERE

For more information on the VMS Mail and Phone utilities, refer to the Digital Equipment *VAX/VMS Utilities Manual*. For more information about DECwindows and FileView, refer to the Digital Equipment *VMS DECwindows User's Guide*.

Chapter 8

Symbols, Data, Expressions and Lexical Functions

As you progress with VMS, you will begin to use many of its advanced features, such as command procedures. Within your command procedures, it is possible to assign an entire command to a single word, manipulate numbers and character strings, and gather information about your working environment. In order to accomplish these tasks, you must first learn how to manipulate data and symbols. In this chapter, you'll learn about:

▼ Symbol creation, deletion and translation
▼ VMS data representation
▼ Expressions
▼ Lexical functions and how they are used

SYMBOLS

A symbol is a name that you choose to represent a string of characters, numeric value or logical value (true or false). A symbol may be used anywhere the value it represents is used. Symbol names may be 1 to 255 characters long and must begin with a character, dollar sign or underscore. Lowercase characters in the symbol name will be translated to uppercase.

Symbol Creation

Symbols are created when you assign them a value in one of the following formats:

symbol_name = *value*   (local symbol)
symbol_name == *value*   (global symbol)

A local symbol may be used at the command level at which you define it. A global symbol may be used at any command level. For example, if you define a local and global symbol in a command procedure, then when the command procedure finishes, the local symbol will be deleted, but the global symbol will remain.

Consider the following example:

```
$ WIDE = "SET TERMINAL/WIDTH = 132"
```

In this example, we assigned the SET TERMINAL command to the symbol "WIDE." Now, anytime we type WIDE at the DCL command level it will execute the command assigned to it. In this case the symbol is being used as a form of shorthand, only one of many applications.

In the next example, the symbol ANSWER contains the result of a simple math operation:

```
$ ANSWER = 9 * (199 - 23)
```

To display the contents of a symbol you can use the DCL command SHOW SYMBOL:

```
$ SHOW SYMBOL ANSWER
        ANSWER = 1584   Hex = 00000630   Octal = 00000006030
```

SHOW SYMBOL uses the local symbol table by default. To display a global symbol, use the /GLOBAL qualifier and the global symbol name. Use the /ALL qualifier to display all local symbols or /GLOBAL/ALL to display all global symbols.

Symbol Deletion

To explicitly delete a symbol, use the DCL command DELETE/ SYMBOL. If the symbol is global, you will have to use the /GLOBAL qualifier. In the following example, the local symbol ANSWER is deleted:

```
$ DELETE/SYMBOL ANSWER
```

NOTE: All symbols, global and local, are deleted when you log out.

Symbol Translation

When a DCL command is executed, symbols in the following positions are automatically translated:

- ▼ At the beginning of the command
- ▼ In a lexical function
- ▼ In a WRITE, IF, EXAMINE or DEPOSIT statement
- ▼ On the right side of an = or == statement
- ▼ Inside brackets on the left side of an assignment statement when you are performing string substitution

If none of these situations is met, you must force translation of the symbol by enclosing it in apostrophes ('symbol'). In the following example, the symbol PARTS is assigned a full file specification. You must then force translation to use it alone or with DCL commands:

```
$ PARTS = "DUB1:[DATABASES]PARTS.DAT"
$ DIRECTORY 'PARTS'
```

Without the apostrophes, the result would have looked like this:

```
$ DIRECTORY PARTS
%DIRECT-W-NOFILES, no files found
```

If you need to force translation of a symbol within a character string, enclose the symbol in double apostrophes, as in this example:

```
$ PP = "PURGE ´´PARTS´"
```

You also might discover that only a single apostrophe is needed at the end of the symbol (e.g., "´´PARTS´").

Common and Practical Symbol Use

Although the most common use of symbols is DCL command shorthand, symbols also may be used effectively to produce mnemonics. In the next example, we'll assign values to three mnemonics, which will be used to clear the display on a VT terminal.

```
$ ESC[Ø,8] = 27        !(value for the <ESCAPE> key)
$ CLEAR = "[J"         !(sequence to clear the display)
$ HOME = "[H"          !(sequence to home the cursor)
$
$ WRITE SYS$OUTPUT ESC,HOME,ESC,CLEAR   !(writes the sequence to
$                                        !the terminal)
```

We could take this one step further and assign the whole command to a symbol:

```
CLR :== WRITE SYS$OUTPUT ESC,HOME,ESC,CLEAR
```

NOTE: You can omit the quotations around a string substitution if you precede the equal signs with a colon, as shown above.

Another practical use for a symbol is to have it execute a command procedure. This allows you to execute a command procedure by typing only the symbol name. For example:

```
$ CD == "@SYS$LOGIN:CD"
```

NOTE: The @ symbol is used to execute a command procedure. For more information on command procedures, refer to Chapter 9.

Finally, you can define a foreign command (a program name not known to DCL) as a symbol. In the following example, the symbol KERMIT is used to execute the program KERMIT.EXE located in the SYS$SYSTEM directory:

```
$ KERMIT :== RUN SYS$SYSTEM:KERMIT
```

Your system manager probably has defined many useful symbols for the users at your site.

VMS DATA REPRESENTATION

When you create a text file, enter information into a database, or supply the computer with data in any way, the computer stores the data as a representation of the type of information with which you are working. The computer can store only binary (base 2) numeric values. It is how the software interprets these numeric values that allows us to use different types of data, such as characters or numbers.

Data is stored in the following ways:

Bit—The basic unit of storage. A bit can only represent a value of 0 or 1, the digits in the binary counting system.

Byte—Equal to eight bits. A byte may range in magnitude from 0 to 255 (unsigned number) or -128 to 127 (signed number).

Word—Equal to two bytes (16 bits).

Longword—Equal to four bytes (32 bits).

Binary number representation—A series of 8, 16 or 32 bits, read right to left, with the right-most bit representing the low-order value.

Binary character representation—A series of 8 bits, read left to right, with the left-most bit representing the low-order value. A standard code, known as the ASCII code, defines the value = to = character association.

To understand this better, let's look at how the VAX stores characters:

Character	ASCII	Binary Representation
A	65	01000001
B	66	01000010
C	67	01000011
D	68	01000100
E	69	01000101
.		
.		
.		
Y	89	01011001
Z	90	01011010

DCL Expressions

DCL expressions are created by combining data elements with operators. Operators are categorized in two groups:

- ▼ Names—.EQ., .GE., .GT., .LE., .LT., .NE., .OR., .AND., and .NOT.; uppercase or lowercase is acceptable.
- ▼ Characters—Plus (+), minus (-), asterisk (*), and slash (/).

See Appendix H for definitions of logical expression operators.

Data elements may be literal values (1,2,3... DOG, CAT...) or symbols. All expressions take one of two forms: logical comparison or operation.

Logical comparison—A logical comparison evaluates the relationship between two components as true or false. True is equivalent to a numeric 1, false to a numeric 0. Consider the following example:

```
$ TEN = 10
$ TRUE_FALSE = TEN .EQ. 10
$ SHOW SYMBOL TRUE_FALSE
TRUE_FALSE = 1 Hex = 000001   Octal = 000001
```

The first command assigns the value 10 to the symbol TEN. The second command says "if the symbol TEN equals (.EQ.) 10, then assign the value of true (TRUE=1) to the symbol TRUE_FALSE; if not, then assign false (FALSE=0)".

Operation—An operation assigns a value to a symbol based on a mathematical evaluation. In this example, two values are multiplied, then assigned to a symbol:

```
$ RESULT = 23 * 2
$ SHOW SYMBOL RESULT
RESULT = 46          Hex = 000002E          Octal = 0000056
```

Sample Expressions
Character string addition (concatenation):

```
$ UNCLE_JOE = "Uncle Joe "
$ UNCLE_JOE = UNCLE_JOE + "is getting fat!"
$ SHOW SYMBOL UNCLE_JOE
  UNCLE_JOE = "Uncle Joe is getting fat!"
$
```

Logical expression:

```
$ TRUE_FALSE = 100 .LT. 20
$ SHOW SYMBOL TRUE_FALSE
  TRUE_FALSE = 0       Hex = 000000    Octal = 000000
$
```

Combined types:

```
$ RESULT = 12 + "12"
$ SHOW SYMBOL RESULT
  RESULT = 24          Hex = 0000018   Octal = 0000030
```

LEXICAL FUNCTIONS

Lexical functions are VMS routines that return process or system information or manipulate user-supplied data. Lexical functions are unique in that the result of the operation is returned in the lexical function name. This enables you to use the lexical function like a symbol.

You invoke a lexical function by typing its name with a list of parameters. All lexical function names begin with F$ and take the form:

F$function_name(parameter, parameter...)

The parameter list must be enclosed in parentheses, with each parameter separated by a comma.

Consider the following simple example, in which the F$SEARCH() lexical function is used:

```
$ FILE = F$SEARCH("DUA1:[...]REMINDERS.DAT")
$ SHOW SYMBOL FILE
  FILE = "DUA1:[BYNON.OFFICE_AUTOMATION]REMINDERS.DAT;1"
$
```

The F$SEARCH() lexical function searches for and returns the name of a file specification supplied as a parameter. If the file specification cannot be found, a null string "" is returned. This is an example of a lexical function that returns system information.

The next example shows a lexical function that manipulates user-supplied data:

```
$ STRING = "For     goodness     sake,     why          me?"
$ STRING = F$EDIT(STRING, "COMPRESS, UPCASE")
$ SHOW SYMBOL STRING
 STRING = "FOR GOODNESS SAKE, WHY ME?"
$
```

Refer to Appendix B for a list and description of VMS lexical functions.

WHERE TO GO FROM HERE

For more information about symbols, data representation, expressions or lexical functions, refer to the Digital Equipment *DCL Dictionary* or to the appendices of this book.

In the next chapter, "Command Procedures," you'll put what you learned in this chapter to work. The true power of symbols and lexical functions is realized when you use them in command procedures.

Chapter 9

Command Procedures

DCL commands are versatile and powerful when used individually. But to realize the full potential and flexibility of VMS and DCL, you must group commands to perform specialized procedures. These procedures are called command procedures.

In this chapter, you'll learn to develop DCL command procedures and how to use the many features of symbols, lexical functions and logical names. Specifically, we'll cover:

▼ Guidelines for creating and invoking command procedures
▼ The use of symbols and lexical functions in command procedures
▼ Input and output
▼ How to put logic in command procedures
▼ How to check for errors and debug command procedures
▼ How to use the VMS batch processor, which enables you to run jobs without tying up your terminal

When you complete this chapter, you'll be able to develop and invoke useful, time-saving command procedures. Many examples in this chapter are portions of sample procedures. You may find it useful to modify these procedures for your own use.

WHAT IS A COMMAND PROCEDURE?

A command procedure is a file containing a sequence of DCL commands that can be executed interactively or as a batch job. Command procedures are used in VMS to perform repetitive or complex tasks, and to save time. With a command procedure, you can execute many complex DCL commands with one simple command.

Saving Time with Command Procedures

To see how command procedures will save you time, assume that you frequently use Kermit, the popular telecommunications program. To use Kermit, you would take these steps:

1. Allocate a modem port for your use.
2. Set the speed of the modem port.
3. Define the port name for Kermit.
4. Run Kermit.
5. Put the port back the way you found it.

To perform these functions as individual commands, you would have to enter a series of DCL commands similar to this:

```
$ ALLOCATE TXA7:
$ SET TERMINAL TXA7: /SPEED=2400 /PERMANENT
$ DEFINE /USER_MODE KER$COMM TXA7:
$ RUN SYS$SYSTEM:KERMIT
$ SET TERMINAL TXA7: /AUTOBAUD /PERMANENT
```

To turn this series of commands into a DCL command procedure, use the EDT or EVE text editor to create a file. Next, enter these same command lines into the file. The file should be given a meaningful name and a file type of .COM, for example, KERMIT.COM. From now on, whenever you want to execute this series of commands, you need only use the @ command followed by the file name, as in this example:

```
$ @KERMIT
```

As you can see, this is faster and easier.

To execute an interactive program, such as EDT or Mail, from within a command procedure, you must redefine where input will come from and where output will go. Input and output are explained fully later in this chapter.

Once you've developed a command procedure, such as the one above, you will not have to enter individual DCL commands to perform the series of commands specified in the procedure. Command procedures generally require little, if any, maintenance.

Your LOGIN Command Procedure

When you log in, a command procedure called LOGIN is executed for you. In most cases, your LOGIN procedure is your responsibility. You can add commands to or delete commands from this procedure as you wish. Your LOGIN command procedure serves a special purpose: it customizes your working environment for you. Any commands that you must execute each time you log in should be put in your LOGIN command procedure. You'll find a sample LOGIN command procedure at the end of this chapter.

Programming in DCL

Command procedures are not bound by simple lists of DCL commands executed one after another. Command procedures can take advantage of a wide range of features, such as labels, lexical functions, symbols, and relational operators, to build sophisticated procedures that act like programs.

Command procedures are flexible. You can write a command procedure that will take specific actions based on a response to a question, or a command procedure that will perform a particular function depending on the time of day or date. Even if you know little or nothing about conventional programming, you'll find it easy to program with DCL command procedures.

GUIDELINES FOR WRITING COMMAND PROCEDURES

Because a command procedure is a file, it follows the same naming conventions as other VMS files. The default file type for a command procedure is .COM. If you use any other file type, you must include the file type when you invoke the procedure.

Use a text editor, such as EDT or EVE, to create and develop a command procedure. If the procedure is short, you can use the CREATE command. Whichever text editor or method you use, the following guidelines will apply.

Command Procedure Structure

The most common structure for a command procedure is as follows:

```
$! introduction, author's name, and other comments
$!
$! comment about the next command(s)
$!
$ command
$ command
$!
$! comment
$!
$ command
data
data
data
$ exit
```

Command Lines

Each new command line must begin with a dollar sign. You can include multiple spaces or tabs after the dollar sign to increase readability. Command lines can be extended past a single line. To do so, end each line to be continued with a hyphen and do not begin the continuation line with a dollar sign. For example:

```
$ SET TERMINAL -
      /ADVANCED_VIDEO -
      /REGIS -
```

```
        /WIDTH=8Ø -
        /PAGE=24 -
        /INSERT
$
```

Program Input

Data input to programs, such as YES or NO responses, must be entered without the dollar sign. Data lines are used by the program running; they are not processed by the DCL command line interpreter. Consider this example, which invokes the Mail utility and enters commands and responses:

`$ MAIL`	← Invokes the Mail utility
`SEND`	← Mail SEND command
`WILLIS,SHIPMAN`	← In response to Mail prompt "To:"
`System schedule...`	← In response to Mail prompt "Subj:"
`Gentlemen,`	← Mail message

```
The system will be down on
Monday, 26 February, from 6am
to 1pm for normal system
maintenance.

David
```
`$`	← Terminates the Mail program
`$ EXIT`	← Terminates the command procedure

Comments and Documentation

You can include comments in your command procedures by preceding them with an exclamation point. The exclamation point causes the DCL command interpreter to ignore everything to the right of it.

It is good programming practice to thoroughly document your command procedures. Comments make command procedures easier to debug or modify at a later date.

1 should limit the number of abbreviated DCL commands you use in complex command procedures. Spelling out the commands helps make a command procedure self-documenting.

Debugging Command Procedures

After you've written a command procedure, you must test it and change any statements that generate DCL errors. You can use the SET VERIFY and SHOW SYMBOL commands to help you with this task.

The SET VERIFY command tells DCL to display each command as it is processed. This enables you to see where an error is generated, and how symbols in strings are translated. Use the SET NOVERIFY command to turn the verify mode off.

The SHOW SYMBOL command displays the contents of a symbol you have defined. In a command procedure, you can use the SHOW SYMBOL command to show a symbol's contents after you define or manipulate it. For example:

```
$ RESULT = 21 * (36/4)
$ SHOW SYMBOL RESULT    !Debug statement
```

INVOKING COMMAND PROCEDURES

There are two methods of invoking command procedures. You can invoke them interactively and as a batch job.

Interactive Command Procedures

To invoke a command procedure interactively, type the at sign (@) followed by the procedure name. If the file type is not .COM, you must include the file type. You also may need to supply parameters as discussed later in this chapter. Command procedures can be invoked at the DCL prompt or from within another command procedure. Invoking a command procedure within another command procedure is called *nesting*.

The following example invokes a command procedure called FUNCTION_KEYS.COM in the user's login directory:

```
$ @SYS$LOGIN:FUNCTION_KEYS
```

SYS$LOGIN is a logical name for your login directory.

Batch Command Procedures

You can invoke a command as a batch job, which executes as a separate job from your interactive process. To do this, use the SUBMIT command. The SUBMIT command places your job in a batch queue, with other jobs waiting to be run.

A command procedure is generally submitted as a batch job when:

▼ You want the procedure to execute at a specific time.
▼ The procedure will take a long time to execute.
▼ A job must run at a reduced priority.

The following command submits the REPORT.COM command procedure to be executed by the batch processor:

```
$ SUBMIT REPORT
Job REPORT (queue SYS$BATCH, entry 106) started on SYS$BATCH
```

The SYS$BATCH queue is used by default, unless you specify another queue with the /QUEUE qualifier. When VMS executes your job, it creates a process with your rights and privileges and executes the procedure.

For more information on using the batch processor and submitting batch jobs, refer to Chapter 10.

USING SYMBOLS AND LEXICAL FUNCTIONS IN COMMAND PROCEDURES

Symbols and lexical functions were introduced in Chapter 8. In this chapter, you'll discover the true power of these tools.

Symbols in Command Procedures

Symbols are either local or global. A local symbol is defined with a single equal sign and is accessible by DCL at the command level at which it was defined and at more deeply nested levels. For example:

```
$ @PROCEDURE_1    ←  Symbols defined in PROCEDURE_2 inaccessible
$ @PROCEDURE_2    ←  Local symbols defined here
$ @PROCEDURE_3    ←  Symbols defined in PROCEDURE_2 accessible
```

A global symbol is defined with two equal signs. It is recognized at any command level (DCL or command procedures).

Use local symbols when the symbol is only necessary for the duration of the command procedure using it. If you want to use a symbol in other command procedures, or for the duration of your login session, define it as a global symbol.

Here is an example of a local symbol:

```
$ COUNT = 30 + 99
```

The following is an example of a global symbol:

```
$ KER*MIT == "@SYS$LOGIN:KERMIT"
```

The * in the symbol definition "KER*MIT" tells the command line interpreter to accept abbreviations of the KERMIT command (e.g., KER, KERM, KERMI or KERMIT). Use this notation when defining lengthy symbol names.

Lexical Functions in Command Procedures

Lexical functions enable you to obtain much of the same information that you can get from DCL SHOW commands. As an example, the following commands would return basically the same information:

```
$ SHOW TIME                     ! DCL SHOW TIME command
  28-FEB-1990 11:38:27
$ WRITE SYS$OUTPUT F$TIME()      ! Lexical function
  28-FEB-1990 11:38:40.37
$
```

In a command procedure, it is easier to capture and manipulate information when it comes from a lexical function. For example, consider the following command procedure:

```
$! SHOW_DATE.COM
$!
$ TIME&DATE = F$TIME()
$ DATE = F$EXTRACT(0,11,TIME&DATE)
$ WRITE SYS$OUTPUT DATE
```

When invoked, this procedure displays only the date portion of the string returned by the lexical function F$TIME(). The lexical function F$EXTRACT() is used to extract a string segment from the supplied string. In this example, the string segment is the first 11 characters of the string contained in the symbol TIME&DATE. The string segment extracted is assigned to a new symbol, called DATE.

```
$ @SHOW_DATE 28-FEB-1990
$
```

Had we used the SHOW TIME command, instead of the lexical function, we could not have assigned the output to a symbol. Extracting the desired string segment would have been difficult and cumbersome as well.

The SHOW_DATE command procedure could have been implemented more efficiently with a single command:

```
$ WRITE SYS$OUTPUT(F$EXTRACT(0,11,F$TIME()))
```

The purpose of the SHOW_DATE example, however, is to demonstrate the use of symbols and lexical functions to collect and manipulate information.

VMS supports lexical functions that:

▼ Return information about the system.

▼ Convert data types.

▼ Return information about your process.

▼ Manipulate text strings.

▼ Return information about files and devices.

▼ Return information about symbols.

▼ Provide information about print and batch queues.

Many of these lexical functions will be demonstrated in the sample command procedures later in this chapter. For more information on lexical functions, refer to Appendix B.

COMMAND PROCEDURE INPUT/OUTPUT

In many cases, command procedures must be able to read data from an external source, such as the keyboard or a file. Similarly, command procedures generate output to be written to a display or file, or passed to another procedure. These activities are called *command procedure input/output (I/O)*. DCL provides a number of methods to perform command procedure I/O. The most common methods are explained below.

Parameters

When you develop command procedures, you will often need to supply data for the procedure to process. Eight reserved symbols (P1 through P8), called parameters, are available to command procedures for this purpose. By using these parameter symbols in your command procedures, you can specify different data each time you execute the procedure.

Parameter specification is done on the command line that invokes the procedure. Unless specifically designed to do so, the command procedure will not prompt you for input parameters. You must know what parameters the procedure needs before you invoke the procedure. A parameter can be a character string, integer or symbol. Each parameter must be separated with a space.

You can specify up to eight parameters on a command line. If you supply two parameters, for example, they will be equated to the symbols P1 and P2. The remaining parameter symbols (P3 through P8) will be equated to null strings (" "). If you wish to skip a parameter, you must specify it as a null string:

```
$ @COMMAND_PROCEDURE P1 P2 "" P4 . . .
```

If you list more than eight parameters, VMS will return an error message, and the command procedure will not be executed.

The following command procedure (MULTIPLY.COM) illustrates the use of parameters. If you supply two numbers on the command line, the procedure will return their product:

```
$! MULTIPLY.COM
$! Command procedure to demonstrate passing parameters
$!
$ WRITE SYS$OUTPUT P1 * P2
$ @MULTIPLY 123 48
5904
```

If your command procedure requires literal text (such as a sentence), you must enclose the parameter in quotation marks. A parameter enclosed in quotes is treated as a single parameter.

Terminal I/O

Most command procedures executed interactively do some text input/output with the terminal. DCL supports terminal I/O with the READ, WRITE, INQUIRE and TYPE commands.

Terminal Output

The WRITE and TYPE commands output data to the terminal. The TYPE command is primarily used to display the contents of a file at the user's terminal. However, it may be used to output lines of text from within a command procedure. The default output device for the TYPE command is the terminal. The TYPE command can only be used to output text.

The WRITE command is much more flexible than the TYPE command. A WRITE command line is processed by DCL; therefore, expressions, symbols and lexical functions are evaluated before the data is sent to the terminal. When using the WRITE command for terminal output, you specify the logical device SYS$OUTPUT as the output file. The output expression must translate to a string; the data, however, may be a string, lexical function, symbol or any combination.

The following example shows some ways you can use the WRITE and TYPE commands to output text to the terminal:

```
$! Writing a simple text string
$!
$ WRITE SYS$OUTPUT "And there you have it..."
$!
$! Use the TYPE command to display multiple lines at your
$! terminal.
$!
$ TYPE SYS$INPUT
WARNING!
        It has been over thirty days
        since you last changed your
        password. Please change it.
$!
$! The TYPE command is primarily used to display the contents of
$! a file.
$!
$ TYPE NOTES.TXT
$!
$! Writing a symbol to your terminal . . . Note: the symbol HI
$! will translate to "HELLO THERE" anywhere it is used as a
$! character string.
$!
$ HI = "HELLO" + "THERE"
```

```
$ WRITE SYS$OUTPUT HI
$!
$! Writing the value of a lexical function to your terminal
$!
$ WRITE SYS$OUTPUT F$DIRECTORY()
$!
$! Writing a list of items to your terminal
$!
$ WRITE SYS$OUTPUT HI," YOU ARE IN DIRECTORY ",F$DIRECTORY()
$!
$! Writing a string that contains a symbol or lexical function
$!
$ WRITE SYS$OUTPUT "´´HI´ YOU ARE IN DIRECTORY ´´F$DIRECTORY()´"
```

Terminal Input

Use the INQUIRE and READ commands to accept data from the terminal keyboard. The INQUIRE command is special because its default input device is the terminal keyboard. The READ command must be told from where to accept data.

The INQUIRE command prompts for input, reads the data and assigns it to a named symbol. All data is accepted as a character string. The character string is converted to uppercase and compressed (i.e., extra blanks and tabs are removed).

The READ command prompts for input (if the /PROMPT qualifier is used), accepts the data from a specified source and assigns it to a named symbol. All data read is accepted as is. No string conversion or compression takes place.

The following example shows some ways you can use the READ and INQUIRE commands to input text from the terminal:

```
$! Accepts whatever you type, and puts it in the symbol NAME.
$!
$ INQUIRE NAME "What is your name"
$ WRITE SYS$OUTPUT "Hello ",NAME
```

```
$ !
$ ! To suppress the colon and space the INQUIRE command adds to the end
$ ! of a prompt, use the /NOPUNCTUATION qualifier.
$ !
$ INQUIRE /NOPUNCTUATION FILENAME "What file would you like to type?"
$ TYPE FILENAME
$ !
$ ! With the READ command you must specify the source, in many cases
$ ! this will be SYS$INPUT. Notice in this example that we evaluated
$ ! an expression in the WRITE statement, while also using the
$ ! expression as a list element.
$ !
$ READ /PROMPT="First value: " SYS$INPUT VALUE_1
$ READ /PROMPT="Second value: " SYS$INPUT VALUE_2
$ WRITE SYS$OUTPUT VALUE_1," + ",VALUE_2," = ",VALUE_1+VALUE_2
```

File I/O

You also may use command procedures with the OPEN, WRITE, READ and CLOSE commands to read and write data to and from files. The basic steps to read and write from files within a command procedure follow:

1. Use the OPEN command to open a file. If the file does not exist, the OPEN command will create it for you.

2. Use the WRITE or READ commands to write or read text records to or from the file.

3. Use the CLOSE command to close the file.

The only files you do not have to explicitly open for reading and writing are SYS$INPUT, SYS$OUTPUT, SYS$ERROR and SYS$COMMAND.

Opening a File for Writing

To open a file for writing, use the /APPEND or /WRITE qualifier. Only one qualifier can be used in any given WRITE command.

The /WRITE qualifier is used to create a new file. The record pointer will be placed at the beginning of the file. If you specify an existing file, the OPEN/WRITE command will create a new version of the same file.

The following example demonstrates how to use the OPEN/WRITE command:

```
$! This command opens a new file named TIME.DAT. OUTPUT_FILE is a
$! logical name for the file. The logical name is required.
$!
$ OPEN/WRITE OUTPUT_FILE TIME.DAT
$!
$! This next command writes the time to the file. Notice that the
$! output is written to the logical name (OUTPUT_FILE), not to
$! the filename.
$!
$ WRITE OUTPUT_FILE "This record was written at: ",F$TIME()
$!
$! When you are finished, close the file...
$!
$ CLOSE OUTPUT_FILE
```

The /APPEND qualifier is used to add records to the end of an existing file. When the file is opened, the record pointer is positioned at the end of the file.

The following example appends a record to the end of TIME.DAT:

```
$ OPEN/APPEND OUTPUT_FILE TIME.DAT
$ WRITE OUTPUT_FILE "This record was written at: ",F$TIME()
$ CLOSE OUTPUT_FILE
```

If you do not close a file when you are finished using it, it will be closed when you log out.

Opening a File for Reading

To open a file for reading, use the /READ qualifier—the default qualifier for the OPEN command. When you open a file for reading, you can only read the file. The record pointer initially will be located at the first record in the file. Each time a record is read, the pointer moves down to the next record. Use the WRITE/ UPDATE command to write over a record.

The following example opens the TIME.DAT file and reads a record:

```
$ OPEN/READ INPUT_FILE TIME.DAT
$!
$! In this READ statement, "RECORD" is a symbol that will
$! contain the record read from the file.
$!
$ READ INPUT_FILE RECORD
$ WRITE SYS$OUTPUT "First record from TIME.DAT — ",RECORD
```

To open a file for reading and writing, you can use both the / WRITE and /READ qualifiers. In this situation, the record pointer will be placed at the first record in the file. A drawback to this method of opening a file is that you may only replace (write over) the most recent record read. In addition, records you replace must be the same length.

REDIRECTING COMMAND PROCEDURE INPUT/OUTPUT

Command procedures can direct or redirect output in various ways. The following sections explain several ways to redirect command procedure I/O.

Redefining SYS$INPUT as Your Terminal

Command procedures often invoke VMS utilities such as Mail. These programs normally obtain input from the logical device SYS$INPUT. While executing a command procedure, the logical name SYS$INPUT is directed to the command procedure. This is

why you can put command and data lines for a utility or program directly in the procedure. By default, the logical name
SYS$COMMAND represents the name of the terminal from which
a command procedure is being executed. By redirecting
SYS$INPUT to SYS$COMMAND, you can interactively use utilities
and other programs from your command procedures. For example:

```
$ DEFINE/USER_MODE SYS$INPUT SYS$COMMAND:
$ EDIT NOTES.DAT
```

NOTE: The /USER_MODE qualifier causes the reassignment to
be in effect only for the next command, in this case, EDIT.

Redirecting Command Procedure Output

Generally, command procedure output is displayed at your terminal. You may redirect output to a file of your choice by using
the /OUTPUT qualifier when you execute a command procedure.
The following example demonstrates:

```
$ @SHOW_DATE/OUTPUT=DATE.DAT
```

Redirecting Messages

By default, DCL error and severe error messages are directed to
the file indicated by the system logical name SYS$ERROR. When
you execute a command procedure interactively, SYS$ERROR
normally is assigned to your terminal. If you want to log these
error messages, you can redirect SYS$ERROR to a file. However,
if you redirect SYS$ERROR without also redirecting SYS$OUTPUT,
DCL will send error messages to both SYS$ERROR and
SYS$OUTPUT. In effect, you will receive the error messages twice
— at your terminal and in the file indicated by SYS$ERROR.

You can completely suppress error messages in two ways. The
first method is to simply redirect both SYS$ERROR and
SYS$OUTPUT to the null device NL:. Anything sent to NL: van-
ishes (the proverbial "bit-bucket"). For example:

```
$! Command procedure segment to suppress error messages.
$!
$ DEFINE/USER_MODE SYS$ERROR NL:
$ DEFINE/USER_MODE SYS$OUTPUT NL:
$!
$! Error messages will be suppressed for the next command.
```

The second method is to use the SET MESSAGE command to turn off all message output. For example:

```
$! This SET MESSAGE command will suppress messages generated
$! by the DCL PURGE command.
$!
$ SET MESSAGE/NOTEXT/NOIDENTIFICATION/NOFACILITY/NOSEVERITY
$ PURGE *.DAT
$!
$! This next SET MESSAGE command turns error messages back on.
$!
$ SET MESSAGE/TEXT/IDENTIFICATION/FACILITY/SEVERITY
```

FLOW CONTROL AND CONDITIONAL PROCESSING

Up to this point we have created command procedures and procedure segments that perform a consecutive series of DCL statements. It also is possible to write command procedures that execute statements based on a particular condition or repeat statements a given number of times.

Before proceeding, you should have an understanding of the following terms:

Variable—A symbol that may be changed each time you perform a task, for example, a symbol being used to hold a count.

Iteration—A command or group of commands that is repeated.

The iteration is the repeat count or, more precisely, the number of times the group of commands has been executed.

Conditional—Describes a command or group of commands that may vary each time the task is performed, for example, a statement that is performed based on the time of day. Time is the condition.

Conditional Statements

You can use DCL IF...THEN statements and conditional operators within command procedures to make your procedures flexible and more intelligent. The IF...THEN statement executes a command based on the evaluation of a condition. The basic usage is either

$ IF *condition* THEN *command*

or

$ IF *condition* THEN *command* ELSE *command* ENDIF

where *condition* is a Boolean expression (a statement that evaluates to true or false), and *command* is any legal DCL command. In the IF-THEN-ELSE-ENDIF format, if the condition is not true, the ELSE command is processed. The following command procedure, TIME.COM, demonstrates the IF...THEN statement:

```
$! TIME.COM
$!
$ TIME = F$TIME()                  !Put the current time in TIME
$ HOUR = F$EXTRACT(12,2,TIME)  !Extract the hour digits into
$                              !HOUR
$ IF HOUR .LT. 12 THEN -
   WRITE SYS$OUTPUT "Good morning!"
$ EXIT
```

In the above example, the IF...THEN statement says: if the hour is less than (.LT.) 12, then say "Good morning!". The mnemonic

Table 9-1. DCL Conditional Operators

Operator	Function
.EQ,/.EQS	Determines whether the two numbers/ character strings are equal
.GE./.GES.	Tests whether the first number/character string is greater than or equal to the second
.GT./.GTS.	Determines whether the first number/ character string is greater than the second
.LE./.LES.	Tests whether the first number/character string is less than or equal to the second
.LT./.LTS.	Determines whether the first number/ character string is less than the second
.NE./.NES.	Tests to see if the two numbers/character strings are not equal
.AND.	Combines two numbers with a logical AND (Boolean algebra addition operation)
.OR.	Combines two numbers with a logical OR (Boolean algebra multiplication operation)
.NOT.	Logically negates a value

.LT. is called a *conditional operator*. DCL supports the conditional operators shown in Table 9-1.

When you write an expression that uses a conditional operator, you must make sure that the two values on which it operates are of the same data type—integer or character string. If you mix data types, DCL will convert the values to the same data type. In most cases, character strings will be converted to an integer value when mixed with numeric values.

Using Labels to Transfer Control

Often you will need to execute multiple commands or go around a segment of commands based on a condition. To do so, use the GOTO command. The GOTO command transfers execution control to a specified label. Labels are markers used by DCL for conditional processing and repetition loops. For example:

```
$ IF condition THEN GOTO GO_AROUND
    .
    .
    .

$ GO_AROUND:
    .
    .
    .

$ EXIT
```

We can expand the TIME.COM procedure using this technique, as follows:

```
$! TIME.COM
$!
$ TIME = F$TIME()
$ HOUR = F$EXTRACT(12,2,TIME)
$ IF HOUR .LT. 12 THEN GOTO MORNING
$ IF HOUR .LE. 17 THEN GOTO AFTERNOON
$ IF HOUR .GE. 18 THEN GOTO EVENING
$ GOTO END
$MORNING:
$ WRITE SYS$OUTPUT "Good morning!"
$ GOTO END
$AFTERNOON:
$ WRITE SYS$OUTPUT "Good afternoon!"
$ GOTO END
$EVENING:
$ WRITE SYS$OUTPUT "Good evening!"
$END:
$ EXIT
```

You should put labels on separate lines to make the labels easier to find. It serves as another form of commenting (if you use descriptive labels). Labels can be 1 to 255 characters long, cannot contain blanks, and must end with a colon.

The use of GOTO commands can make your command procedures difficult to follow. The preferred method of controlling which commands execute is the IF-THEN-ELSE-ENDIF statement. The best way to write the TIME command procedure is as follows:

```
$! TIME.COM
$!
$ HOUR = F$EXTRACT(12,2,F$TIME())
$ IF HOUR .LT. 12
$   THEN
$     WRITE SYS$OUTPUT "Good morning!"
$   ELSE
$     IF HOUR .LE. 17
$       THEN
$         WRITE SYS$OUTPUT "Good afternoon!"
$       ELSE
$         WRITE SYS$OUTPUT "Good evening!"
$       ENDIF
$ ENDIF
$ EXIT
```

As you can see, using the IF-THEN-ELSE-ENDIF statement makes the TIME command procedure shorter and easier to read.

Execution Loops

Execution loops are used to repeat a statement or group of statements until a given condition is met. You can write two kinds of loops: DO WHILE and DO UNTIL. The DO WHILE loop tests for the condition before executing any commands. It takes the form:

```
$ LOOP:
$ IF .NOT. condition THEN GOTO END

    .
    .       !Statements to be executed go here.

    .
$ GOTO LOOP
$ END:
$       EXIT
```

The DO UNTIL loop executes the statements and then tests for the condition:

```
$  LOOP:

    .
    .               !Statements to be executed go here.

    .
$               IF condition THEN GOTO LOOP
$               EXIT
```

Subroutines

The DCL GOSUB command transfers execution control to a label. The RETURN command terminates subroutine execution, returning control to the statement below the GOSUB command.

Subroutines are useful in complex command procedures, where you need to repeat the same series of commands in different parts of your procedure. Subroutines also make your procedures more compact and easier to read.

The following command procedure shows how to use the GOSUB and RETURN commands:

```
$! PERS_INFO.COM
$!
$! Open the personal information file.
$!
```

```
$ OPEN/WRITE OUTPUT_FILE PERSINFO.DAT
$ !
$ ! Collect info
$ !
$ INQUIRE RECORD "Enter your name"
$ GOSUB WRITE_TO_FILE
$ INQUIRE RECORD "Enter your address"
$ GOSUB WRITE_TO_FILE
$ INQUIRE RECORD "Enter your phone number"
$ GOSUB WRITE_TO_FILE
$ CLOSE OUTPUT_FILE
$ EXIT
$ !
$ ! subroutine WRITE_TO_FILE
$ !
$ WRITE_TO_FILE:
$       WRITE OUTPUT_FILE RECORD
$       RETURN
```

HANDLING ERROR CONDITIONS

After DCL has executed a command in a procedure, the command interpreter saves a code that describes the condition of that command. This code indicates a successful termination or an informational error message. After each command is executed, the command interpreter examines the condition code. If an error occurred, the command interpreter prints the message indicated by the condition code.

Unless otherwise directed, the command interpreter will execute an EXIT command if a severe error occurs. The EXIT command will cause the command procedure to terminate, and control will be returned to the previous command level (DCL or command procedure). To prevent this from happening, use the DCL ON command to specify an action for the command interpreter to take.

The ON command supports three keywords: WARNING, ERROR and SEVERE_ERROR. To override error handling for procedure warnings, for example, use a command such as:

```
$ ON WARNING THEN EXIT
```

or

```
$ ON WARNING THEN GOTO label
```

The WARNING keyword causes the command procedure to take the specified action if a warning, error or severe error occurs. The ERROR keyword causes the action to be taken if an error or severe error occurs. The SEVERE_ERROR keyword causes the command procedure to take the specified action only if a fatal error occurs.

Using $STATUS and $SEVERITY to Control Errors

$STATUS and $SEVERITY are reserved DCL global symbols. Each time a command is successfully or unsuccessfully executed, DCL assigns values to these symbols.

The $STATUS symbol holds the full condition code of the last command. The $SEVERITY symbol holds an error severity level. This severity level is the degree of success or failure of the condition code held in $STATUS.

The condition code held in $STATUS is a valid VMS message code. It can be used with the lexical function F$MESSAGE to obtain the actual text message associated with the code. Consider the following:

```
$ SET DEFAULT DUB1:[ACCOUNTING]
$ WRITE SYS$OUTPUT $STATUS
%X00000001
$ WRITE SYS$OUTPUT F$MESSAGE(%X00000001)
%SYSTEM-S-NORMAL, normal successful completion
```

All DCL commands will return a condition code. However, not all condition codes have associated text messages. Condition codes without message text will return the message:

```
"%NONAME-E-NOMSG, Message number (a numeric code)."
```

While the message text may be useful in many applications, it is not useful for making conditional decisions (IF...THEN). It is more useful to use the contents of $SEVERITY, which contains one of five possible values, extracted from the first three bits of $STATUS. Table 9-2 lists the values and their meanings.

NOTE: Odd values (1 and 3) indicate the two levels of success, and even values (0, 2 and 4) indicate various degrees of failure. This is the secret of DCL error handling (i.e., when $STATUS and $SEVERITY are odd, the command was successful; even values indicate an error).

There are two ways to handle errors using the status and severity codes. The first is to treat $STATUS as a Boolean value (true or false), as in this example:

```
$ SET NOON
$ command !                         Your DCL command???
$ IF $STATUS THEN GOTO NO_ERROR     ! Testing $STATUS for T or F

  .
  .                                 ! Handle error
  .

$ NO_ERRORS:

  .
  .                                 ! Continue processing
  .

$ EXIT
```

The second method is to trap the error with an ON WARNING command, then use the severity level to determine what needs to be done about the error. For example:

```
$ SET NOON
$ ON WARNING GOTO ERROR_TRAP
$ command                              ! Your DCL commands???
$ command
$ .
$ .
$ .
$ command
$ EXIT
$!
$! Start of error trap code
$!
$ ERROR_TRAP:
$ SEVERITY = $SEVERITY                 ! Must save the code
$ IF SEVERITY = Ø THEN command...      ! If warning...
$ GOTO ERROR_TAKEN_CARE_OF
$ IF SEVERITY = 2 THEN command...      ! If error...
$ GOTO ERROR_TAKEN_CARE_OF
$ IF SEVERITY = 4 THEN command...      ! If severe error...
$ ERROR_TAKEN_CARE_OF:
    .
    .
    .
$ EXIT
```

Table 9-2. Status Severity Codes

Code	Definition
0	Warning
1	Success
2	Error
3	Information
4	Severe Error

Disabling DCL Error Checking

Error checking can be completely disabled by issuing the DCL SET NOON command. When the SET NOON command is in effect, the command interpreter continues to update condition code status, but does not perform any error condition actions. The DCL SET ON command restores error checking to its normal condition. For example:

```
$ SET NOON
$ RUN MY_PROGRAM
$ SET ON
```

TERMINATING COMMAND PROCEDURES

To correctly terminate a command procedure, use the EXIT or STOP command. The EXIT command terminates the current command procedure and returns control to the command level that called it. The STOP command terminates all command procedures, if nested, and returns control to DCL.

SAMPLE COMMAND PROCEDURES

The following command procedures illustrate some basic concepts involved in programming in DCL.

LOGIN.COM

The following LOGIN.COM procedure will give you a good idea of the things you should consider when using your own login procedure. Notice that at the beginning of the procedure, we check to see if the login is via a network proxy access or the VMS batch processor. This allows us to take a specific action, if required:

```
$! LOGIN.COM
$!
$! This command procedure is executed for you each time you log
$! in.
$!
$! Check for a NETWORK or BATCH log in
```

```
$!
$ IF F$MODE() .EQS. "NETWORK" THEN GOTO NETWORK
$ IF F$MODE() .EQS. "BATCH" THEN GOTO BATCH
$!
$! Define some process permanent symbols
$!
$ SD == "SET DEFAULT"
$ SH == "SET HOST"
$ WI*DE == "SET TERMINAL/WIDTH=132"
$ NA*RROW == "SET TERMINAL/WIDTH=80"
$ DIR*ECTORY == "DIRECTORY/SIZE"
$ PU*RGE == "PURGE/LOG/KEEP=2"
$ HO*ME == "SET DEFAULT SYS$LOGIN:"
$ WHO == "SHOW USERS"
$ EVE == "EDIT/TPU"
$ EDT == "EDIT/EDT/COMMAND=SYS$LOGIN:EDTINI.EDT"
$ BR*OWSE == "TYPE/PAGE"
$!
$! Define special keys
$!
$ DEFINE/KEY/NOLOG/TERM PF1 "DIR"
$ DEFINE/KEY/NOLOG PF2 "EDIT"
$ DEFINE/KEY/NOLOG/TERM/NOECHO PF3 "LOGOUT"
$ DEFINE/KEY/NOLOG/TERM/NOECHO HELP "SHOW KEY/ALL"
$!
$! Modify terminal characteristics
$!
$ SET TERMINAL/INSERT/INQUIRE
$ SET PROMPT = "´´F$USER()´> "
$!
$! Show the time and exit
$!
$ SHOW TIME
$ EXIT
$!
```

```
$! If this is a network log in, simply exit. If you need to
$! perform a special function for a network log in, insert the
$! commands after the "NETWORK:" label.
$!
$NETWORK:
$ EXIT
$!
$! For a batch job log in, you may want to turn verification on.
$!
$ BATCH:
$ SET VERIFY
$ EXIT
```

SUBDIR.COM

SUBDIR illustrates the use of several lexical functions. This procedure demonstrates how to search and parse character strings:

```
$START:
$ WRITE SYS$OUTPUT F$DIRECTORY()+" Subdirectories:"
$ WRITE SYS$OUTPUT ""
$!
$! This loop searches for subdirectory names and displays them
$! on the terminal.
$!
$DIR$LOOP:
$   FILE = F$SEARCH("*.DIR")
$!
$! If DCL returns a null string "", we are finished.
$!
$   IF FILE .EQS. "" THEN GOTO END$DIR$LOOP
$!
$! Find the position of the dot.
$!
$   DOT = F$LOCATE(".",FILE)
$!
$! Find the position of the right bracket.
```

```
$!
$   BRACKET = F$LOCATE("]",FILE)
$!
$! Extract the string between the dot and bracket.
$!
$ FILE = F$EXTRACT(BRACKET+1,DOT-BRACKET-1,FILE)
$!
$! Display the subdirectory name
$!
$ WRITE SYS$OUTPUT " ''FILE'"
$ GOTO DIR$LOOP
$END$DIR$LOOP:
$ EXIT
```

SEAREP.COM

SEAREP.COM uses the EDT editor to search for every occurrence of a given string and replace it with a new string. To accomplish this, SEAREP.COM creates an EDT start-up file with the appropriate commands:

```
$ ON WARNING THEN GOTO CLEANUP
$ FIRST_PASS = 0
$!
$! Create an editor start-up file
$!
$! Get filenames and search/replace strings
$!
$GET_FILE_NAMES:
$ INQUIRE FILES "FILE NAME(S) - SEPARATE BY COMMAS"
$ INQUIRE SEARCH "SEARCH STRING"
$ INQUIRE REPLACE "REPLACE STRING"
$ INQUIRE RANGE "SEARCH RANGE (i.e., 1:80)"
$!
$! Extract one filename from list
$!
$EXT_NAME:
```

```
$ IF F$LOCATE("*",FILES) .NE. F$LENGTH(FILES)
$   THEN
$     IF FIRST_PASS .EQ. Ø
$       THEN
$         PURGE ´FILES´
$         OPEN/WRITE SRLIST SRLIST.DAT
$SRLIST_LOOP:
$         FNAME = F$SEARCH("´´FILES´")
$         IF FNAME .EQS. "" THEN GOTO CLOSE_SRLIST
$         WRITE SRLIST FNAME
$         GOTO SRLIST_LOOP
$CLOSE_SRLIST:
$         CLOSE SRLIST
$         FIRST_PASS = 1
$         OPEN/READ SRLIST SRLIST.DAT
$     ENDIF
$     READ/ERROR=CLEANUP/END=CLEANUP SRLIST FNAME
$   ELSE
$     FNAME = F$EXTRACT(Ø,F$LOCATE(",",FILES),FILES)
$     FILES = FILES - FNAME - ","
$     IF FNAME .EQS. "" THEN GOTO CLEANUP
$   ENDIF
$!
$! Process extracted filename
$!
$ WRITE SYS$OUTPUT ""
$ WRITE SYS$OUTPUT " *** PROCESSING ´´FNAME´ ***"
$ WRITE SYS$OUTPUT ""
$ IF F$SEARCH("´´FNAME´") .EQS. ""
$   THEN
$     WRITE SYS$OUTPUT "´´FNAME´ DOES NOT EXIST, PROCEEDING..."
$     GOTO EXT_NAME
$   ELSE
$     OPEN/WRITE SR SEAREP.EDT
$     WRITE SR "SET MODE LINE
$     WRITE SR "S/´´SEARCH´/´´REPLACE´/´´RANGE´"
```

```
$     WRITE SR "EXIT"
$     CLOSE SR
$     WRITE SYS$OUTPUT "NOW PROCESSING ''FNAME'..."
$     EDIT/EDT/COMMAND=SEAREP.EDT 'FNAME'
$     DELETE SEAREP.EDT;
$   ENDIF
$ GOTO EXT_NAME
$!
$CLEANUP:
$ IF F$LOCATE("*",FILES) .NE. F$LENGTH(FILES)
$   THEN
$     CLOSE SRLIST
$     DELETE SRLIST.DAT;*
$   ENDIF
$ EXIT
```

MENU

MENU is a menu for DCL commands and utilities. MENU supports 10 options, of which four are defined. You can add or remove as many options as you like:

```
$! MENU.COM
$!
$ SAY = "WRITE SYS$OUTPUT"
$!
$! Define Video Terminal Escape Sequences
$! To enter the escape character with EDT, press:
$! <PF1><2><7><SPECINS>
$!
$ ESC = "<ESC>" ! ESCAPE character, ASCII 27
$ AUXKP = ESC + "="
$ BOTTOM = ESC + "[24;1H"
$ BLDON = ESC + "[1m"
$ BLDOFF = ESC + "[0m"
$ CLS = ESC + "[2J"
$ CURLF = ESC + "[1D"
```

```
$ CURRT = ESC + "[1C"
$ CURUP = ESC + "[1A"
$ CURDN = ESC + "[1B"
$ HOME = ESC + "[1;1H"
$ DBLHTT = ESC + "#3"
$ DBLHTB = ESC + "#4"
$ DBLWD = ESC + "#6"
$ EREOL = ESC + "[ØK"
$ EREOS = ESC + "[ØJ"
$ NUMKP = ESC + ">"
$ PF1 = ESC + "OP"
$ PF2 = ESC + "OQ"
$ RPCUR = ESC + "[6n"
$ RVIDON = ESC + "[7m"
$ RVIDOFF = ESC + "[Øm"
$ SNGWD = ESC + "#5"
$ UNDRL = ESC + "[4m"
$ RESET_SCROLL_REGION = ESC + "[Ør"
$ SETUP_SCROLL_REGION1 = ESC + "[4;24r"
$ ERASE_SCROLL_REGION1 = ESC + "[4;1H" + EREOS
$ SETUP_SCROLL_REGION2 = ESC + "[6;24r"
$ ERASE_SCROLL_REGION2 = ESC + "[6;1H" + EREOS
$!
$! Define Menu Option Text Strings
$!
$ OPTION1 = " ''BLDON'1 ''BLDOFF' Mail"
$ OPTION2 = " ''BLDON'2 ''BLDOFF' Phone"
$ OPTION3 = " ''BLDON'3 ''BLDOFF' "
$ OPTION4 = " ''BLDON'4 ''BLDOFF' "
$ OPTION5 = " ''BLDON'5 ''BLDOFF' "
$ OPTION6 = " ''BLDON'6 ''BLDOFF' "
$ OPTION7 = " ''BLDON'7 ''BLDOFF' "
$ OPTION8 = " ''BLDON'8 ''BLDOFF' "
$ OPTION9 = " ''BLDON'9 ''BLDOFF' Change Password"
$ OPTION10 = " ''BLDON'10 ''BLDOFF' Log out"
$!
```

```
$ DEASSIGN SYS$OUTPUT
$!
$! Set up error handlers
$!
$ SET ON
$ SET CONTROL=Y
$ ON CONTROL_Y THEN GOTO MENU
$ ON WARNING THEN GOTO MENU
$!
$MENU:
$!
$! Output menu header
$!
$ SAY HOME, CLS
$ SAY HOME, DBLHTT,    " DCL Menu"
$ SAY DBLHTB,   " DCL Menu"
$ SAY "
$ SAY "
$!
$! Menu Choice
$!
$ SAY OPTION1
$ SAY OPTION2
$ SAY OPTION3
$ SAY OPTION4
$ SAY OPTION5
$ SAY OPTION6
$ SAY OPTION7
$ SAY OPTION8
$ SAY OPTION9
$ SAY OPTION10
$ SAY " ´´BLDON´CTRL/Z ´´BLDOFF´Exit Menu"
$ SAY ""
$!
$! Read input from user
$!
```

```
$GET_OPTION:
$ READ /PROMPT="Your selection? " -
        /END=EXIT_PROCEDURE SYS$COMMAND CHOICE
$ IF CHOICE .EQS. "" THEN GOTO OPTION_ERROR
$ CHOICE = F$INTEGER(CHOICE)
$ IF CHOICE .LT. 1 .OR. CHOICE .GT. 10 THEN GOTO OPTION_ERROR
$ GOTO CHOICE´CHOICE´
$OPTION_ERROR:
$ TYPE SYS$INPUT

        Valid choices are 1 to 10, or <CTRLZ> to exit.

$ WAIT 0:0:3
$ SAY CURUP,CURUP,CURUP,CURUP,CURUP,EREOS
$ GOTO GET_OPTION
$!
$! Menu Option 1 — VMS MAIL
$!
$CHOICE1:
$ ON CONTROL_Y THEN GOTO EXIT_PROCEDURE
$ SAY HOME,CLS,BLDON,"VMS MAIL",BLDOFF
$ DEFINE/USER_MODE SYS$INPUT SYS$COMMAND
$ MAIL
$ GOTO MENU
$!
$! Menu Option 2 — VMS PHONE
$!
$CHOICE2:
$ ON CONTROL_Y THEN GOTO EXIT_PROCEDURE
$ SAY HOME,CLS,BLDON,"VMS Phone",BLDOFF
$ DEFINE/USER_MODE SYS$INPUT SYS$COMMAND
$ PHONE
$ GOTO MENU
$!
$! Menu Option 3
$!
```

```
$CHOICE3:
$ ON CONTROL_Y THEN GOTO EXIT_PROCEDURE
$ SAY HOME,CLS
$ SAY BLDON,"Option 3",BLDOFF
$ GOTO MENU
$!
$! Menu Option 4
$!
$CHOICE4:
$ ON CONTROL_Y THEN GOTO EXIT_PROCEDURE
$ SAY HOME,CLS
$ SAY BLDON,"Option 4",BLDOFF
$ GOTO MENU
$!
$! Menu Option 5
$!
$CHOICE5:
$ ON CONTROL_Y THEN GOTO EXIT_PROCEDURE
$ SAY HOME,CLS
$ SAY BLDON,"Option 5",BLDOFF
$ GOTO MENU
$!
$! Menu Option 6
$!
$CHOICE6:
$ ON CONTROL_Y THEN GOTO EXIT_PROCEDURE
$ SAY HOME,CLS
$ SAY BLDON,"Option 6",BLDOFF
$ GOTO MENU
$!
$! Menu Option 7
$!
$CHOICE7:
$ ON CONTROL_Y THEN GOTO EXIT_PROCEDURE
$ SAY HOME,CLS
$ SAY BLDON,"Option 7",BLDOFF
```

```
$ GOTO MENU
$!
$! Menu Option 8
$!
$CHOICE8:
$ ON CONTROL_Y THEN GOTO EXIT_PROCEDURE
$ SAY HOME,CLS
$ SAY BLDON,"Option 8",BLDOFF
$ GOTO MENU
$!
$! Menu Option 9 - SET PASSWORD
$!
$CHOICE9:
$ ON CONTROL_Y THEN GOTO EXIT_PROCEDURE
$ SAY HOME,CLS,BLDON,"Change Password",BLDOFF
$ SAY ""
$ DEFINE/USER_MODE SYS$INPUT SYS$COMMAND
$ SET PASSWORD
$ GOTO MENU
$!
$! Menu Option 10 - LOGOUT
$!
$CHOICE10:
$ ON CONTROL_Y THEN GOTO EXIT_PROCEDURE
$ SAY HOME,CLS
$ SAY HOME,CLS,BLDON,"LOGOUT",BLDOFF
$ EXIT
$!
$EXIT_PROCEDURE:
$ EXIT
```

WHERE TO GO FROM HERE

For detailed information on writing and using command procedures, refer to the *Digital Equipment Guide to Using DCL and Command Procedures on VAX/VMS*. Refer to Appendices A and B in this book for a quick reference to DCL commands and lexical functions.

Chapter 10

Advanced VMS Features

This chapter is for readers who feel they have mastered the commands and ideas presented in previous chapters. In this chapter, you'll be introduced to subprocesses, batch jobs, DECnet features, VAXclusters and several utilities. Specifically, you'll learn how to:

- ▼ Use the SPAWN and ATTACH commands.
- ▼ Use the SUBMIT command to process jobs in a batch queue.
- ▼ Use DECnet to access other VAX systems.
- ▼ Use the Backup utility to save and restore your files.
- ▼ Use the Sort and Library utilities.

WORKING WITH SUBPROCESSES

One benefit of the VMS operating system is its multiprocessing capability. Multiprocessing is not limited to multiple users logged in and using the system; VMS users can create (spawn) subprocesses from their main process. From each subprocess, a command or program can be run.

The SPAWN Command

The SPAWN command is used to create a subprocess. By default, SPAWN creates a subprocess with the attributes of its parent process (default directory, privileges, quota, and so forth). The following example demonstrates:

```
$ SPAWN
%DCL-S-SPAWNED, process BYNON_1 spawned
%DCL-S-ATTACHED, terminal now attached to process BYNON_1
$
```

In this example, the parent process is put into hibernation and the subprocess is given control of the keyboard. Notice that we are left at the DCL command level. You are free to execute any DCL commands, utilities or other programs. To return to your parent process and subsequently delete the subprocess, enter LOGOUT:

```
$ LOGOUT
   Process BYNON_1 logged out at 13-SEP-1990 10:33:33.60
$DCL-S-RETURNED, control returned to process BYNON
```

To suppress the informational messages SPAWN creates, use the SPAWN qualifier /NOLOG.

You can directly execute DCL commands, command procedures and VMS utilities with SPAWN by entering the correct syntax for the command or procedure after the SPAWN command. For example:

```
$ SPAWN/NOLOG MAIL
MAIL> EXIT
$
$ SPAWN/NOLOG @CLEANUP
$
$ SPAWN/NOLOG KERMIT
Kermit> EXIT
$
```

If you have a task that can be executed without user intervention, such as a program compile, you can spawn a task to run as a background process to your current process:

```
$ SPAWN/NOWAIT FORTRAN WHO
%DCL-S-SPAWNED, process BYNON_1 spawned
```

The SPAWN qualifier /NOWAIT spawns the task to run concurrently (in parallel) with your parent process. Both processes will share the terminal. Any messages from the background task will be displayed at your terminal. To prevent any possible conflicts, use the /OUTPUT qualifier. For example:

```
$ SPAWN/NOWAIT/OUTPUT=COMPILE.LOG FORTRAN WHO
%DCL-S-SPAWNED, process BYNON_1 spawned
```

When the job in the subprocess is complete, it terminates (logs out) and is removed from the system.

The ATTACH Command

The ATTACH command enables you to connect your keyboard to any process or subprocesses that you have created. ATTACH is an alternative method of exiting from a subprocess. The following example shows how to shift keyboard and screen focus from process BYNON_2 to process BYNON:

```
$ ATTACH BYNON
%DCL-S-RETURNED, control returned to process BYNON
```

When you shift keyboard and screen control with ATTACH, the process you leave behind hibernates. You can later attach to the process from which you exited and continue to work.

Interrupting Processes

Often, you will want to stop what you are doing, start something else, then continue with your original activity. The key combination allows you to do this by interrupting your current process. The <CTRL/Y> combination has two purposes. First, it allows you to cancel a command abruptly. Second, after pressing <CTRL/Y>, you can use the SPAWN and ATTACH commands to create and access your subprocesses. When you return from the subprocess (back to the interrupted one), use the CONTINUE command to re-sume the interrupted program. For example:

```
$ BACKUP [BYNON...]*.*;* DUA3:[*...]
<CTRL/Y> *INTERRUPT*
$ SPAWN MAIL
%DCL-S-SPAWNED, process BYNON_1 spawned
%DCL-S-ATTACHED, terminal now attached to process BYNON_1


You have 1 new message.

MAIL> READ
   .
   .
   .
MAIL> EXIT
%DCL-S-RETURNED, control returned to process BYNON
$ CONTINUE
$
```

When you use <CTRL/Y>, the program currently executing will be interrupted and control will return to DCL (you will get your prompt back). The program is temporarily suspended so that one or more built-in DCL commands (SPAWN, ATTACH and CON-TINUE) can be used. If you enter any command other than SPAWN, ATTACH or CONTINUE, the interrupted program image will be canceled.

To spawn a subprocess while using the EDT editor, first go to command mode (type <CTRL/Z>). If you fail to return directly to your edit session after you have finished with your spawned process, you will have to recover your edit session.

Some VMS utilities, such as Mail, intrinsically support SPAWN. In other words, you can spawn a process from within these utilities by entering the SPAWN command.

Other Process Control-Key Commands

The <CTRL/C> key combination interrupts the execution of built-in commands and most program images. Program images, however, may define what action is taken when you press <CTRL/C>. Many programs treat a <CTRL/C> interrupt as if <CTRL/Y> was pressed. Others, such as the TYPE command, define <CTRL/C> as a cancel command. In the case of the TYPE command, <CTRL/C> tells TYPE to quit displaying the file it is processing and move on to the next file.

It often is necessary to get statistical information about your process while a program image or command procedure is executing. The <CTRL/T> key combination performs this function. When you press <CTRL/T>, the executing command is interrupted and a status line is displayed. The status line provides information about your current process.

Many times, you will execute a command or run a program that sends large quantities of information to your screen. There are three control-key combinations that allow you to control the flow of this information: <CTRL/O>, <CTRL/S> and <CTRL/Q>.

Press <CTRL/O> to toggle screen output off and on for the program image currently executing. The messages "Output off" and "Output on" are displayed as appropriate. When you press <CTRL/O> to turn display output off, the program image continues to process, but the display information is lost. The <CTRL/O> control-key combination is useful if large quantities of messages are being sent to your display; you can shut off the display to speed processing.

If you want to suspend terminal output so you can read what is on your screen, use <CTRL/S> and <CTRL/Q> (or the <HOLD SCREEN> key). <CTRL/S> suspends program output and <CTRL/Q> lets the output resume. No output information will be lost.

SUBMITTING JOBS TO BATCH QUEUES

In Chapter 9, the DCL SUBMIT command was introduced. In this section we will go into detailed usage of the SUBMIT command and cover the basics of working with batch jobs.

A batch job is one or more DCL command procedures that execute from a detached process with your privileges and quotas. The controller of this process is called the *batch queue*. Jobs enter the batch queue via the SUBMIT command. The benefit of submitting a batch job is that it executes without your interaction; the batch job permits you to use your terminal for interactive work while the system executes the batch job (command procedure). Typically, you will submit jobs to a batch queue that take a long time to execute, use a high level of system resources, or need to be scheduled to execute at a specific time.

The SUBMIT Command

Use the DCL SUBMIT command to enter jobs into a batch queue. If you do not specify a queue name, with the /QUEUE qualifier, SUBMIT will enter the job into the default batch queue named SYS$BATCH. For example:

```
$ SUBMIT MAIL_SCHEDULE
Job MAIL_SCHEDULE (queue SYS$BATCH, entry 207) started on SYS$BATCH
```

When you submit a command procedure for batch execution, it is given a job name. The default name of the batch job is the name of the command procedure submitted. In addition to being given a name, the job also is assigned an entry number. This entry number will become important when you need to control the job.

Controlling Your Batch Jobs

You can specify a name for your batch jobs by using the /NAME qualifier, as in this example:

```
$ SUBMIT BACKUP /NAME=DAILY_BACKUP
Job DAILY_BACKUP (queue SYS$BATCH, entry 208) started on SYS$BATCH
```

When issuing the SUBMIT command, you may list more than one command procedure to be executed by separating the procedure names with a comma. For example:

```
$ SUBMIT SORT_DATA,REPORT /NAME=WEEKLY_REPORT
Job WEEKLY_REPORT (queue SYS$BATCH, entry 29) started on SYS$BATCH
```

In the above example, the SORT_DATA and REPORT procedures were submitted for execution under a single job name, WEEKLY_REPORT.

In many cases, it may be necessary to schedule a job's execution for a specific time. This is possible by using the /AFTER=*time* qualifier. When you use /AFTER, your job will remain in queue until the specified time; the command procedure will then be executed. The following command demonstrates this:

```
$ SUBMIT CLEANUP /AFTER=11:40
Job CLEANUP (queue SYS$BATCH, entry 31) holding until 1-FEB-1987 11:40
```

Notice that the date defaults to the current day. If you want the job to be held past the current date and time, you must specify a date and time.

In addition to a timed release, you may hold a job in queue to be released at a later time with the /HOLD qualifier. To release a batch job being held or a batch job pending a timed release, issue the DCL SET QUEUE/ENTRY=*n*/RELEASE command. The following commands demonstrate:

```
$ SUBMIT REMINDER /HOLD
Job REMINDER (queue SYS$BATCH, entry 32) holding
$
$ SET ENTRY 32 /RELEASE SYS$BATCH
```

On most VMS systems, multiple batch queues with various characteristics are established. The system manager does this to balance the system's workload. For example, the system manager may establish two classifications of queues: fast and slow. The fast queue may be set up with a higher execution priority and the ability to execute multiple jobs at one time. This queue would be used for short, non-resource-intensive jobs. In comparison, the slow queue might be set up to execute jobs at a much lower priority, one job at a time. A queue such as this would be used for long CPU-, I/O- or memory-intensive jobs.

To send a job to a specific queue, use the /QUEUE qualifier. For example:

```
$ SUBMIT COMPILE /QUEUE=SLOW
Job COMPILE (queue SLOW, entry 110) started on SLOW
$
```

It also is possible to assign your own execution characteristics to the jobs you submit. For instance, if you know the job you are submitting is CPU-intensive, you may lower the job's execution priority to prevent degradation of the system's performance. The following example demonstrates:

```
$ SUBMIT CRUNCH /PRIORITY=2
Job CRUNCH (queue SYS$BATCH, entry 109) started on SYS$BATCH
```

Additional qualifiers, such as /CPUTIME, /WSDEFAULT, /WSQUOTA and /WSEXTENT, are available to control other resources a job may consume.

For some command procedures, it may be necessary to pass parameters, just as you would if you invoked the procedure at the DCL command level. This is possible if you use the /PARAMETERS qualifier. The parameter list must be enclosed within parentheses, as in this example:

```
$ SUBMIT COMPILE /PARAMETERS=(WINDOWS,MISC,DISP_IO)
Job COMPILE (queue SYS$BATCH, entry 201) started on SYS$BATCH
```

Logging and Printing Batch Jobs

When you submit a batch job, a log of that job is sent to the system print device SYS$PRINT. To disable this action, use the /NOPRINT qualifier when you submit your procedure.

If you wish to keep a log file of a job's execution, use the /LOG_FILE qualifier to send the output to a file. For example:

```
$ SUBMIT BUILD /NOPRINT /LOG_FILE=DUA2:[BYNON]
Job BUILD (queue SYS$BATCH, entry 211) started on SYS$BATCH
```

In this example, a log file with the name DUA2:[BYNON] BUILD.LOG, is created. If the /NOPRINT qualifier had not been specified, the log file would have been printed and then deleted. To print and keep a specified log file, you must use the /KEEP qualifier with the /LOG_FILE qualifier.

Controlling Batch Jobs in Queue

After a procedure has been submitted to a batch queue, you can monitor its status and modify its job characteristics. To monitor a job in queue, use the SHOW QUEUE command. For example:

```
$ SHOW QUEUE SYS$BATCH
Batch queue SYS$BATCH, on BIFF::

  Jobname      Username      Entry      Status
   BUILD       BYNON         211        Executing
$
```

This command displays the name, entry number and status of the jobs you have in queue. This command has two useful qualifiers, /ALL and /FULL. The /ALL qualifier displays all jobs you have the privilege to know about. The /FULL qualifier provides additional information about batch jobs, such as their operating characteristics and submission time.

Before a job starts to execute, you can modify operating characteristics, such as execution priority (/PRIORITY), the job name (/NAME), the release of a held job (/RELEASE), or the delay of the job's execution (/AFTER). To do so, use the SET ENTRY command with the appropriate qualifier, as in this example:

```
$ SET ENTRY 212 /PRIORITY=2 SYS$BATCH
```

This command lowers the operating priority of job 212 to 2.

You can delete batch jobs from a queue before or during execution by using the DCL DELETE/ENTRY command. For example, the following command deletes a job from the queue named fast:

```
$ DELETE /ENTRY=18 FAST
```

For more information on batch jobs, refer to the Digital Equipment VAX/VMS *DCL Dictionary* and *Guide to Using DCL and Command Procedures on VAX/VMS*.

DECNET

Chapter 1 introduced you to DECnet through the DCL SET HOST command. The SET HOST command allows you to use your terminal and local VAX system as a terminal interface to a host VAX computer on your network. In Chapter 4, you learned about a VMS file specification. The first part of a VMS file specification is the VAX node name. By using the node name in a file specification, you can access files and directories on other systems.

This section will introduce you to the major facilities of DECnet. You will explore copying files between systems, task-to-task communication, and the idea of a DECnet proxy.

Accessing Remote Files

VMS and DECnet are highly integrated. As such, they provide transparency for most user file operations. DECnet uses the standard VMS file specification for remote file access. In addition to a remote node specification, you also may include access control information (username and password). The following example is a typical remote file specification:

```
BIFF"SCOTT MRBILL"::DUA6:[SCOTT]SCHEDULE.TXT
```

Notice that the access control information is in quotes. When used in a command which must access a remote system, the access control information permits a remote connect request. The local system actually logs in to the remote system under your account. If you do not supply explicit access control information, a default DECnet account or proxy must exist on the remote system. The following examples demonstrate VMS file operations on a remote system:

```
$ DIRECTORY BIFF"SCOTT MRBILL"::DUA6:[SCOTT]
$ EDIT BIFF"SCOTT MRBILL"::DUA6:[SCOTT]SCHEDULE.TXT
$ DELETE BIFF"SCOTT MRBILL"::DUA6:[SCOTT]SCHEDULE.TXT;*
$ PURGE BIFF"SCOTT MRBILL"::DUA6:[SCOTT]
$ COPY BIFF"SCOTT MRBILL"::DUA6:[SCOTT]SCHEDULE.TXT *.*
```

You can use the same file commands that you use on your local system on a remote system across DECnet. These remote file operations are preferable to connecting directly to the host (via SET HOST) because they use fewer resources.

Proxy Access

Including access control information in a command string is a burden and a security risk. Because of this, Digital Equipment provides a mechanism known as *proxy access* or *proxy log in*. Proxy access works by keeping a database of users and their hosts who may gain access to the local system via DECnet. The proxy database format is as follows:

```
SYSTEM::REMOTE_USERNAME LOCAL_USERNAME
```

This information lets DECnet say, "If I have a request to access system resources from user X on system Y, I can give him or her access to local account Z." Proxy access is the secure and easy way to perform DECnet operations. Ask your system manager if a proxy database entry is in place for your account.

Task-to-Task Communication

Task-to-task communication is a feature of DECnet that allows programs executing on different systems to communicate with each other. Consider the DCL TYPE command. TYPE provides a way of injecting commands, in a command procedure, to the input stream of a remote process. The command procedure must reside in your account on the remote system. To execute the procedure, use the TYPE command with the "TASK=*procedure*" parameter. For example:

```
$ TYPE BIFF::"TASK=SHOW_USERS"
```

To show users logged in to a remote node, for example, you use a command such as the following:

```
$! SHOW_USERS.COM
$!
$ IF F$MODE() .NES. "NETWORK"
$   THEN
$     SHOW USERS
$     EXIT
$   ELSE
$     DEFINE/USER_MODE SYS$OUTPUT SYS$NET
$     SHOW USERS
$ ENDIF
```

Notice that because this command procedure produces output to the terminal, SYS$OUTPUT was redirected to SYS$NET. This redirects the output to your terminal over the DECnet network.

Task-to-task communication can be simple or as complex as two or more programs passing data, such as bank transactions.

Remote Printing

If your DECnet network includes a local area network (LAN), such as Ethernet, chances are you will share a printer with other nodes on the network. There are several ways to use a remote printer.

The first method is to copy your file directly to the print device. This works well as long as the device is spooled and set up with world write privileges. For example:

```
$ COPY WEEKLY.RPT BIFF::LCA0:
```

In this example, the file WEEKLY.RPT is copied to the device LCA0: on node BIFF.

Another way to print remotely is to use the DCL PRINT/REMOTE command. To do so, however, requires that the file to be printed is located on the remote system. This is inconvenient if the file you want to print is on your local system. However, you often will require the services of the queue manager and therefore will need to use this command. For example:

```
$ COPY WEEKLY.RPT BIFF::[BYNON]
$ PRINT/REMOTE BIFF::[BYNON]WEEKLY.RPT
   Job WEEKLY (queue SYS$PRINT, entry 547) started on LCA0
$ DELETE BIFF::[BYNON]WEEKLY.RPT;1
```

For more information, refer to the Digital Equipment *Guide to Networking on VAX/VMS*.

VAXCLUSTERS

A VAXcluster is a highly integrated group of VAX systems that communicate over a high-speed communications link. The primary purposes of VAXcluster systems are to provide high processor availability, shared resources, and a single security and management domain.

The following sections will acquaint you with the operational differences between VAXcluster systems and a single VAX system. You will learn the various ways to gain access to VAXcluster systems and their shared resources.

Types of VAXclusters

There are two generic types of VAXclusters, homogeneous and heterogeneous. The fundamental difference between these types of VAXclusters is how they share resources, primarily the VMS operating system environment.

In a homogeneous VAXcluster, the VMS operating environment is identical on each VAX computer. This is achieved by using a common system disk for all VAX computers in the cluster. In this configuration, user accounts, system files, queues and mass storage devices are shared. Each computer behaves the same way.

In a heterogeneous VAXcluster, the working environment on each system is unique. Each VAX has its own system disk, user accounts and system files. Queues and mass storage devices may or may not be shared. Users work in different operating environments driven by the system they are working on.

VAXcluster Access

In most cases, VAXcluster access is via a terminal server (see Figure 10-1). Using a terminal server, you can establish a terminal session with any available VAXcluster member. The connection is indistinguishable from the connection of a directly connected terminal. However, unlike a directly connected terminal, the terminal server supports simultaneous sessions to several nodes, load balancing at login time, and login failover if a system fails.

It is possible to have a VAXcluster with directly connected terminals. In such a case, if you need to access another system in the VAXcluster, you must use the SET HOST command.

VAXcluster Storage Devices

In a VAXcluster, each VAX system can use the same mass storage devices to store files. To use a VAXcluster system efficiently, it is important to understand the conventions used to identify storage devices. Each storage device in a VAXcluster is identified by a unique name in the following format:

node_name$device_name:

This convention provides an accurate way to access any device in the cluster. "*Node_name*" is the name of the cluster member to which the device is connected, and "*device_name*" is the standard physical device name.

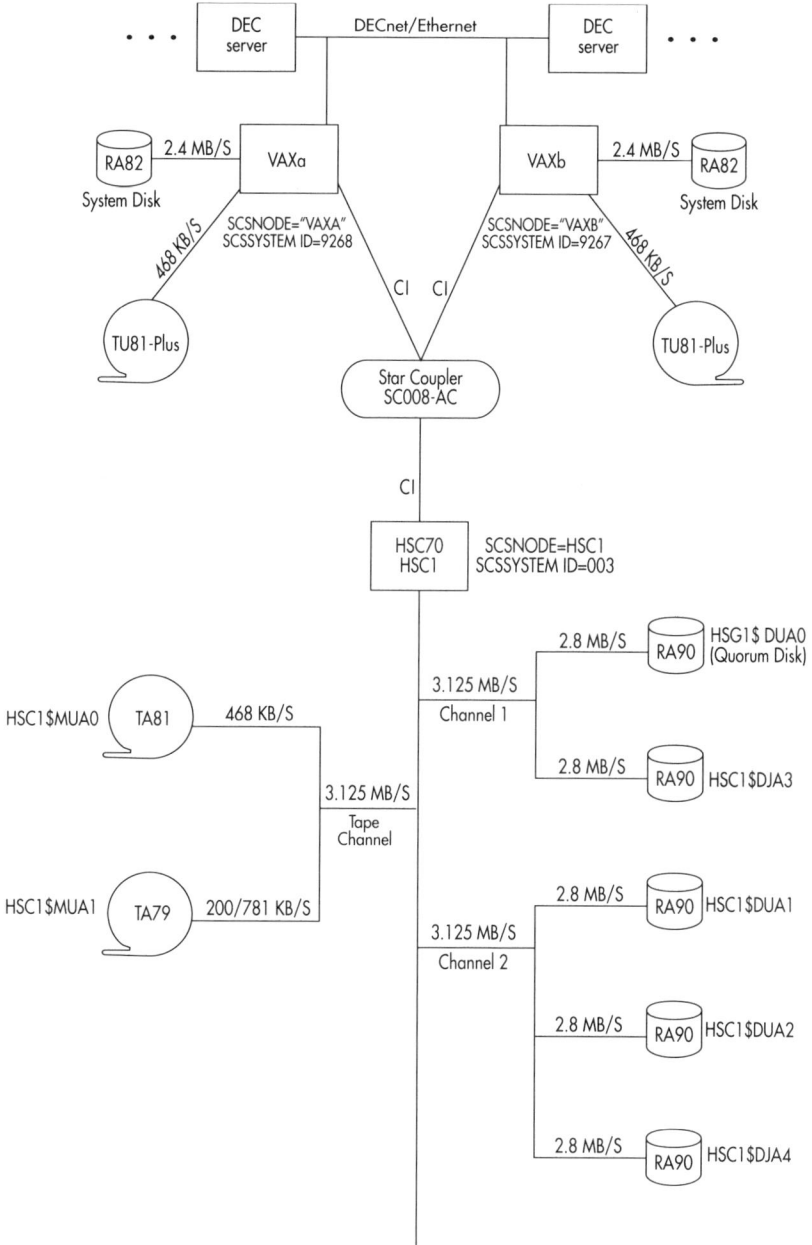

Figure 10-1. VAXcluster with Terminal Servers

There are several methods of configuring disks to make them available to the cluster, such as the following:

▼ Dual-ported MASSBUS disks (dual-pathed)
▼ Hierarchical Storage Controller (HSC)-based disks (may be dual-pathed)
▼ Mass Storage Control Protocol (MSCP)-served disks

How the devices are configured will make a difference in the way you access them. For example, an MSCP-served disk is a disk connected directly to a VAXcluster member, but is available to all VAXcluster members. When accessing this device on the VAX that owns it, you can use the local device name (e.g., DUA0:). If you are using another node in the VAXcluster, you must use that node's cluster name (e.g., BIFF$DUA0:). Use the DCL SHOW DEVICE command to list the devices known to a VAX system.

Most large VAXcluster installations use a Hierarchical Storage Controller (HSC40, HSC50 or HSC70). An HSC is a computer that connects a group of tape and disk drives to all members of a VAXcluster. An HSC is a nonparticipating VAXcluster member. (It provides no interactive user services.) Devices connected to an HSC are made available to all VAX members of the VAXcluster. The cluster device-naming convention applies to HSC-based devices. For example, if your HSC node name is R2D2, then all devices controlled by that HSC would be accessed by the name R2D2$*device_name*.

HSC and dual-ported MASSBUS disks may be dual-pathed, which means that there are two physical links to the device. This is possible when two HSCs are configured to control the same set of devices, and when two VAX members of a VAXcluster share a MASSBUS disk through separate physical connections.

Disks that are dual-pathed are identified differently than explained above. This is because the path used to access a dual-ported device is arbitrary; no specific path to a dual-ported device is ever guaranteed. Since the path to a dual-ported device is chosen without use of a cluster member node name, another convention, *allocation class*, was devised.

Allocation class is a mechanism used to distinguish the relationship between dual-pathed devices and VAXcluster members. The allocation class designator is used in place of a node name when addressing these devices. An allocation class is a number between 1 and 255 preceded by a dollar sign, such as 1DUA2: or 4DJA1:. Use the DCL SHOW DEVICE command to list the devices available on your system.

VAXcluster Queues

In a VAXcluster, VAX systems can share processing resources through the use of print and batch queues. These queues are called clusterwide print and batch queues. On some VAXcluster systems, a node may be singled out to process batch jobs only. Consult with your system manager about your particular configuration.

You use clusterwide queues the same as standard VMS queues. The only special information you need are the queue names. Use the DCL SHOW QUEUE command to list all queues established in the cluster.

When you submit a job to a print or batch queue in a VAXcluster, you must ensure that the node that will execute the job has access to the file you want printed or the command procedure you want processed.

THE BACKUP UTILITY

The Backup utility is frequently used by VAX system managers and operators to back up system disks. This ensures that a recent copy of all data on the disk drives is available and can be used if data on the system disks is lost or becomes unreadable.

Generally, the contents of the system disk and any user disks on a multidisk VAX system are backed up to magnetic tape for safekeeping. On VAX systems configured with removable disks, the contents of one disk may be backed up to a removable disk pack. In this case, the disk pack containing the backup copy of the files is removed from the disk drive and stored in a secure location.

A full system backup can be performed only by individuals whose accounts have the privileges to read all files on the system. However, users can use the Backup utility on files in their own accounts. You will find the utility useful when you want to make copies of files for safekeeping, for transfer to another system, or for offline storage.

Backup Methods

The Backup utility has qualifiers that influence the way it operates and the files it affects. When you use Backup, you must decide what you want to back up, and how you want it backed up. You have the following options:

Selective—The Backup utility can back up files on a selective basis, according to specified criteria such as a date, file type or version number. Backup qualifiers (such as /DATE) and file specifications (such as *.TXT) are used to specify the selective files.

File-by-file—The Backup utility can copy individual files or entire file directories. In this mode, Backup provides file copy facilities (directory creation during copy) that the VMS COPY command does not.

Incremental—An incremental backup saves files created since the most recent backup operation. In general, incremental backups are done by your VAX system manager or operator.

Physical—A physical backup operation saves an exact duplicate of a volume. All file structures are ignored. The copy is a bit-by-bit duplicate.

Image—An image backup creates a functionally equivalent copy of the original volume. Image backups are typically done on bootable volumes, such as the VAX system disk.

Volume Initialization

In most cases, you will have to initialize a tape or disk volume before you can use it for the first time. Tape volume names can be one to six characters long, and disk volume names can be up to 12 characters. For example:

```
$ INITIALIZE MUA0: TAPE
$ INITIALIZE DJA1: MYDISK
```

When you initialize a tape or disk, all files are effectively erased. A volume only needs to be initialized the first time you want to use it, or when you decide the files it contains are no longer needed. Be careful not to initialize a volume that might have files you want to keep.

Before you can use a volume, it must be mounted and writable. For backup purposes, volumes are mostly mounted foreign to accommodate the Backup utility's special save set format. To mount a tape or disk device as foreign, issue a command such as the following:

```
$ MOUNT/FOREIGN MUA0:
```

or

```
$ MOUNT/FOREIGN DJA1:
```

For save set backup operations, the Backup utility will mount the output volume for you if it is not mounted.

Single File Copy

To copy a single file, enter a command in the format:

```
$ BACKUP file_spec file_spec
```

The first file specification is the source file and the second is the destination. If you specify the destination as simply a directory, the Backup utility will assume a wildcard file specification and retain the original name.

For example, to copy your LOGIN.COM file to a directory named [SHIPMAN], enter the following command:

```
$ BACKUP LOGIN.COM [SHIPMAN]
```

or

```
$ BACKUP LOGIN.COM [SHIPMAN]EXAMPLE_LOGIN.COM
```

If you specify a new filename in the destination file specification, the file will be renamed. For example:

```
$ BACKUP LOGIN.COM [SHIPMAN]EXAMPLE_LOGIN.COM
```

Multiple File Copy

You can copy multiple files by using wildcards or file lists in the source specification. For example:

```
$ BACKUP *.TXT [BYNON.MEMOS]
$ BACKUP NOTES.TXT,TRAVEL.TXT,EVENTS.TXT [WILLIS.TEXT]
```

If the destination directories do not exist, the Backup utility will create them for you. This is one of the primary benefits of the Backup utility over the DCL COPY command.

Copying a Directory Tree

To copy an entire directory tree, use the following Backup format:

```
$ BACKUP [directory]file_spec [directory]file_spec
```

All files and directories represented by the ellipses ([...]) will be copied from the source specification. For example:

```
$ BACKUP [BYNON...]*.FOR DUA2:[SOURCES.FORTRAN]
```

or

```
$ BACKUP USER$DISKS:[SWEET...]*.* USER$DISK2:[*...]
```

Saving Disk Files to Tape

When you save files on tape using Backup, the output is called a save set. The save set name always is followed by the /SAVE_SET qualifier. You can select any valid VMS filename and type for a save set name.

If you are backing up multiple save sets to a single tape, assign a different name to each save set on the tape. This avoids confusion when you restore the files.

The following example demonstrates how to back up files from a single directory to a save set on tape:

```
$ MOUNT/FOREIGN MSA0:
 MOUNT-I-MOUNTED, BYNON mounted on _MSA0:
$ BACKUP DUA2:[BYNON.XWIN]*.*;* MSA0:XWIN.BAK/SAVE_SET
```

This command backs up all files in the directory [BYNON.XWIN] to the tape mounted on MSA0:. The save set name is XWIN.BAK.

To back up an entire directory tree, use the ellipses wildcard:

```
$ MOUNT/FOREIGN MUA0:
 MOUNT-I-MOUNTED, TAPE mounted on _MUA0:
$ BACKUP DUB0:[SHIPMAN...] MUA0:SHIPMAN.BAK/SAVE_SET
```

This command backs up all files in user Shipman's login directory and all its subdirectories.

Restoring Backup Files from Tape

At some point, you may need to restore the files you have saved to tape. This also is done with the Backup utility. The procedure is called a *tape-to-disk file restore*.

To restore files from a backup tape volume to a disk volume, determine whether you want to restore a single file or an entire save set, then use the appropriate BACKUP command. The following examples demonstrate the restoration of a single file and a backup save set:

```
$ MOUNT/FOREIGN MUA0:
 MOUNT-I-MOUNTED, SHIPMAN mounted on _MUA0:
$ BACKUP MUA0:MYFILES.BAK/SAVE_SET -
_$ /SELECT=[SHIPMAN]LOGIN.COM *.*
```

This command restores the LOGIN.COM file to the current device and directory. Note that the /SELECT qualifier is used to specify the individual file that is to be restored from the save set.

If you need to restore an entire backup save set to disk, specify the tape drive and the save set name as the source, and the destination disk and directory names. Following the directory name with an ellipsis tells the Backup utility that you want files restored to the root directory and any subdirectories beneath it. For example:

```
$ MOUNT MUA0: SHIPMAN
$ BACKUP MUA0:SHIPMAN.BAK/SAVE_SET DUA1:[*...]
```

This command restores all files in the save set to the original root directory and all its subdirectories.

Listing a Backup Save Set

There will be times when you need to know the contents of a backup save set. For example, you might want to restore a few files from a tape but can't remember their names. By listing the contents of a save set, you can determine the size and name of the files you want to restore.

To get a listing of a backup save set, you must mount the tape containing the save set as a foreign volume. Then enter the BACKUP command with the /LIST qualifier as shown in the example:

```
$ MOUNT/FOREIGN MUA0:
 MOUNT-I-MOUNTED, SHIPMAN mounted on MUA0:
$ BACKUP/LIST *.*/SAVE_SET
```

After information about the backup save set is displayed, each file in the save set will be listed. The save set information includes the directory, filename, file type, version number, block size, and creation date for each file listed.

THE LIBRARY UTILITY

It is often easier to maintain a single file than a group of related files. The VMS Library utility helps you create and maintain a specially formatted file in which you can store groups of files called *modules*. Predefined libraries include text, help, object, sharable image and macro. Many VMS utilities and commands, such as HELP and LINK, are capable of processing library files.

Library Applications

Libraries have many applications. However, unless you are a programmer or system manager, you probably will use only text and help libraries. Here are some of the types of libraries available:

   ▼ Personal help library
   ▼ Program source code libraries
   ▼ Technical document reference libraries
   ▼ Archive transaction libraries

Creating Libraries

Libraries are created and manipulated with the Library utility. To create a library, use the LIBRARY commands type qualifier and the /CREATE qualifier. The type qualifiers are:

/TEXT	/HELP	/OBJECT
/MACRO	/SHARE	

The following command creates a text library named INTROVMS.TLB:

```
$ LIBRARY/TEXT/CREATE INTROVMS
```

When you create a library, you may specify a list of files to be included in the library. This saves you from entering another command. For example, the following command will create a text library and load it with four text files:

```
$ LIBRARY/TEXT/CREATE INTROVMS CHAP1,CHAP2,CHAP3,CHAP4
```

Listing Library Modules

To list the names of modules contained in a library, use the /LIST qualifier. For example:

```
$ LIBRARY/TEXT/LIST INTROVMS

Directory of TEXT library INTROVMS.TLB;1 on 27-FEB-1990 16:21:50

CHAP1
CHAP2
CHAP3
CHAP4
```

To display a history of updates made to the library, use the /HISTORY qualifier in conjunction with /LIST.

Adding Library Modules

To add modules to a library, use the /INSERT qualifier. The /INSERT qualifier will not add a module if a module with the same name exists. The following command adds the file CHAP5.TXT to the library INTROVMS:

```
$ LIBRARY/TEXT/INSERT INTROVMS CHAP5
```

Updating Library Modules

To update a module in a library, follow these steps:

1. Extract the module to be updated with the /EXTRACT qualifier.

2. Make the necessary modifications.

3. Write over the old module with the /REPLACE qualifier.

For example:

```
$ LIBRARY/TEXT/EXTRACT INTROVMS CHAP2
$ EDIT CHAP2.TXT
  .
  .   (edit session)
  .
$ LIBRARY/TEXT/REPLACE INTROVMS CHAP2
```

For further information on the Library utility, refer to the Digital Equipment *VAX/VMS Utilities Manual*.

THE SORT UTILITY

The DCL SORT command invokes the VMS Sort utility. This utility enables you to reorganize records within a file. A number of parameters and qualifiers may be appended to the SORT command. In its simplest form, the Sort utility sorts records in ascending alphabetical sequence. For example, assume your directory contains a text file called DEPARTMENT.NAMES composed of the following eight records:

```
ED
DAVE
BOB
GREY
CATHY
DEBBIE
CHUCK
DAVID
```

To sort these records in ascending alphabetical order and display the reordered file, type the command strings shown below:

```
$ SORT DEPARTMENT.NAMES SORTED.NAMES
$ TYPE SORTED.NAMES

BOB

CATHY

CHUCK

DAVE

DAVID

DEBBIE

ED

GREY

$
```

By default, the Sort utility sorts on the first character of the first field in each record contained in the input file. Each record can be considered analogous to a line or sentence. If there is more than one field or column in each record, the entire record is moved into alphabetic sequence, not just the first field.

There will be times when you want to sort on a specific field, perform a numeric sort, or sort in descending order. Continuing with the previous example, let's add a field to each record in the DEPARTMENT.NAMES file and sort it in descending numeric sequence based on the contents of the second field, phone extension. This two-character field starts in position 9 of the file. As the command line in the following example shows, you must supply this information to the utility so it can properly sort the file.

Here is how the unsorted DEPARTMENT.NAMES file looks with its additional field:

```
ED        12
DAVE      44
BOB       21
GREY      08
CATHY     02
DEBBIE    18
CHUCK     13
DAVID     25
```

Here is the SORT command line and the newly sorted file:

```
$ SORT/KEY=(POSITION=9,SIZE=2,DESCENDING) DEPT.NAME SORTED.NAME
$ TYPE SORTED.NAMES
```

```
DAVE      44
DAVID     25
BOB       21
DEBBIE    18
CHUCK     13
ED        12
GREY      08
CATHY     02
```

The extensive list of parameters and qualifiers available in the Sort utility permits you to select complex sort specifications.

WHERE TO GO FROM HERE

VMS is filled with advanced features, such as multiprocessing, batch processing, DECnet networks and VAXclusters. Although these features are among the most important in the DEC computing philosophy, there are many others.

For more information about DECnet, VAXclusters, and DCL commands, refer to the following Digital Equipment documentation:

▼ *VAX/VMS Guide to DECnet*
▼ *VAX/VMS Guide to VAXclusters*
▼ *VAX/VMS Utilities and Commands*

DCL Commands

This appendix briefly describes DCL commands and their major functions. Not all DCL commands are presented. For a complete list and description, refer to the *VAX/VMS DCL Dictionary*.

= (Assignment statement)   Assigns an expression to a symbol.

symbol =[=] expression
symbol[bit_position,size] =[=] expression

: = (Assignment statement)   Assigns a string expression to a symbol.

symbol :=[=] string
symbol[offset,size] :=[=] string

@ file_spec [p1 p2...p8]   Executes a DCL command procedure.

Qualifier:
/OUTPUT=file_spec

ALLOCATE device_name: [logical_name]   Provides exclusive use of a device and optionally establishes a logical name for that device. While a device is allocated, other users may not access the device until you DEALLOCATE it or log out.

Qualifier:
/GENERIC

ANALYZE/IMAGE file_spec[,...]   Analyzes the contents of an executable image or a shareable image, and checks for obvious errors.

ANALYZE/OBJECT file_spec[,...]   Analyzes the contents of an object file and checks for obvious errors.

ANALYZE/PROCESS_DUMP dump_file   Invokes the VMS Debugger for analysis of a process dump file that was created when an image failed during execution. You must use the /DUMP qualifier with the RUN or SET PROCESS command to generate a dump file.

ANALYZE/RMS_FILE file_spec[,...]   Invokes the VMS Analyze/ RMS_File Utility to analyze the internal structure of a VAX RMS file.

APPEND input_file_spec[,...] output_file_spec   Adds the contents of one or more input files to the end of a file.

Qualifiers:

/ALLOCATION	/BACKUP
/BEFORE	/BY_OWNER
/CONFIRM	/CONTIGUOUS
/CREATED	/EXCLUDE
/EXPIRED	/EXTENSION
/LOG	/MODIFIED
/NEW_VERSION	/READ_CHECK
/SINCE	/WRITE_CHECK

ASSIGN equivalence_name logical_name   Equates a logical name to a physical device name, file specification or another logical name.

ATTACH [process_name]   Enables you to transfer control from the current process to another process created by you (see SPAWN).

Qualifier:
/IDENTIFICATION

BACKUP input_spec output_spec   Invokes the VAX/VMS Backup utility to perform one of the following file operations:

▼ Copy disk files.
▼ Save disk files as a save set (a single data file) on a disk or magnetic tape volume.
▼ Restore files from a save set.
▼ Compare files.
▼ Display information about files contained in a save set.

Qualifiers:

/BACKUP	/BEFORE
/BLOCK_SIZE	/BRIEF
/BUFFER_COUNT	/COMMENT
/COMPARE	/CONFIRM
/CRC	/CREATED
/DELETE	/DENSITY
/EXCLUDE	/EXPIRED
/FAST	/FULL
/GROUP_SIZE	/IGNORE
/IMAGE	/INCREMENTAL
/INITIALIZE	/INTERCHANGE
/JOURNAL	/LABEL
/LIST	/LOG
/MODIFIED	/NEW_VERSION
/OVERLAY	/OWNER_UIC
/PHYSICAL	/PROTECTION
/RECORD	/REPLACE
/REWIND	/SAVE_SET
/SELECT	/SINCE
/TRUNCATE	/VERIFY
/VOLUME	

CALL label [p1 p2...p8]   Transfers command procedure control to a labeled subroutine in the procedure.

Qualifier:
/OUTPUT

CLOSE logical_name   Closes a file opened for input/output with the OPEN command, and deassigns the logical name created for the file.

Qualifiers:

/ERROR	/LOG

CONTINUE   Resumes execution of a DCL command, program or command procedure interrupted by pressing <CTRL/Y> or <CTRL/C>. You can abbreviate the CONTINUE command to the letter C.

COPY input_file_spec[,...] output_file_spec   Creates a new file from one or more existing files. The COPY command can be used to:

   ▼ Copy an input file to an output file, optionally changing its name and location.
   ▼ Copy a group of input files to a group of output files.
   ▼ Concatenate two or more files into a single new file.

Qualifiers:

/ALLOCATION	/BACKUP
/BEFORE	/BY_OWNER
/CONCATENATE	/CONFIRM
/CONTIGUOUS	/CREATED
/EXCLUDE	/EXPIRED
/EXTENSION	/LOG
/MODIFIED	/OVERLAY
/PROTECTION	/READ_CHECK
/REPLACE	/SINCE
/TRUNCATE	/VOLUME
/WRITE_CHECK	

CREATE file_spec   Creates one or more sequential disk files from records that follow in the input stream (i.e., the keyboard, a modem, and so on). To terminate input and close the file, enter <CTRL/Z>.

Qualifiers:

/LOG	/OWNER_UIC
/PROTECTION	/VOLUME

CREATE/DIRECTORY directory_spec[,...]   Creates a new directory or subdirectory for cataloging files.

Qualifiers:

/LOG	/OWNER_UIC
/PROTECTION	/VERSION_LIMIT
/VOLUME	

CREATE/FDL=fdl_file_spec [file_spec]   Invokes the FDL (File Definition Language) utility to use the specifications in a definition file to create a new (empty) data file.

Qualifier:
/LOG

DEALLOCATE device_name: Releases a previously allocated device to the pool of available devices.

Qualifier:
/ALL

DEASSIGN logical_name[:]   Deletes logical name assignments made with the ALLOCATE, ASSIGN, DEFINE or MOUNT command.

Qualifiers:

/ALL	/EXECUTIVE_MODE
/GROUP	/JOB
/PROCESS	/SUPERVISOR_MODE
/SYSTEM	/TABLE
/USER_MODE	

DEBUG   Invokes the VAX/VMS Debugger.

DEFINE logical_name equivalence_name[,...]   Creates a logical name entry and assigns an equivalence string, or a list of equivalence strings, to the specified logical name.

Qualifiers:

/CHARACTERISTIC	/EXECUTIVE_MODE
/FORM	/GROUP
/JOB	/KEY
/LOG	/NAME_ATTRIBUTES
/PROCESS	/SUPERVISOR_MODE
/SYSTEM	/TABLE
/TRANSLATION_ATTRIBUTES	/USER_MODE

DEFINE/KEY key_name string Associates a character string and a set of attributes with a function key.

Qualifiers:

/ECHO	/ERASE
/IF_STATE	/LOCK_STATE
/LOG	/SET_STATE
/TERMINATE	

DELETE file_spec[,...] Deletes one or more files from a mass storage device.

Qualifiers:

/BACKUP	/BEFORE
/BY_OWNER	/CONFIRM
/CREATED	/ERASE
/EXCLUDE	/EXPIRED
/LOG	/MODIFIED
/SINCE	

DELETE/ENTRY=(queue_entry_number[,...]) queue_name[:]
Deletes one or more job entries from the named queue.

DELETE/KEY key_name Deletes a key definition established by the DEFINE/KEY command.

Qualifiers:

/ALL	/LOG
/STATE	

DELETE/SYMBOL symbol_name Removes a symbol definition from a local or global symbol table or removes all symbol definitions in a symbol table.

Qualifiers:

/ALL	/GLOBAL
/LOCAL	/LOG

DIFFERENCES master_file_spec [revision_file_spec]
Compares the contents of two disk files and creates a listing of those records that do not match.

Qualifiers:

/CHANGE_BAR	/COMMENT_DELIMITER
/IGNORE	/MATCH
/MAXIMUM_DIFFERENCES	/MERGED
/MODE	/NUMBER
/OUTPUT	/PARALLEL
/SEPARATED	/SLP
/WIDTH	/WINDOW

DIRECTORY [file_spec[,...]]   Provides a list of files or information about a file or group of files.

Qualifiers:

/ACL	/BACKUP
/BEFORE	/BRIEF
/BY_OWNER	/COLUMNS
/CREATED	/DATE
/EXCLUDE	/EXPIRED
/FILE_ID	/FULL
/GRAND_TOTAL	/HEADING
/MODIFIED	/OUTPUT
/OWNER	/PRINTER
/PROTECTION	/SECURITY
/SELECT	/SINCE
/SIZE	/TOTAL
/TRAILING	/VERSIONS
/WIDTH	

DISCONNECT   Disconnects a physical terminal from a virtual terminal that has been connected to a process. The virtual terminal, and its associated process, will remain on the system when the physical terminal is disconnected from it.

Qualifier:
/CONTINUE

DISMOUNT device_name[:]   Dismounts a disk or magnetic tape volume that was previously mounted with a MOUNT command.

Qualifiers:

/ABORT	/CLUSTER
/UNIT	/UNLOAD

DUMP file_spec [,...]   Displays the contents of files or volumes in ASCII, decimal, hexadecimal or octal representation.

Qualifiers:

/ALLOCATED	/BLOCKS
/BYTE	/DECIMAL
/FILE_HEADER	/FORMATTED
/HEADER	/HEXADECIMAL
/LONGWORD	/NUMBER
/OCTAL	/OUTPUT
/PRINTER	/RECORDS
/WORD	

EDIT/ACL file_spec   Invokes the Access Control List editor to create or update access control list information for a specified object.

Qualifiers:

/JOURNAL	/KEEP
/MODE	/OBJECT
/RECOVER	

EDIT/EDT file_spec   Invokes the VMS EDT text editor. The /EDT qualifier is not required because EDT is the default editor.

Qualifiers:

/COMMAND	/CREATE
/JOURNAL	/OUTPUT
/READ_ONLY	/RECOVER

EDIT/FDL file_spec   Invokes the VMS FDL (File Definition Language) editor to create or modify File and FDL file.

Qualifiers:

/ANALYSIS	/CREATE
/DISPLAY	/EMPHASIS
/GRANULARITY	/NOINTERACTIVE
/NUMBER_KEYS	/OUTPUT
/PROMPTING	/RESPONSES
/SCRIPT	

EDIT/TPU file_spec   Invokes the VMS Text Processing Utility (TPU). EVE (Extensible VAX Editor) is the default interface for TPU. To invoke TPU with the EDT Emulator interface, define the logical TPUSECINI to point to the section file for the EDT interface as follows:

```
$ DEFINE TPUSECINI EDTSECINI
```

Qualifiers:

/COMMAND	/CREATE
/DISPLAY	/JOURNAL
/OUTPUT	/READ_ONLY
/RECOVER	/SECTION

EOD   Signals the end of an input stream when a command, program or utility is reading data from an input device other than a terminal.

EXIT [status_code]   Terminates the current command procedure. If the command procedure was executed from within another command procedure, control will return to the calling procedure.

GOSUB label   Transfers command procedure control to a labeled subroutine.

GOTO label   Transfers control to a labeled statement in a command procedure.

HELP   Invokes the VMS Help utility to display information about a VMS command or topic.

Qualifiers:

/INSTRUCTIONS	/LIBLIST
/LIBRARY	/OUTPUT
/PAGE	/PROMPT
/USERLIBRARY	

IF expression THEN command   Tests the value of a logical expression and executes the command following the THEN key word if the test is true.

IF expression THEN commands ELSE commands ENDIF
Tests the value of a logical expression and executes the commands following the THEN keyword if the test is true. If the test is false, the commands following the ELSE clause are executed. The command must be written as follows:

```
$ IF expression
$  THEN [command]
$       command
$        .
$        .
$  ELSE [command]
$       command
$        .
$        .
$ ENDIF
```

INITIALIZE device_name[:] volume_label Formats and writes a label on a mass storage volume.

Qualifiers:

/ACCESSED	/BADBLOCKS
/CLUSTER_SIZE	/DATA_CHECK
/DENSITY	/DIRECTORIES
/ERASE	/EXTENSION
/FILE_PROTECTION	/GROUP
/HEADERS	/HIGHWATER
/INDEX	/LABEL
/MAXIMUM_FILES	/OVERRIDE
/OWNER_UIC	/PROTECTION
/SHARE	/STRUCTURE
/SYSTEM	/USER_NAME
/VERIFIED	/WINDOWS

INQUIRE symbol_name [prompt] Provides interactive assignment of a value for a local or global symbol in a command procedure.

Qualifiers:

/GLOBAL	/LOCAL
/PUNCTUATION	

LIBRARY library_file_spec [input_file_spec[,...]] Invokes the VMS Library utility to create, modify or describe a macro, object, help, text or shareable image library.

Qualifiers:

/BEFORE	/COMPRESS
/CREATE	/CROSS_REFERENCE
/DATA	/DELETE
/EXTRACT	/FULL
/GLOBALS	/HELP
/HISTORY	/INSERT
/LIST	/LOG
/MACRO	/MODULE
/NAMES	/OBJECT
/ONLY	/OUTPUT
/REMOVE	/REPLACE
/SELECTIVE_SEARCH	/SHARE
/SINCE	/SQUEEZE
/TEXT	/WIDTH

LINK file_spec[,...]   Invokes the VMS Linker to link object modules into a VMS program image.

Qualifiers:

/BRIEF	/CONTIGUOUS
/CROSS_REFERENCE	/DEBUG
/EXECUTABLE	/FULL
/HEADER	/IMAGE
/INCLUDE	/LIBRARY
/MAP	/OPTIONS
/PROTECT	/SELECTIVE_SEARCH
/SHAREABLE	/SYMBOL_TABLE
/SYSLIB	/SYSSHR
/SYSTEM	/TRACEBACK
/USERLIBRARY	

LOGOUT   Terminates an interactive terminal session with VMS.

Qualifiers:

/BRIEF	/FULL
/HANGUP	

MACRO file_spec[,...]   Invokes the VMS MACRO assembler to assemble MACRO assembly language source programs.

Qualifiers:

/CROSS_REFERENCE	/DEBUG
/DISABLE	/ENABLE
LIBRARY	/LIST
/OBJECT	/SHOW
/UPDATE	

MAIL [file_spec] [recipient_name] Invokes the VMS Personal Mail utility, which is used to send messages to, and receive messages from, other system users.

Qualifiers:
/EDIT   /SELF
/SUBJECT

MERGE input_file_spec1,input_file_spec2[,...] output_file_spec Invokes the VAX/VMS Sort utility to combine up to 10 similarly sorted input files. The input files to be merged must be in sorted order before invoking MERGE.

Qualifiers:
/ALLOCATION   /BUCKET_SIZE
/CHECK_SEQUENCE   /COLLATING_SEQUENCE
/CONTIGUOUS   /DUPLICATES
/FORMAT   /INDEXED_SEQUENTIAL
/KEY   /OVERLAY
/RELATIVE   /SEQUENTIAL
/SPECIFICATION   /STABLE
/STATISTICS

MESSAGE file_spec[,...] Invokes the VMS Message utility to compile message definition files.

Qualifiers:
/FILE_NAME   /LIST
/OBJECT   /SYMBOLS
/TEXT

MOUNT device_name[:][,...] [volume_label[,...]] [logical_name[:]] Invokes the VMS Mount utility to make a disk or tape volume available for use.

Qualifiers:
/ACCESSED   /ASSIST
/AUTOMATIC   /BIND
/BLOCKSIZE   /CACHE
/CLUSTER   /COMMENT
/CONFIRM   /COPY
/DATA_CHECK   /DENSITY
/EXTENSION   /FOREIGN
/GROUP   /HDR3
/INITIALIZE   /LABEL
/MESSAGE   /MOUNT_VERIFICATION
/OVERRIDE   /OWNER_UIC

/PROCESSOR	/PROTECTION
/QUOTA	/REBUILD
/RECORDSIZE	/SHADOW
/SHARE	/SYSTEM
/UNLOAD	/WINDOWS
/WRITE	

ON condition THEN_command   Defines the DCL command to be executed when a command or program executed within a command procedure encounters an error condition or is interrupted by the user pressing <CTRL/Y>. See Chapter 9 for more information.

OPEN logical_name[:] file_spec   Opens a file for input/output. The OPEN command assigns a logical name to the file and places the name in the process logical name table.

Qualifiers:

/APPEND	/ERROR
/READ	/SHARE
/WRITE	

PHONE [phone_command]   Invokes the VMS Phone utility. The PHONE command provides the facility for you to communicate with other users on your system or any other VAX/VMS system connected to your system via a DECnet network.

Qualifiers:

/SCROLL	/SWITCH_HOOK
/VIEWPORT_SIZE	

PRINT file_spec[,...]   Puts one or more files in a queue for printing.

Qualifiers:

/AFTER	/BACKUP
/BEFORE	/BURST
/BY_OWNER	/CHARACTERISTICS
/CONFIRM	/COPIES
/CREATED	/DELETE
/DEVICE	/EXCLUDE
/EXPIRED	/FEED
/FLAG	/FORM
/HEADER	/HOLD
/IDENTIFY	/JOB_COUNT

/LOWERCASE	/MODIFIED
/NAME	/NOTE
/NOTIFY	/OPERATOR
/PAGES	/PARAMETERS
/PASSALL	/PRIORITY
/QUEUE	/REMOTE
/RESTART	/SETUP
/SINCE	/SPACE
/TRAILER	/USER

PURGE [file_spec[,...]]   Deletes all but the highest versions of the specified files.

Qualifiers:

/BACKUP	/BEFORE
/BY_OWNER	/CONFIRM
/CREATED	/ERASE
/EXCLUDE	/EXPIRED
/KEEP	/LOG
/MODIFIED	/SINCE

READ logical_name[:] symbol_name   Inputs a single record from the specified input file and assigns the contents of the record to the specified symbol name.

Qualifiers:

/DELETE	/END_OF_FILE
/ERROR	/INDEX
/KEY	/MATCH
/NOLOCK	/PROMPT
/TIME_OUT	

RECALL [command_specifier]   Recalls previously entered commands for reprocessing or correcting.

Qualifiers:

/ALL	/ERASE

RENAME input_file_spec[,...] output_file_spec   Modifies the file specification in an existing disk file or disk directory.

Qualifiers:

/BACKUP	/BEFORE
/BY_OWNER	/CONFIRM
/CREATED	/EXCLUDE

/EXPIRED	/LOG
/MODIFIED	/NEW_VERSION
/SINCE	

REQUEST "message"   Writes a message on the system operator's terminal and optionally requests a reply.

Qualifiers:

/REPLY	/TO

RETURN [status_code]   Terminates a GOSUB statement and returns control to the command following the calling GOSUB command.

RUN   Places an image into execution in the process, and creates a subprocess or detached process to run a specified image.

SEARCH file_spec[,...] search_string[,...]   Searches one or more files for the specified strings and lists all the lines in which the strings occur.

Qualifiers:

/EXACT	/EXCLUDE
/FORMAT	/HEADING
/LOG	/MATCH
/NUMBERS	/OUTPUT
/REMAINING	/STATISTICS
/WINDOW	

SET ACL object_name   Allows you to modify the access control list of a VMS object.

Qualifiers:

/ACL	/AFTER
/BEFORE	/BY_OWNER
/CONFIRM	/CREATED
/DEFAULT	/DELETE
/EDIT	/EXCLUDE
/JOURNAL	/KEEP
/LIKE	/LOG
/MODE	/NEW
/OBJECT_TYPE	/RECOVER
/REPLACE	/SINCE

SET BROADCAST=(class_name[,...]) Allows you to block out various terminal messages from being broadcast to your terminal.

SET COMMAND [file_spec[,...]] Invokes the VMS Command Definition utility to add, delete or replace commands in your process command table or a specified command table file.

Qualifiers:

/DELETE	/LISTING
/OBJECT	/OUTPUT
/REPLACE	/TABLE

SET [NO]CONTROL[=(T,Y)] Indicates whether control will pass to the command language interpreter when <CTRL/Y> is pressed and whether process statistics will be displayed when <CTRL/T> is pressed.

SET DEFAULT device_name:directory_spec Changes the default device or directory specification. The new default is used with all subsequent file operations that do not explicitly include a device or directory name.

SET DIRECTORY directory_spec[,...] Modifies directory characteristics.

Qualifiers:

/BACKUP	/BEFORE
/BY_OWNER	/CONFIRM
/CREATED	/EXCLUDE
/EXPIRED	/LOG
/MODIFIED	/OWNER_UIC
/SINCE	/VERSION_LIMIT

SET DISPLAY When DECwindows is installed, this command defines the display server.

Qualifiers:

/CREATE	/NODE
/PERMANENT	/TRANSPORT

SET FILE file_spec[,...] Modifies file characteristics.

Qualifiers:

/BACKUP	/BEFORE
/BY_OWNER	/CONFIRM
/CREATED	/DATA_CHECK
/END_OF_FILE	/ENTER
/ERASE_ON_DELETE	/EXCLUDE
/EXPIRATION_DATE	/EXTENSION
/GLOBAL_BUFFER	/LOG
/NODIRECTORY	/OWNER_UIC
/PROTECTION	/REMOVE
/SINCE	/STATISTICS
/TRUNCATE	/UNLOCK
/VERSION_LIMIT	

SET HOST node_name   Connects your terminal to another processor in a DECnet network or to an asynchronous terminal port.

Qualifiers:

/DTE	/DUP
/HSC	/LOG

SET KEY   Changes the current key definition state. Keys are defined by the DEFINE/KEY command.

Qualifiers:

/LOG	/STATE

SET MESSAGE [file_spec]   Specifies the format of messages, or overrides or supplements system messages.

Qualifiers:

/DELETE	/FACILITY
/IDENTIFICATION	/SEVERITY
/TEXT	

SET [NO]ON   Controls command interpreter error checking. If SET NOON is in effect, the command interpreter will ignore errors in a command procedure and continue processing.

SET OUTPUT_RATE[=delta_time]   Defines the rate at which output will be written to a batch job log file.

SET PASSWORD Permits users to change their password to a VMS account.

Qualifiers:
/GENERATE   /SECONDARY
/SYSTEM

SET PRINTER printer_name[:] Defines characteristics for a line printer.

Qualifiers:
/CR   /FALLBACK
/FF   /LA11
/LA180   /LOG
/LOWERCASE   /LP11
/PAGE   /PASSALL
/PRINTALL   /TAB
/TRUNCATE   /UNKNOWN
/UPPERCASE   /WIDTH
/WRAP

SET PROCESS [process_name] Modifies execution characteristics associated with the named process for the current login session. If a process is not specified, changes are made to the current process.

Qualifiers:
/CPU   /DUMP
/IDENTIFICATION   /NAME
/PRIORITY   /PRIVILEGES
/RESOURCE_WAIT   /RESUME
/SUSPEND   /SWAPPING

SET PROMPT[=string] Defines a new DCL prompt for your process. The default prompt is the dollar sign.

Qualifier:
/CARRIAGE_CONTROL

SET PROTECTION[=(code)] file_spec[,...] Modifies the protection applied to a particular file or group of files. The protection limits the access available to various groups of system users.

When used without a file specification, it establishes the default protection for all the files subsequently created during the login session.

It also may be used to modify the protection of a non-file-oriented device.

Qualifiers:

/CONFIRM	/DEFAULT
/DEVICE	/LOG
/PROTECTION	

SET QUEUE queue_name   Modifies the current status or attributes of a queue, or changes the current status or attributes of a job that is not currently executing in a queue.

Qualifiers:

/BASE_PRIORITY	/BLOCK_LIMIT
/CHARACTERISTICS	/CPUDEFAULT
/CPUMAXIMUM	/DEFAULT
/DISABLE_SWAPPING	/ENABLE_GENERIC
/ENTRY	/FORM_MOUNTED
/JOB_LIMIT	/OWNER_UIC
/PROTECTION	/RECORD_BLOCKING
/RETAIN	/SCHEDULE
/SEPARATE	/WSDEFAULT
/WSEXTENT	/WSQUOTA

SET RESTART_VALUE=string   Defines a test value for restarting portions of a batch job after a system failure.

SET RMS_DEFAULT   Sets default values for the multiblock and multibuffer counts, network transfer sizes, prologue level, and extends quantity used by Record Management Services (RMS) for file operations.

Qualifiers:

/BLOCK_COUNT	/BUFFER_COUNT
/DISK	/EXTEND_QUANTITY
/INDEXED	/MAGTAPE
/NETWORK_BLOCK_COUNT	/PROLOG
/RELATIVE	/SEQUENTIAL
/SYSTEM	/UNIT_RECORD

SET SYMBOL   Controls access to local and global symbols within command procedures.

Qualifier:
/SCOPE

SET TERMINAL [device_name[:]]   Modifies interpretation of various terminal characteristics.

Qualifiers:

/ADVANCED_VIDEO	/ALTYPEAHD
/ANSI_CRT	/APPLICATION_KEYPAD
/AUTOBAUD	/BLOCK_MODE
/BRDCSTMBX	/BROADCAST
/CRFILL	/DEC_CRT
/DEVICE_TYPE	/DIALUP
/DISCONNECT	/DISMISS
/DMA	/ECHO
/EDIT_MODE	/EIGHT_BIT
/ESCAPE	/FALLBACK
/FORM	/FRAME
/FULLDUP	/HALFDUP
/HANGUP	/HARDCOPY
/HOSTSYNC	/INQUIRE
/INSERT	/LFFILL
/LINE_EDITING	/LOCAL_ECHO
/LOWERCASE	/MANUAL
/MODEM	/NUMERIC_KEYPAD
/OVERSTRIKE	/PAGE
/PARITY	/PASTHRU
/PERMANENT	/PRINTER_PORT
/PROTOCOL	/READSYNC
/REGIS	/SCOPE
/SECURE_SERVER	/SET_SPEED
/SIXEL_GRAPHICS	/SOFT_CHARACTERS
/SPEED	/SWITCH
/SYSPASSWORD	/TAB
/TTSYNC	/TYPE_AHEAD
/UNKNOWN	/UPPERCASE
/WIDTH	/WRAP

SET [NO]VERIFY [=([NO]PROCEDURE, [NO]IMAGE)]   Controls whether command and data lines in a command procedure are displayed as they are processed.

SET WORKING_SET   Sets the default working set size for the current process, or sets an upper limit to which the working set size can be changed by an image that the process executes.

Qualifiers:
/ADJUST   /EXTENT
/LIMIT   /LOG
/QUOTA

SHOW ACL   Displays the access control list of a VAX/VMS object.

Qualifier:
/OBJECT_TYPE

SHOW BROADCAST   Displays message classes that currently are affected by the SET BROADCAST command.

Qualifier:
/OUTPUT

SHOW DEFAULT   Displays the current default device and directory specification, along with any equivalence strings that have been defined.

SHOW DEVICES [device_name[:]]   Displays the status of a device on the running VAX/VMS system.

Qualifiers:
/ALLOCATED   /BRIEF
/FILES   /FULL
/MOUNTED   /OUTPUT
/SERVED   /SYSTEM
/WINDOWS

SHOW ENTRY [entry_number,...]   Displays information about a users's batch or print jobs.

Qualifiers:
/BATCH   /BRIEF
/BY_JOB_STATUS   /DEVICE
/FILES   /FULL
/GENERIC   /OUTPUT
/USER_NAME

SHOW KEY [key_name]   Displays the key definition for the specified key.

Qualifiers:

/ALL	/BRIEF
/DIRECTORY	/FULL
/STATE	

SHOW LOGICAL [logical_name[:],[...]]   Displays logical names from one or more logical name tables, or displays the equivalence strings assigned to the specified logical names.

Qualifiers:

/ACCESS_MODE	/ALL
/DESCENDANTS	/FULL
/GROUP	/JOB
/OUTPUT	/PROCESS
/STRUCTURE	/SYSTEM
/TABLE	

SHOW NETWORK   Displays node information about the DECnet network of which your host processor is a member.

Qualifier:
/OUTPUT

SHOW PRINTER device_name[:]   Displays characteristics defined for a system printer.

Qualifier:
/OUTPUT

SHOW PROCESS [process_name]   Displays information about a process and its subprocesses.

Qualifiers:

/ACCOUNTING	/ALL
/CONTINUOUS	/IDENTIFICATION
/MEMORY	/OUTPUT
/PRIVILEGES	/QUOTAS
/SUBPROCESSES	

SHOW PROTECTION   Displays the file protection that will be applied to all new files created during the current login session.

SHOW QUEUE [queue_name]   Displays information about queues and the jobs currently in queue.

Qualifiers:

/ALL	/ALL_JOBS
/BATCH	/BRIEF
/BY_JOB_STATUS	/CHARACTERISTICS
/DEVICE	/FILES
/FORM	/FULL
/GENERIC	/SUMMARY
/OUTPUT	

SHOW QUOTA   Displays the disk quota authorized for a specific user on a specific disk.

Qualifiers:

/DISK	/USER

SHOW RMS_DEFAULT   Displays the default multiblock count, multibuffer count, network transfer size, prologue level and extend quantity that Record Management Services (RMS) will use for file operations.

Qualifier:
/OUTPUT

SHOW STATUS   Displays status information for the current process.

SHOW SYMBOL [symbol_name]   Displays the value of a local or global symbol.

Qualifiers:

/ALL	/GLOBAL
/LOCAL	/LOG

SHOW TERMINAL [device_name[:]]   Displays the characteristics of a specified terminal.

Qualifiers:

/OUTPUT	/PERMANENT

SHOW TIME   Displays the system date and time.

SHOW TRANSLATION logical_name   Searches logical name tables for a specified logical name, then returns the first equivalence name of the match found.

Qualifier:
/TABLE

SHOW USERS [username]   Displays a list of users currently using the system, their terminal names, usernames and process identification codes.

Qualifier:
/OUTPUT

SHOW WORKING_SET   Displays the current working set limit, quota and extent assigned to the current process.

Qualifier:
/OUTPUT

SORT input_file_spec[,...] output_file_spec   Invokes the VMS Sort utility to reorder records in a file into a defined sequence.

Qualifiers:

/COLLATING_SEQUENCE	/DUPLICATES
/FORMAT	/KEY
/PROCESS	/SPECIFICATION
/STABLE	/STATISTICS
/WORK_FILES	

Output File Qualifiers:

/ALLOCATION	/BUCKET_SIZE
/CONTIGUOUS	/FORMAT
/INDEXED_SEQUENTIAL	/OVERLAY
/RELATIVE	/SEQUENTIAL

SPAWN [command_string]   Creates a subprocess to the current process.

Qualifiers:

/CARRIAGE_CONTROL	/CLI
/INPUT	/KEYPAD
/LOG	/LOGICAL_NAMES
/NOTIFY	/OUTPUT
/PROCESS	/PROMPT
/SYMBOLS	/TABLE
/WAIT	

STOP process_name   Specifies the name of a process to be deleted from the system. If the /IDENTIFICATION qualifier is used, the process name is ignored.

Qualifier:
/IDENTIFICATION

SUBMIT file_spec[,...]   Enters a command procedure into a batch queue.

Qualifiers:

/AFTER	/BACKUP
/BEFORE	/BY_OWNER
/CHARACTERISTICS	/CLI
/CONFIRM	/CPUTIME
/CREATED	/DELETE
/EXCLUDE	/EXPIRED
/HOLD	/IDENTIFY
/KEEP	/LOG_FILE
/MODIFIED	/NAME
/NOTIFY	/PARAMETERS
/PRINTER	/PRIORITY
/QUEUE	/REMOTE
/RESTART	/SINCE
/USER	/WSDEFAULT
/WSEXTENT	/WSQUOTA

SYNCHRONIZE [job_name]   Places the process issuing the command into a wait state until the specified job completes execution.

Qualifiers:

/ENTRY	/QUEUE

TYPE file_spec[,...]   Displays the contents of a file or group of files on the current output device (normally your terminal screen).

Qualifiers:

/BACKUP	/BEFORE
/BY_OWNER	/CONFIRM
/CREATED	/EXCLUDE
/EXPIRED	/MODIFIED
/OUTPUT	/PAGE
/SINCE	

WAIT delta_time   Places the current process in a wait state until a specified period of time has elapsed.

WRITE logical_name expression[,...]   Writes the specified data record to the output file indicated by the logical name.

Qualifiers:

/ERROR	/SYMBOL
/UPDATE	

Lexical Functions

This appendix briefly describes the VMS lexical functions. Parameters for the lexicals are listed in parentheses after the function name. Parentheses are required whether or not the lexical function requires parameters.

F$CVSI(bit_position,width,string)   Extracts bit fields from a character string. The result is converted to a signed integer value.

F$CVTIME(input_time,output_time,field)   Converts absolute or combination time to the format "yyyy-mm-dd hh:mm:ss.cc". The F$CVTIME function also can be used to return information about an absolute, combination or delta time string.

F$CVUI(bit_position,width,string)   Extracts bit fields from a character string and converts the result to an unsigned integer value.

F$DIRECTORY()   Returns the default directory name as a character string. The F$DIRECTORY function has no arguments.

F$EDIT(string, edit_list   Edits a character string based on the parameters specified in the edit_list.

F$ELEMENT(element_number, delimiter, string) Extracts an element from a character string in which the elements are separated by some specified delimiter.

F$ENVIRONMENT(item Returns information about the DCL command environment.

F$EXTRACT(offset,length,string) Extracts a substring from a character string. For example:

```
$ DATE = F$EXTRACT(0,11,F$TIME())
$ WRITE SYS$OUTPUT "Today is "DATE'"
Today is 14-APR-1989
```

F$FAO(control_string[,arg1,arg2...arg15]) Calls the $FAO system service to convert a specified control string to formatted ASCII. This function may be used to:

- ▼ Insert variable character string data into an output string.
- ▼ Convert integer values to ASCII and substitute the result into the output string.

F$FILE_ATTRIBUTES(file_spec,item) Returns attribute information for the specified file.

F$GETDVI(device, item) Calls the $GETDVI system service to return an item of information on a specified device. This function allows a process to obtain information for a device to which the process has not necessarily allocated or assigned a channel.

F$GETJPI(pid,item) Calls the $GETJPI system service to return accounting, status and identification information on a specified process.

F$GETQUI(function,[item],[object_id],[flags]) Invokes the $GETQUI system service to return information about queues and jobs.

F$GETSYI(item [,node])   Calls the $GETSYI system service to return status and identification information about the running system or about a node in the VAXcluster (if your system is a member of a VAXcluster).

F$IDENTIFIER(identifier,conversion_type)   Converts an identifier to its integer equivalent, or vice versa. An identifier is a name or number that identifies a category of users of a data resource. The system uses identifiers to determine user access to a system resource.

F$INTEGER(expression)   Returns the integer value of the result of the specified expression.

F$LENGTH(string)   Returns the length of a specified character string.

F$LOCATE(substring,string)   Locates a character or character substring within a string and returns its offset within the string. If the character or character substring is not found, the function returns the length of the string that was searched.

F$MESSAGE(status_code)   Returns a character string containing the message associated with a system status code.

F$MODE()   Returns a character string displaying the mode in which a process is executing. The F$MODE function has no arguments.

F$PARSE(file_spec[,related_spec][,field][,parse_type])   Calls the $PARSE RMS service to parse a file specification and return either its expanded file specification or a particular file specification field that you have specified.

F$PID(context_symbol)   Returns a process identification number (PID), and updates the context symbol to point to the current position in the system's process list.

F$PRIVILEGE(priv_states)   Returns a value of true or false, depending on whether your current process privileges match the privileges listed in the parameter argument.

F$PROCESS()   Obtains the current process name as a character string. The F$PROCESS function requires no arguments.

F$SEARCH(file_spec[,stream_id])   Calls the $SEARCH RMS service to search a directory and return the full file specification for a specified file.

F$SETPRV(priv_states)   Returns a list of keywords indicating current user privileges. This function also may be used to call the $SETPRV system service to enable or disable specified user privileges. The return string indicates the status of the user privileges before any changes have been made with the F$SETPRV function.

F$STRING(expression)   Returns the character string equivalent of the result of the specified expression.

F$TIME()   Returns the current date and time string. The F$TIME function has no arguments.

F$TRNLNM(logical_name [,table] [,index] [,mode] [,case] [,item])   Translates a logical name to its equivalence name string, or returns the requested attributes of the logical name. The equivalence string is not checked to determine if it is a logical name or not.

F$TYPE(symbol_name)   Returns the data type of a symbol.

F$USER()   Returns the user identification code (UIC), in named format, for the current user. The F$USER function has no arguments.

F$VERIFY([procedure_value] [,image_value])   Returns an integer value that indicates whether procedure verification mode is on or off. If used with arguments, the F$VERIFY function can turn verification mode on or off. You must include the parentheses after the F$VERIFY function whether or not you specify arguments.

Terminal Functions and Control Keys

The following table defines common VMS function and control keys.

Key	Function
<RETURN>	Used to input data or a command string typed at the terminal. This key acts like a period, indicating the end of a command or data string. All commands and data that you type at the terminal must be followed by <RETURN> or the computer will never see the information.
<DELETE>	Used to rub out errors as you are typing a command. If you hold the key down it will continue to erase characters on the line from right to left.
	Note that on a hardcopy terminal any deleted characters will appear within

Key	Function
<DELETE> (cont.)	backslashes (\ \) in the reverse of the order in which they were entered. The deleted characters contained within the backslashes are invisible to the computer.
<TAB>	Moves the cursor to the next tab stop position. If pressed while in an editing session, this key will move the text element before the cursor to the next tab stop.
<HOLD SCREEN>	Toggles output to the display ON/OFF. Use this key when text is scrolling too fast for you to read. It provides the same function as the <CTRL/S> and <CTRL/Q> keys. (Use <NO SCROLL> on VT100 terminals.)
<CTRL/A>	Allows you to insert, rather than overstrike, characters on a DCL command line that you are editing. *See* <CTRL/B>.
<CTRL/B> or <UP ARROW>	Displays DCL commands that you previously entered into the system.
<CTRL/C> or <F6>	Interrupts the command being processed or the program being executed.
<CTRL/E>	Positions the cursor at the end of the line.
<CTRL/H>	Positions the cursor at the beginning of the line.
<CTRL/I>	Duplicates the function of the <TAB> key.
<CTRL/O>	Alternately suppresses and continues the display of output at the terminal.
<CTRL/Q>	Resumes (toggles on) output to the display after <CTRL/S> has been pressed.

Key	Function
<CTRL/R>	Retypes the current input line and repositions the cursor at the end of the retyped line.
<CTRL/S>	Suspends (toggles off) output to the display until <CTRL/Q> is pressed.
<CTRL/T>	Displays process statistics.
<CTRL/U>	Discards the current input line and performs a carriage return.
<CTRL/W>	Refreshes the screen.
<CTRL/X>	Flushes the type-ahead buffer.
<CTRL/Y>	Interrupts command or program execution and returns control to the DCL command line interpreter.
<CTRL/Z> or <F10>	Indicates the end of a file for data entered from the terminal.
<DOWN ARROW>	Recalls the next command in the recall buffer.

Default VMS File Types

The following is a list of default VMS file extensions. These file types are conventions set by Digital Equipment Corporation and might not be followed by other software vendors.

File Type	Contents
ANL	Output file from the ANALYZE command
BAS	Source input file for BASIC compiler
CLD	Command line interpreter command description file
COM	Command procedure file that may be executed using the @ symbol, or submitted for batch execution with the SUBMIT command
DAT	Data input or output file
DIF	Output file created by the DIFFERENCES command

File Type	Contents
DIR	Subdirectory
DIS	Mail distribution list
DMP	Output file created by the DUMP command
EDT	EDT editor initialization file
EXE	VAX/VMS executable program image created by the LINK command
FDL	File definition language file created with the EDIT/FDL or ANALYZE/RMS/FDL command
FOR	Source input file for FORTRAN compiler
HLB	Help text library
HLP	Help text file most commonly used as source input to a help text library file
JNL	EDT editor journal file
LIS	List file created by an assembler or compiler
LOG	Information file created by one of many VAX/VMS elements, such as a batch job or DECnet
MAI	Electronic mail storage file

File Type	Contents
MAR	Source input file for Macro assembler
MLB	Macro source library
OBJ	Intermediate object file created by a compiler or an assembler
OLB	Object module library
OPT	Option input file for the LINK command
PS	PostScript
STB	Symbol table
SYS	System image
TJL	Journal file created by the TPU editor
TLB	Text library
TMP	General-purpose temporary file
TPU	Command input file for the TPU editor
TXT	Text

VMS Device Names

The following table lists common VMS device codes and corresponding device types.

Device Code	Device Type
CS	Console boot/storage device
DA	RC25 (25 Mb fixed/25 Mb removable)
DB	RP05, RP06 disks
DD	TU58 tape
DI	RF disks compatible with DSSI
DJ	RA60 disk
DK	SCSI disk
DL	RL02 disk
DR	RM03, RM05, RM80, RP07 disks
DU	RA80, RA81, RA82 disks
DX	RX01 floppy
DY	RX02 floppy
LC	Line printer device on DMF32
LP	Line printer device on LP11
LT	Local area terminal (LAT)
MB	Mailbox device
MF	TU78 magnetic tape drive
MS	TS11 magnetic tape drive

Device Code	Device Type
MT	TU45, TU77, TE16 magnetic tape drives
MU	TK50, TA78, TA81, TU81 magnetic tape drives
NL	Null device (proverbial bit-bucket)
OP	Operators console device
RT	Remote terminal (via DECnet)
TT	Interactive terminal device
TX	Interactive terminal device
VT	Virtual terminal
XE	DEUNA
XQ	DEQNA

VT Escape Sequences

This appendix describes the terminal escape sequences used with DEC VT terminals. At the end of this appendix is a command procedure that demonstrates how to use these escape sequences with DCL.

CHARACTER SETS

DEC terminals have three character sets to choose from: US (default), UK and GRAPHIC. The US and UK character sets are identical except for the pound sign (number sign). The GRAPHIC character set displays an assortment of line drawing characters and special symbols.

The following table lists escape sequences for changing character sets:

Character Set	Escape Sequence
US (ASCII)	<ESC>(B
UK National	<ESC>(A
GRAPHIC	<ESC>(0

CURSOR MOVEMENT

The next table lists escape sequences VT terminals support for positioning the cursor. (Substitute the character *n* for the number of lines or character positions. If you omit *n*, the command will default to 1.)

Escape Sequence	Cursor Function
<ESC>[M	Moves the cursor up (scrolls within the defined scrolling region)
<ESC>[nA	Moves the cursor up (without scrolling)
<ESC>D<LF>	Moves the cursor down (scrolls within the defined scrolling region)
<ESC>[nB	Moves the cursor down (without scrolling)
<ESC>[nC	Moves the cursor to the right
<ESC>[nD	Moves the cursor to the left
<ESC>E	Positions the cursor at the beginning of the next line
<ESC>[r;cH	Positions the cursor at row r and column c
<ESC>7	Saves the cursor's column position and character attributes
<ESC>8	Restores the cursor's column position and character attributes

SCREEN ERASING

The following table defines escape sequences that enable you to clear specified positions on the display. After erasing screen text, the cursor will be where the erasing completed.

Escape Sequence	Erase Function
<ESC>[OK	Erases from the cursor to the end of the line
<ESC>[1K	Erases from the beginning of the line to the cursor
<ESC>[2K	Erases the entire line
<ESC>[OJ	Erases from the cursor to the end of the screen
<ESC>[1J	Erases from the bottom of the screen to the cursor
<ESC>[2J	Erases the entire screen

SCROLLING REGIONS

A scrolling region is a horizontal portion of the display in which text scrolls. Text lines above and below the scrolling region are protected from the scrolling text; they remain stationary. The following table lists escape sequences used to define scrolling regions.

Escape Sequence	Scrolling Function
<ESC>[t;br	Defines a scrolling region in which the top line = t and the bottom line = b

Escape Sequence	Scrolling Function
<ESC>[?6h	Sets cursor position 0,0 equal to the upper left corner of the scrolling region
<ESC>[?61	Sets cursor position 0,0 equal to the upper left corner of the defined scrolling region

DISPLAY CHARACTERISTICS

The following table defines the escape sequences that enable you to modify display characteristics.

Escape Sequence	Display Characteristic Function
<ESC>[0m	Reset normal characteristics
<ESC>[1m	Bold characters
<ESC>[4m	Underline characters
<ESC>[5m	Blinking characters
<ESC>[7m	Reverse video characters
<ESC>#3	Double-height characters (top half)
<ESC>#4	Double-height characters (bottom half)
<ESC>#5	Single-width characters (default)
<ESC>#6	Double-width characters

TERMINAL CHARACTERISTICS

This table defines the escape sequences that permit you to set various terminal attributes.

Escape Sequence	Terminal Characteristic Function
<ESC>[?3l	Sets terminal to 132-column mode
<ESC>[?3h	Sets terminal to 80-column mode
<ESC>H	Sets tab stop at current column posiion
<ESC>[g	Clears tab stop at current column
<ESC>[3g	Clears all tab stops

EXAMPLE COMMAND PROCEDURE

```
$! VT_ESC.COM
$!
$! Define VT advanced video modes
$!
$ esc[0,8] = %X9b            ! ASCII escape
$ erase = "[J"               ! VT100 erase screen seq
$ home = "[H"                ! VT100 home cursor seq
$ dhl1 = "''esc'#3"          ! Double-height line seq 1
$ dhl2 = "''esc'#4"          ! Double-height line seq 2
$ swl = "''esc'#5"           ! Single-width line
$ dwl = "''esc'#6"           ! Double-width line
$ rev = "''esc'[7m"          ! Reverse video
$ norm = "''esc'[0m''esc'5"  ! Normal mode
$ bold = "''esc'[1m"         ! Bold characters
$ blink = "''esc'[5m"        ! Blinking characters
$ under = "''esc'[4m"        ! Underscored characters
```

```
$!
$!      CURSOR SYNTAX:    CURSOR,"DISTANCE",DIRECTION
$!
$ cursor = "write sys$output esc,""["""
$ up = "A"
$ down = "B"
$ forward = "C"
$ back = "D"
$!
$!      GOxy SYNTAX:      SAY GOxy,"LINE#;COLUMN#",END_GO
$!
$ goXY = "write sys$output esc,""["""
$ end_go = "H"
$!
$!      DEFINE SPECIAL COMMANDS
$!
$ CLR = "write sys$output esc,home,esc,erase"     ! Clear screen
$ SAY = "write sys$output"          ! Output a string
$ CLB = "write sys$output esc,""[12;1H""",esc,""[J""" ! Clear bottom only
$ GRA = "write sys$output ESC,""(0"""! Invoke line graphics mode
$ TXT = "write sys$output ESC,""(B"""      ! Invoke text mode
$
$! EXAMPLES
$ clr
$ say "Line drawing set..."
$ gra
$ say "abcdefghijklmnopqrstwxyz"
$ txt
$ say bold,"this is a bold line",norm
$ say dhl1,"this is a double line"
$ say dhl2,"this is a double line",norm
$ say blink,"this is a blinking line",norm
```

VMS Error Messages

VMS errors are displayed in the format:

%facility-code-ident, text

Facility is the name of the VMS facility that produced the error, for example the Command Language Interpreter (CLI).

Code is a one-letter code indicating the severity of the error. The severity codes are:

I — Informational
S — Success
W — Warning
E — Error
F — Severe error

Ident is an abbreviation for the message name.

Text is a brief description of the error.

VMS Logical Expression Operators

The following table lists the VMS logical expression operators for use in DCL statements.

Operator	Evaluation Precedence	Description
+	1	Indicates a positive number
-	1	Indicates a negative number
/	2	Divides two numbers
*	2	Multiplies two numbers
+	3	Adds two numbers or concatenates two character strings
-	3	Subtracts two numbers or character strings

Operator	Evaluation Precedence	Description
.EQS.	4	Tests two character strings for equality
.GES.	4	Tests the first string for being greater than or equal to the second
.GTS.	4	Tests the first character string for being greater than the second
.LES.	4	Tests the first character for being less than or equal to the second
.LTS.	4	Tests the first character string for being less than the second
.NES.	4	Tests two character strings for being unequal
.EQ.	4	Tests two numbers for equality
.GE.	4	Tests the first number for being greater than or equal to the second number
.GT.	4	Tests the first number for being greater than the second number
.LE.	4	Tests the first number for being less than or equal to the second number

Operator	Evaluation Precedence	Description
.LT.	4	Tests the first number for being less than the second number
.NE.	4	Tests two numbers for being unequal
.NOT.	5	Logically negates a value
.AND.	6	Applies the logical AND operation to two numbers
.OR.	7	Applies the logical OR operation to two numbers

Many of the terms defined in this glossary are specific to Digital Equipment Corporation and may have different meanings to other groups or computer manufacturers. For your convenience, these terms are marked with a "(d)" at the end of the definition.

ACCESS In computer terminology, a verb meaning to get, find or look up the contents of, to gain admittance to, or to obtain the use of. Access of data may be direct, random or sequential.

ACCESS CONTROL LIST A list of entries that define the types of access that can be granted or denied to users of an object. Generally, the object is a device, directory, file or mailbox. (d)

ACCESS VIOLATION An attempt to reference an address that has not been mapped into virtual memory, or an attempt to reference an address that is not accessible in the current access mode. For example, an attempt to address a Kernel-privileged address while in the User access mode would result in an access violation. (d)

ACCOUNT The VMS entity that permits access to the computer system. You must have an account, or be able to log in to an account, to access and use the computer. An account is a unit of system accounting. (d)

ACCOUNT NAME A name specified by the system manager in the User Authorization File to identify a given account. Statistics on the user resources consumed by a job are accumulated and charged to the account name. An exception to this rule involves disk quota, which is charged to the user's user identification code. *See* Disk Quota and User Identification Code. (d)

ACP (ANCILLARY CONTROL PROCESS) A VMS process that interfaces a VAX I/O device driver with the user software requiring the use of the device. If your program writes data to magnetic tape, the program will access the MTAACP (Magtape Ancillary Control Process) in the process of transferring and writing data to the tape drive. The F11ACP (Files-11 Ancillary Control Process) handles read/ write operations on VAX Files-11 structured disks.

ADDRESS A hexadecimal (base 16) number used by VMS and user-supplied software that identifies a storage location in the system. Addresses may be virtual or physical. (d)

ADDRESS SPACE The set of all possible addresses available to a given process. Address space may be virtual or physical. (d)

ALLOCATE The act of reserving a given hardware device for the exclusive use of a given process. If you want to allocate a tape drive to copy disk files onto a magnetic tape, you enter a DCL command such as ALLOCATE MUA0:. You may only allocate a device when that device is not already allocated to another user or process. If you attempt to allocate a previously allocated device, VMS returns an error message informing you that the device is allocated to another user. (d)

ALPHANUMERIC CHARACTER A standard ASCII decimal digit (0 through 9), an uppercase or lowercase alphabetic character, the dollar sign or the underscore character. Alphanumeric characters are valid for filenames, account names and passwords.

ALPHANUMERIC UIC A user identification code that consists of either a member identifier or a group and member identifier specified in alphanumeric form. In an alphanumeric user identification code, the group and member identifiers may be up to 31 characters long and must contain at least one alphabetic character. (d)

ASCII. Acronym for American Standard Code for Information Interchange. The standard code by which DEC computers, such as the VAX, represent alphabetic and numeric characters and other symbols. Each ASCII character is an 8-bit binary number. This code contrasts Extended Binary Coded Decimal Code (EBCDIC), the representation used on IBM hardware.

ASSIGNMENT STATEMENT A statement that defines a symbol name to be used in place of a numeric value or character string. Symbols may be defined as synonyms for system commands; they also may serve as variables in DCL command procedures.

BASE PRIORITY The processing priority established in and assigned from the User Authorization File when a process is created. In VMS, priorities range from 0 to 15 for interactive processes and from 16 to 31 for real-time processes. The higher the base priority of a process, the more rapidly the process will be executed (the more attention the CPU will pay to it). With sufficient privilege you can alter the base priority of a running process. (d)

BATCH The processing mode in which you submit a job to the computer through a batch queue, using the DCL SUBMIT command. Your job will execute when the jobs preceding it in the queue have completed. In the batch mode, you do not have two-way communication with the computer system. Your commands are submitted to the system as a file.

BINARY Pertaining to base 2 numeric representation. The decimal number 7 is represented as 111 in the binary numbering system.

BIT Contraction for *binary digit*. May indicate a single character in a binary number, or the smallest unit of capacity for information storage in a computer system.

BREAK-IN ATTEMPT An attempted breach of security in which an unauthorized user tries to penetrate a computer system. Break-in attempts can take many forms but are often perpetrated by unauthorized individuals who try to penetrate a computer system by dialing in and attempting to guess valid usernames and passwords.

BUFFER A temporary storage area for text or data.

BYTE Eight consecutive bits of data starting on an addressable boundary. The bits are numbered 0 through 7, from the right. One byte stores an ASCII character.

CAPTIVE ACCOUNT A type of VMS account that limits the activities of a user. The account works by locking the user in to a command procedure during login. The user is restricted to the menu of commands provided in the captive account. Captive accounts are often employed to allow users to perform privileged tasks, such as system backup, without granting them these privileges for their own purposes. (d)

CENTRAL PROCESSING UNIT (CPU) The portion of a computer system that contains the arithmetic, logical and control circuits needed for the interpretation and execution of instructions.

COMMAND An instruction that directs the command interpreter to perform a given task. The instruction may be typed in at a terminal or entered by invoking a command procedure. In VMS, commands are generally issued in Digital Command Language (DCL), a set of English-like verbs.

COMMAND FILE *See* Command Procedure.

COMMAND LINE INTERPRETER (CLI) A system procedure that accepts commands, examines them for validity and syntax, and directs the computer to execute the commands. The default command line interpreter for VMS systems is the Digital Command Language (DCL) interpreter. (d)

COMMAND PROCEDURE A file, usually created by a computer user, containing a predefined series of commands and data that the command line interpreter will accept and process. By using a command procedure, you avoid typing each individual command, data element and response. Command procedures may be invoked interactively with the DCL @ statement, or they can be submitted to the batch processor. (d)

COMMAND STRING A DCL command verb and any parameters and qualifiers associated with it. (d)

COMPILER A programming language processor that translates high-level statements from a source program into a machine-readable object module. Programs written in languages like FORTRAN and Pascal must be compiled before they can be linked and executed.

CONCATENATE To link together or join, as in a chain. Records and files may be concatenated.

CONTIGUOUS Consecutively numbered, physically adjacent units. In computer terminology, this refers to data elements.

CONTINUATION CHARACTER A hyphen entered at the end of a line of a long command string, indicating that the command string is to be continued on the next line rather than submitted to the computer via the <RETURN> key. The first character of a line succeeding a line ending with a hyphen is a slash. (d)

CONTROL CHARACTER Any character having an ASCII value of less than 32. Included are such characters as backspace (<CTRL/H> or ASCII 8), bell (<CTRL/G> or ASCII 7) and escape (<ESC> or ASCII 27).

CURSOR A flashing block or bar of light that appears on the screen of a video terminal. It indicates where the next character entered will be displayed on the screen.

DATA A general term used to denote raw or processed information in the form of letters, numbers and symbols. On a VMS system, data is stored in fields within records within files.

DATA ELEMENT A single item of information. *See* Field.

DATA FILE A specific file that contains related data stored in the fields of records.

DCL Acronym for Digital Command Language. (d)

DEBUG To detect, locate and correct errors in a computer program, or to find and repair malfunctions in computer hardware.

DEBUGGER An interactive VMS utility that permits you to display and modify variables in a program as the program is being executed, or to step through a program line by line to locate and correct programming errors. (d)

DECNET Digital Equipment Corporation software that enables DEC computer users to access information and resources on remote computer systems via telecommunication lines. (d)

DEFAULT The action taken by a computer system or program if no specific command or response is given. The device or file that is referred to by the system unless you specify another one. The assumption of predetermined values or actions.

DEFAULT DISK The disk on a VAX system that stores all your files when you do not state a different device name in your file specifications. Your default disk is established in the User Authorization File entry for your account. (d)

DELIMITER A character that organizes or separates individual elements of a file specification or character string. Periods, commas, colons and semicolons are delimiters.

DETACHED PROGRAM A VMS program that operates without a terminal. A detached program cannot communicate with a user until it is attached to a terminal. (d)

DEVICE The general name for any physical or logical entity connected with a computer that is capable of transmitting, receiving or storing data. Terminals and modems are called communication devices, whereas disk and tape drives are mass storage devices.

DEVICE INDEPENDENCE The characteristic of a system, file or program that allows it to operate on any type of device. In the case of VMS programs and files, device independence is achieved through the use of logical names. (d)

DEVICE NAME The name used in a file specification or program to identify a device on which information is stored. In Digital terminology, a device name consists of a mnemonic code. The code takes the form *ddcu:*, where *dd* is the device type, *c* is the controller identifier, *u* is the unit number, and the colon is a terminator. A logical name like SYS$INPUT, which is equated with a physical device like your terminal, also is considered a device name. (d)

DIGITAL COMMAND LANGUAGE (DCL) The standard VMS command interpreter and the collection of valid English-like keywords or verbs that it interprets and acts on. (d)

DIRECTORY A master file with a file type of .DIR that catalogs your files on a given device. It also can be a file used to locate subsidiary files on a volume. A directory contains the filename, file type, version number, protection code and other internal information for each file it catalogs. (d)

DIRECTORY NAME The field in a file specification that identifies the directory in which a given file is listed. In VMS, a directory name can consist of up to nine alphanumeric characters. The name begins with a left bracket ([) and ends with a right bracket (]). When you create a directory, VMS automatically supplies the default file type and extension .DIR;1. (d)

DISK A flat circular platter or stack of platters coated with a magnetic substance. Data is stored on the platter or platters by the selective magnetization of surface portions. The data is read from and written to these rapidly spinning surfaces by movable read/write heads. Because of the speed at which the disk rotates and the speed at which the read/write heads can be positioned, disk drives are considered high-speed random-access mass storage devices.

DISK QUOTA The number of blocks of disk space that the files in your account may occupy. Your disk quota will normally include a permanent quota and an overdraft amount. Disk quota is established by the Diskquota utility, which is run by the system manager. If you exceed your quota, you will be unable to create new files or add to existing ones. You should delete obsolete files regularly, because disk space is almost always at a premium. (d)

DISK SCAVENGING Any method of obtaining data from a disk that is presumed to have been erased.

DRIVE The portion of a mass storage device on which the media (magnetic tape reel, disk or disk pack) is mounted. The drive contains the electromechanical units that rotate the media. These units also perform the reading and writing of data from or onto the media.

DUMP A print-out of all or part of the contents of a storage device or of the physical memory of a computer system. The only way a programmer can read the contents of an executable program (.EXE) file is by dumping the file. (d)

ECHO The display of characters on a terminal screen or hardcopy media as the characters are entered at the keyboard. Characters are echoed by default on a VMS system except when you are entering or changing your password.

EDIT To create or modify the form or format of data; to revise text material; to invoke a Digital editor such as EDT, TPU, SLP, SOS or TECO.

EDITOR A program used to create or modify files. The default VMS editor is EDT.

EQUIVALENCE NAME The string associated with a logical name in a logical name table. The equivalence name can be another logical name or a device name. For example, the equivalence name "DUA0:" (a device name) could be equated with "USER$DISK" (a logical name). (d)

ERROR MESSAGE The message VMS displays when an action you have directed to take place fails. (d)

EVENT In VMS, the occurrence of an activity or the change in the status of a process that affects that process. Because VMS is event-driven, when an event relative to a process is reported to the VMS scheduler, the ability of that process to execute or continue execution may be affected. (d)

EXECUTABLE IMAGE An image that can be run within the context of a process. When the command is given to run an executable image, the image is read into a process from an executable image (.EXE) file. The process then runs the image. (d)

EXECUTE To perform a routine or carry out an instruction. To run a program or an executable image.

EXECUTIVE The collection of VMS software that controls and monitors the functioning of the operating system. (d)

EXTENSION An alternate name for the file type in a file specification. On a disk, an extension is the amount of space added to the end of a file when an addition to the file exceeds the allocated length of the file. (d)

EXTENT Contiguous disk space containing a file or a portion of a file. An extent may consist of one or more clusters. *See* Cluster. (d)

FIELD A specified number of contiguous character positions capable of holding a single element of data. A field is a subdivision of a record.

FILE An organized collection of related data stored on a tape or disk volume. In most cases, files consist of a number of records, each of which contains several fields. The use of records and files aids in the logical and coherent storage of data.

FILENAME The portion of a file specification preceding the file type. It gives the file a logical name. (d)

FILE SPECIFICATION The unique identification of a file on a mass storage volume. It describes the physical location of the file as the filename and file type identifiers. A complete file specification includes the node name, device name, directory name, filename, file type and version number. File specifications have the format:

NODE::DEVICE:[DIRECTORY]FILENAME.TYPE;VERSION NUMBER

Each complete file specification must be unique—there can be only one occurrence of any particular full file specification at any one time. You usually need to concern yourself only with the filename, file type and version number. (d)

FILE TYPE The portion of a file specification that follows the filename and precedes the version number. The file type often describes the nature or use of the file. (d)

GLOBAL SYMBOL Any symbol defined by an assignment statement that will be recognized by any command procedure executed in any account on a system. Contrast global symbol with local symbol. (d)

GROUP In the VMS file protection scheme, a group is one of the four classes of users definable to a VMS system. Specifically, a group is a set of users who have access to each other's directories and the files contained within those directories.

GROUP IDENTIFIER The group of characters in a two-part alphanumeric user identification code entry. Users who share the same group identifier are in the same user identification code group. (d)

GROUP NUMBER The first group of digits in a numeric user identification code. Users who share the same group number are in the same user identification code group. (d)

HARDCOPY Printed computer output produced by a printer or hardcopy terminal.

HARDWARE The physical devices and equipment associated with a computer system. Contrast with software, the operating system and programs used within the system.

HELP FILE A text file associated with the VMS HELP command. You can add entries to the help file supplied with the VMS operating system. The help file can provide up to eight levels of information beneath each main topic. (d)

HIGH-LEVEL LANGUAGE A programming language that consists of English-like statements. This type of language is generally machine-independent. Each high-level program statement is translated into several machine language instructions when the program is compiled and linked.

IMAGE Procedures and data bound together by the linker, often the end result of compiling and linking a program on the system. VMS supports three kinds of images—executable (e.g., executable program), shared and system. (d)

INPUT The process of transferring external data into main memory or an intermediate storage device. Input also is defined as the data that is transferred.

INPUT/OUTPUT Input, output or both. Commonly referred to as I/O.

INTERACTIVE A mode of system operation. In the interactive mode, you use a terminal for two-way communication with the system. The opposite of the interactive mode of operation is the batch mode of operation.

INTERRUPT An event other than a program instruction that changes the normal flow of execution of a program or process. When the interrupt occurs, it usually is external to the executing program or process. An interrupt may be generated by a device or by system software.

INVOKE To call up or run a program or compiler, or to execute a command procedure with the @ symbol. (d)

JOB From a VMS standpoint, a job is the accounting unit equated with a process. Because certain processes may spawn or create subprocesses, a job may contain a number of processes. Jobs are classified as batch or interactive. When you log in to the system, an interactive job is created to handle your requests and processes. If you submit a program to a batch queue for processing, a batch job is created. (d)

JOB CONTROLLER The VMS process that establishes the process context of a job, handles the login and logout facilities, maintains accounting records, and terminates processes. (d)

KEYPAD On Digital Equipment VT200 and VT300 terminals, the two groups of keys to the right of the main keyboard. (d)

KEYWORD In DCL, a valid command, option or qualifier. (d)

LINKER The VMS facility that creates an executable program image from one or more object modules output by a compiler or assembler. The linking process involves the establishment of virtual addresses for portions of the image, acquisition of system services referenced by the program, and accumulation of data that will be needed for image execution. Using the linker, you can link a VAX BASIC object program with a MACRO-32 object program, and end up with an executable program containing the BASIC and MACRO-32 object modules. (d)

LOCAL SYMBOL Any symbol defined by an assignment statement that is recognized only within the DCL command procedure in which it has been defined. Contrast with global symbol. (d)

LOGICAL NAME A name that you specify as a substitute for a file specification or a portion of a file specification. You can assign logical names to frequently used devices or files to save keystrokes. For example, if you frequently use a given terminal for data entry, you can assign the logical name "read" to the equivalence name (such as DRA0:TTD7) of that terminal. (d)

LOGICAL NAME TABLE An area in the system containing the set of logical names and equivalence names for a particular process, a particular group or the entire system. (d)

LOG IN The act of initiating a terminal session with a computer. When you log in, VMS establishes default terminal characteristics and creates a process in your account in which images can run.

LOGIN FILE Also referred to as LOGIN.COM, the command procedure that executes automatically when you log in to the system or submit a batch job. It is used to tailor your account environment to meet your needs. You can write your own LOGIN.COM or the system manager can assign a preset LOGIN.COM to your account in the User Authorization File. (d)

LOG OUT The act of terminating a terminal session with a computer. When you log out, your account is disabled and accounting information that has accumulated during the session is stored in the system accounting file.

LONGWORD 32 bits or four contiguous bytes beginning on a byte boundary. The longword is the unit required for addressing virtual space in a 32-bit computer such as the VAX. (d)

MACHINE LANGUAGE A computer program expressed in binary numbers. An executable image consists of machine language instructions.

MACRO A statement that requests a language processor such as MACRO-32 to generate a predefined series of instructions. Macros can save an assembly language programmer much time. For example, division is done in assembly language by repetitive subtraction. Using the macro DIV, the programmer can perform a division operation without writing the subtraction routine.

MAGNETIC TAPE A mass storage medium consisting of tape coated with a metallic oxide. Data can be recorded and stored in the form of magnetically polarized spots on this tape. Although information on magnetic tape cannot be accessed as rapidly as data on disks, magnetic tape is a much less expensive medium. Files stored on disks often are copied or backed up to magnetic tape for archival storage and safekeeping.

MASS STORAGE DEVICE A hardware device capable of reading and writing large amounts of data on mass storage media such as magnetic tape reels, disk packs or floppy disks.

MEMBER IDENTIFIER The entry in a one-part alphanumeric user identification code or the second half of a two-part alphanumeric user identification code. It identifies the user who has been assigned the code. (d)

MEMBER NUMBER The second number in a numeric user identification code. (d)

MEMORY MANAGEMENT VMS functions that include page mapping and protection within the processor, and the VMS pager, swapper and image activator. (d)

MOUNT A VOLUME To place a disk pack or magnetic tape on a drive, ready the drive for operation, and place the drive online. Also to issue the MOUNT command in order to logically associate a volume with the hardware unit on which it has been physically mounted.

NETWORK A collection of individual but interconnected computer systems linked by a communications protocol such as DECnet. Networked computer systems can share files and other resources with each other.

NIBBLE Half a byte—either the low-order or high-order 4 bits of a byte.

NODE An individual computer within a network. Each system can communicate with some or all the other computers in the network, depending on the communications protocol and the configuration of the network. (d)

NODE SPECIFICATION A portion of a file specification that identifies the location of a particular computer, or node, within a computer network. Node specifications are terminated with two colons (::). (d)

NULL PROCESS A small VMS process that accumulates idle computer time for accounting purposes. It functions at the lowest priority within the system and occupies an entire priority class. (d)

NUMERIC Pertaining to numbers or to representation by numbers. In field definition, a numeric field is one in which only numbers may be stored.

OBJECT MODULE Designated by the file type .OBJ, an object module is the binary output from a program compiler or assembler. This output is input to the linker. An object module is not readable or executable. (d)

OFFLINE Refers to peripheral equipment or devices not currently under direct control of the computer system. (d)

OPEN ACCOUNT A VMS account that does not require a password for login. (d)

OPERATING SYSTEM An organized collection of techniques and procedures that control the overall operation of a computer system. In other words, the operating system acts as a supervisor. It is supplied by the computer vendor as the system software. On Digital Equipment VAX computers, the operating system is VMS.

OPERATOR'S CONSOLE Usually the hardcopy terminal designated as the system operator's terminal (OPA0:), but it can be any terminal designated as an operator console by the DCL REPLY/ENABLE command. It is possible to respond to OPCOM messages and to start up and shut down the computer system from any terminal designated as the operator's console. A temporary operator's terminal can be disabled with the DCL REPLY/DISABLE command. (d)

OUTPUT Data that has been processed, or the process of transferring data from an internal or mass storage device to an output device such as a printer or terminal.

OWNER In the VMS file protection scheme, the owner is the member of a group to whom a file belongs. *See* User Identification Code and Member Number. (d)

PAGE The basic unit VMS uses for establishing working set sizes, transferring data between memory and disk storage, and memory mapping. A page consists of 512 contiguous byte locations beginning on an even 512-byte boundary. (d)

PAGE FAULT An exception that occurs when a page that is not currently within a process working set is referenced. When a page fault occurs in a process, the process is suspended until the system writes "used" pages back out to the disk and replaces them by reading in the pages that the process working set requires. (d)

PAGER One of the VMS memory management facilities. The pager is a set of privileged kernel mode instructions that reads in a required page cluster when a page fault occurs. This permits the image that generated the page fault to resume execution. In VMS, a process can page only against itself. Thus, a page fault generated by one user's process cannot affect the working set of any other user's process.

PAGING The action of bringing pages of an executing process into physical memory when the process image is first activated, or when requested by a page fault.

PARAMETER The object of a command; the noun associated with a DCL command verb within a command string. A parameter can be a symbol value passed to a command procedure, a word defined by DCL, or a file specification. For example, in the DCL PRINT MYFILE.DAT command string, MYFILE.DAT is a parameter.

PARSE To break a command string into its elements so it can be interpreted. When a command string is parsed, it is broken into the DCL command verb, its parameters and qualifiers.

PASSWORD The protective keyword associated with an account.

PERIPHERAL A hardware device in a computer system that is not a functional part of the CPU (e.g., a printer or disk drive).

PHYSICAL ADDRESS The address VMS uses to identify a specific location in physical memory or on a disk drive. (d)

PHYSICAL MEMORY The tangible memory boards or modules within a computer containing data and instructions that the computer can directly fetch and execute. Also, elements of the operating system or any other data that the processor must manipulate to function. Physical memory also is referred to as main memory.

PRIORITY A numeric rank assigned to an image, process or account to determine its precedence in obtaining system resources such as CPU time or disk access. In VMS, processing priorities range from 0 to 15 for interactive processes, and from 16 to 31 for real-time processes. VMS can dynamically raise and lower the priority of processes, but it cannot lower a process' priority beneath the base priority established in the User Authorization File. (d)

PRIVILEGES In VMS, the 35 keywords identifying special system functions that can be granted or denied to system users. Privileges are categorized by their potential to affect the computer system or its resources. They are granted or denied in a manner consistent with the needs of users and the need to maintain the integrity of the system. (d)

PROCESS The basic entity that can be scheduled by VMS. A process provides the context in which an image executes. A process includes software and hardware contexts and an address space. (d)

PROGRAM A sequence of instructions and routines that solves a problem on a computer system.

PROMPT A word, words or symbol used by the computer system as a cue to assist you in making a response, or to inform you that the system is waiting for a response.

PROTECTION CODE In VMS, the protection code specifies what type of file access different categories of users may have. Four types of access (Read, Write, Execute and Delete) may be granted or denied to four categories of users (System, Owner, Group and World). An additional type of access, Control, can be specified in an access control list. (d)

QUALIFIER A portion of a command added to a DCL command verb. It modifies the verb or command parameter by specifying one of several options. For example, if you issue the DIRECTORY command with the /SIZE qualifier (DIRECTORY/SIZE), the /SIZE qualifier will indicate to the DCL interpreter that you want to know the size (in blocks) of a file. (d)

QUEUE A waiting line in the computer system. The system has certain areas set aside for input, output and special device queues. With sufficient privileges, you can create, start, modify, stop and delete specific queues. A typical queue on a VMS system is SYS$BATCH, the default batch queue.

QUEUE MANAGER A VMS system program that provides orderly processing of batch and print jobs. (d)

QUOTA The total amount of a reusable system resource that a job is permitted to use during a given period of time. Quotas are established in the User Authorization File. They can be used to set limits on working set size, virtual address space, and CPU time consumable by a process. *See* Disk Quota. (d)

RAM Acronym for random access memory. A read/write memory device.

RANDOM ACCESS A technique by which the computer can find one data element as rapidly as any other, regardless of its location in storage, without requiring a sequential search.

RECORD A meaningful collection of related information (data elements) organized into fields and treated as a single unit by the computer. Records are composed of fields; one or more records comprise a data file.

RECORD MANAGEMENT SERVICES (RMS) A set of system routines that opens, closes, reads from, extends and deletes files. When you invoke a DCL command that deletes files, such as the PURGE command, RMS is the system service that performs the file deletion. (d)

REGISTER A storage location in the CPU that is not considered a portion of main memory. Registers are accessible by programmers and the VMS operating system.

RESOURCE A physical portion of the computer system such as a tape drive or memory. Also, a reusable operating system-specific entity, such as working set size or maximum virtual page count.

RESPONSE TIME The time that elapses between when you press <RETURN> after entering data or a command into the computer and your receipt of output from the computer. Response time on VMS systems is affected by the number of users on the system, the jobs that are running, and the availability of system devices.

REVERSE VIDEO On Digital Equipment VT terminals, a reverse of the normal video contrast. If the default is amber lettering on a black screen, reverse video displays black lettering on an amber screen. The EDT editor and some user programs use reverse video to highlight text or information.

RIGHTS DATABASE A file that lists users and special identifiers associated with them. This associative file is used in the access control list system. (d)

RIGHTS LIST In the access control list system, a list associated with each process that contains all the identifiers that the process holds. (d)

RWED Refers to the VMS file access scheme of Read, Write, Execute and Delete. (d)

SCROLLING On a video terminal, the process that makes new information appear at the bottom of the screen. Simultaneously, the old information is pushed up to the top of the screen until it disappears.

SECURE TERMINAL SERVER An optional VMS feature that ensures that you can only log in to a terminal that already has been logged out. To log in to a terminal that is protected with the secure server you must first press the <BREAK> key. This will automatically halt any process that might be executing from the terminal and log out the terminal. This technique is a deterrent to password grabber programs. (d)

SOFTWARE The sum total of assemblers, compilers, programs, utilities and commands available within a computer system. System software includes system-specific utilities, subprograms and the operating system used by the processor.

SOURCE PROGRAM A program written in an assembly or high-level language. A source program must be assembled or compiled and then linked before it can be executed by a computer.

SPOOLING A method of using a high-speed mass storage device as an intermediate buffer to hold data passing from a low-speed device, such as a terminal, to memory, or passing from memory to a line printer.

STRING A specific sequence of characters. The characters and words in a DCL command often are referred to as a command string.

SUBDIRECTORY A directory file that is cataloged in a higher-level directory in an account. It lists additional files that belong to the directory owner. In VMS, a subdirectory is denoted by a period preceding its name. The subdirectory name is concatenated to the name of the higher-level directory that lists it.

SUBPROCESS A process created, or spawned, by a parent process. The creator process owns the subprocess; the subprocess inherits the quotas and limits imposed on the creator process. Once a subprocess is spawned, you have no further control over its execution. Subprocesses may be created or spawned with the DCL SPAWN command. When the creating process exits the system, all its subprocesses are deleted. (d)

SUBROUTINE In a program, a routine that can be called and used by another routine to accomplish a specific task.

SWAPPER The swapper performs memory scheduling and execution throughout the computer system. Based on priorities and the degree of system usage, the swapper removes processes from the balance set (swaps them out), creates shells for new processes, and enters processes that have been waiting for execution into the balance set. (d)

SWAPPING The act of sharing memory resources among several processes by writing an entire working set to secondary storage (swapping out) and reading another working set into physical memory (swapping in).

SYMBIONT A system process that transfers record-oriented data to or from mass storage devices such as disk drives. The system symbionts are functions of spooling and queuing. An example of a symbiont is the print symbiont, which transfers a print file from disk to the line printer. (d)

SYMBOL A user-defined name that can be equated with a command, character string or arithmetic value through the DCL ASSIGN statement. A symbol must be defined or given a meaning so that it can be used.

SYNTAX The structure of expressions in a language or a command language; the rules governing the structure of a programming language or the form that a command must follow to be valid.

SYSTEM PASSWORD A password that must be entered at a terminal before the system will initiate the login procedure and display the username prompt. (d)

SYSTEM SERVICES User-callable procedures provided by VMS. They include memory management, logical name, change mode, I/O and process control services. Most system services are provided and executed for users by VMS, but some services may be called and used by application programmers. (d)

TERMINAL A peripheral device used for interactive communication with a computer. It consists of a typewriter-like keyboard and a printer or video screen.

TIMESHARING A scheme in which each user of a computer is allocated a fair share of computer time and resources in rotation.

USER AUTHORIZATION FILE (UAF) A file maintained by the system manager containing important information on every user who is authorized to access the system. Each UAF entry contains, at the very least, the username, password, user identification code, privileges, default account and directory, quotas, and limits for each individual authorized to use the system. (d)

USER IDENTIFICATION CODE (UIC) A code consisting of two numbers or two alphanumeric identifiers enclosed in brackets and separated by a comma in the form [group,member]. An alphanumeric user identification code may optionally consist of a single member identifier. The user identification code identifies the group and member of a given user or file and is used by VMS to permit or deny file access. (d)

USERNAME The name associated with your account that you type at a terminal to log in to the system. (d)

UTILITY A general-purpose program or facility provided by an operating system to perform common or generic tasks. On a VMS system, Phone, Mail and Sort are considered utilities.

VAX Acronym for Virtual Address Extension, a high-performance, multiprocessing computer based on a 32-bit architecture. VAX is made by Digital Equipment Corporation. (d)

VERSION NUMBER The numeric field that follows the file type and terminates a file specification. It begins with a semicolon and is followed by a number. Each time a new file version is created, the system automatically assigns it a new version number incremented by one. This number uniquely identifies a file; no two duplicate file specifications can have the same version number. (d)

VIRTUAL ADDRESS A 32-bit integer that identifies the location of a given byte in virtual address space. When needed, the VMS memory management system will translate a virtual address to a physical address within the memory of the computer.

VIRTUAL ADDRESS SPACE The set of all virtual addresses that are available within VMS. This space can be conceived of as a linear array of 4,294,967,296 byte addresses. (d)

VIRTUAL MEMORY The set of storage locations on disk and in physical memory that virtual addresses refer to. To the user, the storage locations on disk appear to be located in physical memory and can be used as such. The maximum size of virtual memory in a computer system is contingent upon available physical memory and the amount of disk space that can be used to store virtual memory addresses. (d)

VMS Abbreviation for Virtual Memory System, the operating system for VAX computers. (d)

VOLUME The largest logical unit of the file structure. Examples of volumes are disk packs and reels of magnetic tape.

WILDCARD CHARACTER An asterisk or percent sign used within or in place of a filename, file type, directory name or version number in a file specification to indicate "all" for the given field or portion of the field. (d)

WORD 16 bits or 2 contiguous bytes beginning on a byte boundary. This is the unit required for addressing locations in a Digital Equipment PDP-11 or other 16-bit computer. (d)

WORKING SET The number of pages in physical memory to which a process can refer without incurring a page fault. The larger the working set size, the fewer page faults the process will generate. However, as working set sizes increase, the number of processes in the balance set decreases. VMS permits the establishment of a minimum working set size, a working set quota, and a maximum size to which a working set can grow as long as it does not interfere with other processes. You can obtain a display of your current working set size by issuing the DCL SHOW WORKING_SET command. (d)

WORLD In the System, Owner, Group, World scheme, World refers to all users of the system, including the system manager, operators and members of an owner's group, as well as members of other groups. (d)

Index

E

F

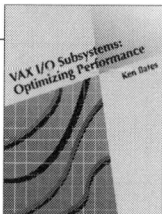

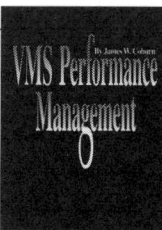

CBM Books Order Form

**To order by phone, call (215) 957-4265 or FAX (215) 957-1050.
Also available through CompuServe mail — user ID 76702,1565.**

Title			Quantity	Subtotal
Introduction to VAX/VMS, 3rd Edition				
1-5 books	$35 each			
6-15 books	$29.75 each	SAVE 15%		
16-49 books	$24.50 each	SAVE 30%		
50+ books	$21 each	SAVE 40%		
Mastering VMS $40				
VAX I/O Subsystems: Optimizing Performance $49				
The Hitchhiker's Guide to VMS $35				
VMS Performance Management $30				
The Complete Guide to Pathworks $39				
PA residents add 6% sales tax.				
UPS shipping: $4 for the first book, $1 for each additional book. Outside the U.S., please call (215) 957-4265 for shipping information.				
TOTAL ORDER				

Name _____

Title _____

Company _____

Address _____

City _____ State _____ Zip _____

Country _____

Telephone (_____) _____ FAX (_____) _____
Street address required.

☐ Check enclosed for $_____. (Checks payable to Cardinal Business Media, Inc.)

Charge to: ☐ MasterCard MasterCard ☐ VISA VISA ☐ American Express American Express

Account #: _____ Exp. Date _____

Signature _____ Date _____

Please send me a free CBM Books catalog.

Mail to:
CBM Books
101 Witmer Road, P.O. Box 446
Horsham, PA 19044

IVBI0793